EXCEL 2020

FOR BEGINNERS

THE COMPLETE DUMMY TO EXPERT ILLUSTRATIVE GUIDE WITH EXAMPLES THAT TEACHES EVERYTHING YOU NEED TO KNOW ABOUT MICROSOFT EXCEL 2020 (FORMULAS AND FUNCTIONS INCLUSIVE)

JAMES JORDAN

ALL RIGHT RESERVED

This manuscript may not be reproduced in part or in full or stored in a retrieval system or transmitted in any form or in any means; electronic, mechanical, photocopying, recording or otherwise except for brief quotation in critical articles or review-without the prior written consent of the copyright owner and the publisher.

This book is sold subject to the condition that it should not by way of trade or otherwise be lent, hired out or otherwise circulated without the copyright owner consent, in any form of binding or cover that in which it is published and this condition being imposed on the subsequent purchaser.

ISBN: 9798706675158
Copyright © 2021 **JAMES JORDAN**

CONTENTS

PREFACE XII
INTRODUCTION... XIII
CHAPTER ONE 1
INTRODUCTION TO MICROSOFT EXCEL 2020 1
    WHAT IS EXCEL? 1
    USES OF EXCEL 2
    WHAT'S NEW IN EXCEL 2020? 3
    MICROSOFT EXCEL TERMINOLOGIES 4
    EXCEL TOOLS 9
    EXCEL FILE TYPES 10
    WHERE CAN I GET MICROSOFT EXCEL? 11
CHAPTER TWO 13
THE BASIC OPERATIONS ON EXCEL 2020 13
    LAUNCHING AND QUITTING EXCEL 2020 FROM THE WINDOW 13
    STARTING YOUR EXCEL FROM WINDOW 10 13
    QUITTING EXCEL 14
    EXCEL'S START SCREEN 15
    EXCEL'S RIBBON USER INTERFACE 16
    UNDERSTANDING THE WORKBOOK 18
    CREATING A NEW WORKSHEET 18
    RENAMING A WORKSHEET 19
    INSERTING A NEW WORKSHEET 20
    DELETING A WORKSHEET 20
    COPYING OR MOVING A WORKSHEET 21
    CHANGING THE WORKSHEET COLOUR 21
    SAVING YOUR DOCUMENT 22
    HOW TO RECOVER YOUR DOCUMENT USING AUTOSAVE 23
    EXPORTING WORKBOOKS 24
    HOW TO SHARE EXCEL WORKBOOK 25
    UNDERSTANDING THE CELL 26
    WHAT'S A CELL? 27
    INSERTING CONTENTS IN A CELL 28
    HOW TO DELETE A CELL 28
    COPYING AND PASTING CELL CONTENT 29
    DRAGGING AND DROPPING THE CELL 30
    USING THE FILL HANDLE IN A CELL 30
    FORMATTING THE CELL 32
    CHANGING THE FONT 32
    CHANGING THE FONT SIZE 33
    CHANGING THE FONT COLOR 34

USING THE BOLD, ITALICS, AND UNDERLINED COMMANDS 35
ADDING BACKGROUND COLOR USING THE FILL COLOR 35
ADDING BORDERS TO CELLS 36
CHANGING THE TEXT ALIGNMENT OF YOUR BORDER 37
MODIFYING THE COLUMNS, ROWS, AND CELL IN A WORKSHEET 38
MODIFYING THE COLUMN WIDTH 38
MODIFYING THE ROW HEIGHT 39
INSERTING NEW ROW 40
INSERTING NEW COLUMN 40
DELETING OF ROWS AND COLUMNS 40
HOW TO HIDE AND UNHIDE ROWS OR COLUMNS 41
WRAPPING TEXT AND MERGING CELLS 42
CUSTOMIZING THE DEFAULT WORKBOOK 44
HOW TO CHANGE THE WORKSHEET THEME 44
HOW TO CHANGE THE WORKSHEET THEME COLOUR 44
HOW TO CHANGE THE WORKSHEET THEME EFFECTS 45
ZOOMING IN OR OUT OF THE SPREADSHEET 46
ADDING MORE WORKSHEETS TO THE WORKBOOK 46

CHAPTER THREE 48

EXCEL TABLES AND CHARTS 48

WHAT IS AN EXCEL TABLE? 48
CREATING A TABLE 48
SORTING A TABLE 49
FILTERING A TABLE 50
CREATING PIVOT TABLE AND CHARTS IN EXCEL 50
THE PIVOTTABLE 50
THE PIVOT CHART 52
USING SLICER ON TABLES OR PIVOT TABLES 53
WORKING WITH CHARTS 55
TYPES OF EXCEL CHART 55
HOW TO INSERT A CHART IN EXCEL 57
HOW TO ADD TITLE TO A CHART 58
HOW TO CHANGE CHART TYPE IN EXCEL 60
HOW TO CHANGE CHART STYLE IN EXCEL 61
HOW TO CHANGE CHART LAYOUT IN EXCEL 62
HOW TO SWITCH ROWS AND COLUMNS OF DATA IN A CHART 63
HOW TO MOVE A CHART 64
HOW TO RESIZE A CHART ON YOUR WORKSHEET 65

CHAPTER FOUR 66

CELL REFERENCING IN EXCEL 66

MEANING OF CELLS REFERENCING 66
TYPES OF CELL REFERENCING 66
RELATIVE REFERENCES 66

ABSOLUTE AND MULTIPLE CELL REFERENCE 68
HOW TO CREATE AND COPY A FORMULA USING THE ABSOLUTE REFERENCE 68
REFERENCES TO OTHER WORKSHEET 70
REFERENCES TO WORKSHEETS IN OTHER WORKBOOK 71

CHAPTER FIVE 73

INTRODUCTION TO EXCEL FORMULAS & FUNCTIONS 73

WHAT'S A FORMULA? 73
HOW TO INSERT FORMULAS IN EXCEL 2020 73
WHAT'S A FUNCTION? 75
HOW TO INSERT A FUNCTION 75
INTRODUCING THE FORMULAR TAB 78
THE FORMULA BAR 79
WHERE IS THE FORMULA BAR LOCATED IN MICROSOFT EXCEL? 80
EXPANDING THE FORMULA BAR 80
CONTRACTING THE FORMULA BAR 81
ENTERING AND EDITING DATA IN THE FORMULA BAR 81
THE INSERT FUNCTION DIALOGUE BOX 81
THE FUNCTION ARGUMENT DIALOG BOX 82
CONTROLLING THE DISPLAY OF THE FORMULA BAR 82
WHAT TYPE OF DATA DOES THE EXCEL FORMULA ACCEPT? 83
METHODS OF ENTERING AND EDITING OF FORMULAS 84
METHODS OF ENTERING OR INSERTING FORMULAS 84
EDITING A FORMULA 85
USING THE FORMULA OPERATORS 86
ORDER OF FORMULA OPERATORS PRECEDENCE 89
THE NESTED PARENTHESES 89
WORKING WITH FUNCTIONS 90
WHY SHOULD YOU USE FUNCTIONS? 90
THE FUNCTION ARGUMENTS 90
USING FUNCTIONS WITH NO ARGUMENTS 91
USING FUNCTION WITH ONE OR MORE ARGUMENTS 91
USING FUNCTIONS WITH BOTH REQUIRED AND OPTIONAL ARGUMENT 91
LOCATING A FUNCTION'S ARGUMENTS 92
ERRORS IN FORMULAS AND FUNCTIONS 93
DIFFERENCES BETWEEN AN EXCEL FORMULA AND FUNCTION 94
USING CALCULATION OPERATORS IN EXCEL FORMULAS 95
MATHEMATICAL ORDER OF OPERATION IN EXCEL 96
ARITHMETIC IN EXCEL 96

CHAPTER SIX 99

MUST KNOW EXCEL FORMULAS & FUNCTIONS 99

MATH FUNCTIONS 99
THE SUM FUNCTION 99
USING THE SUM FUNCTION 100

THE SUMIF FUNCTION	101
USING THE SUMIF FUNCTION	101
THE SUMIFS FUNCTION	105
USING THE SUMIFS FUNCTION	105
THE MOD FUNCTION	107
USING THE MOD FUNCTION	107
RANDBETWEEN FUNCTION	108
USING THE RANDBETWEEN FUNCTION	108
THE ROUND FUNCTION	109
USING THE ROUND FUNCTION	110
THE ROUNDUP FUNCTION	111
USING THE ROUNDUP FUNCTION	111
THE ROUNDDOWN FUNCTION	113
USING THE ROUNDDOWN FUNCTION	113
THE SORT FUNCTION	115
USING THE SORT FUNCTION	116

CHAPTER SEVEN **118**

STATISTICAL FUNCTIONS **118**

THE COUNT FUNCTION	118
USING THE COUNT FUNCTION	118
THE COUNTIF FUNCTION	120
USING THE COUNTIF FUNCTION	120
THE COUNTIFS FUNCTION	122
USING THE COUNTIFS FUNCTION	122
THE COUNTA FUNCTION	124
USING THE COUNTA FUNCTION	124
THE COUNTBLANK FUNCTION	125
USING THE COUNTABLANK FUNCTION	126
The AVERAGE Function	127
USING THE AVERAGE FUNCTION	127
THE AVERAGEIF FUNCTION	129
USING THE AVERAGEIF FUNCTION	129
THE AVERAGEIFS FUNCTION	131
USING THE AVERGAEIFS FUNCTION	131
THE MIN FUNCTION	133
USING THE MIN FUNCTION	133
THE MAX FUNCTION	135
USING THE MIN FUNCTION	135
THE MEDIAN FUNCTION	137
USING THE MEDIAN FUNCTION	137

CHAPTER EIGHT **139**

THE FINANCIAL FUNCTION **139**

THE PV FUNCTION	139

USING THE PV FUNCTION	140
THE FV FUNCTION	141
USING THE FV FUNCTION	142
THE NPV FUNCTION	143
USING THE NPV FUNCTION	143
THE PMT FUNCTION	145
USING THE PMT FUNCTION	146
THE SLN FUNCTION	147
USING THE SLN FUNCTION	148
The SYD Function	149
USING THE SYD FUNCTION	150
THE DB FUNCTION	151
USING THE DB FUNCTION	152
THE DDB FUNCTION	153
USING THE DDB FUNCTION	154
THE SEARCH FUNCTION	155
THE FIND FUNCTION	157

CHAPTER NINE 159

LOGICAL FUNCTIONS 159

THE IF FUNCTION	159
USING THE IF FUNCTION	160
THE NESTED IF FUNCTION	161
THE IFS FUNCTION	163
USING THE IFS FUNCTION	163
The IFFEROR Function	164
USING THE IFERROR FORMULAS	165
THE AND FUNCTION	166
USING THE AND FUNCTION	166
THE OR FUNCTION	168
USING THE OR FUNCTION	168

CHAPTER TEN 170

LOOKUP AND REFERENCE FUNCTIONS 170

THE VLOOKUP FUNCTION	170
USING THE VLOOKUP FUNCTION	171
THE HLOOKUP FUNCTION	174
USING THE HLOOKUP FUNCTION	174
THE CHOOSE FUNCTION	177
USING THE CHOOSE FUNCTION	177
THE MATCH FUNCTION	178
USING THE MATCH FUNCTION	179
THE TRANSPOSE FUNCTION	180
USING THE TRANSPOSE FUNCTION	181
THE FORMULATEXTS FUNCTION	183

USING THE FORMULATEXT FUNCTION 183
THE COLUMN FUNCTION 185
USING THE COLUMN FUNCTION 185
THE ROW FUNCTION 188
USING THE ROW FUNCTION 188
THE INDEX FUNCTION... 191
THE ARRAY FORMAT OF THE INDEX FUNCTION 191
USING THE ARRAY FORMAT OF THE INDEX FUNCTION 192
THE REFERENCE FORMAT OF THE INDEX FUNCTION 193
USING THE REFERENCE FORMAT OF THE INDEX FUNCTION 194

CHAPTER ELEVEN 197

LOGICAL FUNCTIONS 197

THE IF FUNCTION.. 197
USING THE IF FUNCTION 198
THE NESTED IF FUNCTION 199
THE IFS FUNCTION 201
USING THE IFS FUNCTION.. 201
THE IFFEROR FUNCTION 202
USING THE IFERROR FORMULAS 203
THE AND FUNCTION 204
USING THE AND FUNCTION 204
THE OR FUNCTION... 205
USING THE OR FUNCTION 206

CHAPTER TWELVE 208

LOOKUP AND REFERENCE FUNCTIONS 208

THE VLOOKUP FUNCTION.. 208
USING THE VLOOKUP FUNCTION 209
THE HLOOKUP FUNCTION.. 212
USING THE HLOOKUP FUNCTION 212
THE CHOOSE FUNCTION 215
USING THE CHOOSE FUNCTION.. 215
THE MATCH FUNCTION 216
USING THE MATCH FUNCTION 217
The TRANSPOSE Function 218
USING THE TRANSPOSE FUNCTION 219
THE FORMULATEXTS FUNCTION 221
USING THE FORMULATEXT FUNCTION 221
THE COLUMN FUNCTION 223
USING THE COLUMN FUNCTION 223
THE ROW FUNCTION 226
USING THE ROW FUNCTION 226
THE INDEX FUNCTION... 229
The Array Format of The INDEX Function 229

USING THE ARRAY FORMAT OF THE INDEX FUNCTION 230
THE REFERENCE FORMAT OF THE INDEX FUNCTION 231
USING THE REFERENCE FORMAT OF THE INDEX FUNCTION 232

CHAPTER THIRTEEN 235

TEXT FUNCTIONS 235

THE FIND FUNCTION 235
USING THE FIND FUNCTION 235
CONCATENATE FUNCTION 238
USING THE CONCATENATE FUNCTION IN EXCEL 238
ADDING SPACE, COMMA, QUOTATION MARK, HYPHEN USING THE CONCATENATE FUNCTION 239
THE TEXTJOIN FUNCTION 241
USING THE TEXTJOIN FUNCTION 241
TRIM FUNCTION 242
USING THE TRIM FUNCTION 243
THE UPPER FUNCTION 244
USING THE UPPER FUNCTION 244
THE LOWER FUNCTION 245
USING THE LOWER FUNCTION 245
THE PROPER FUNCTION 246
USING THE PROPER FUNCTION 247
LEN FUNCTION 248
USING THE LEN FUNCTION 248
THE LENB FUNCTION 249
USING THE LENB FUNCTION 249
MID Function 250
USING THE MID FUNCTION 251
THE MIDB FUNCTION 252
USING THE MIDB FUNCTION 252
LEFT FUNCTION 253
USING THE LEFT FUNCTION 253
THE LEFTB FUNCTION 254
USING THE LEFTB FUNCTION 255
THE RIGHT FUNCTION 256
USING THE RIGHT FUNCTION 256
THE RIGHTB FUNCTION 257
USING THE RIGHTB FUNCTION 258

CHAPTER FOURTEEN 260

DATE AND TIME FUNCTION 260

THE DATE FORMAT 260
DATA PARAMETER 261
CUSTOMIZING A DATE 261
THE DAY FUNCTION 262

ix

- USING THE DAY FUNCTION...262
- THE MONTH FUNCTION..263
- USING THE MONTH FUNCTION 263
- THE YEAR FUNCTION 264
- USING THE YEAR FUNCTION 265
- THE DATE FUNCTION 266
- USING THE DATE FUNCTION 266
- THE DATEDIF FUNCTION..268
- USING THE DATEDIF FUNCTION 269
- THE DAYS FUNCTION 271
- USING THE DAYS FUNCTION 271
- THE EDATE FUNCTION 272
- USING THE EDATE FUNCTION...273
- THE DATEVALUE FUNCTION..275
- USING THE DATEVALUE FUNCTION 275
- THE NETWORKDAYS FUNCTION 277
- USING THE WORKDAYS FUNCTION 277
- THE NOW FUNCTION 278
- USING THE NOW FUNCTION...279
- THE TODAY FUNCTION 279
- USING THE TODAY FUNCTION 280
- THE TIME FUNCTION 281
- USING THE TIME FUNCTION 281

CHAPTER FIFTEEN 284

THE EXCEL POWER QUERY..284

- WHAT IS POWER QUERY?...284
- WHERE IS THE POWER QUERY LOCATED?..284
- What Can Power Query Do?...284
- SOURCES OF POWER QUERY DATA 285
- IMPORTING DATA SOURCE USING POWER QUERY 285
- IMPORTING A SINGLE DATA SOURCE FROM THE WORKBOOK 285
- IMPORTING DATA FROM MULTIPLE DATA SOURCES IN A WORKBOOK.......286
- IMPORTING DATA FROM A CSV FILE 288
- IMPORTING DATA FROM A TEXT FILE 289
- POWER QUERY EDITOR 290

CHAPTER SIXTEEN..291

EXCEL SHORTCUTS, TIPS & TRICKS 291

- EXCEL SHORTCUTS...291
- EXCEL TIPS AND TRICKS 296
- HOW TO USE IDEAS 296
- HOW TO REMOVE BLANKS FROM A WORKSHEET..297
- HOW TO REMOVE DUPLICATE DATA FROM EXCEL WORKBOOK..................299
- TRANSPOSING ON YOUR WORKSHEET 300

HOW TO ADD TEXT TO COLUMNS... 301
HOW TO INSERT SCREENSHOT TO YOUR EXCEL WORKBOOK 302
HOW TO INSERT MULTIPLES ROWS 303
HOW TO CREATE PEOPLE GRAPH.. 304
HOW TO HIGHLIGHT TEXT AND NUMBERS 305
HOW TO HIGHLIGHT CELLS THAT HAVE FORMULAS... 308
HOW TO GET DATA FROM THE INTERNET 310
RENAMING A SHEET WITH A DOUBLE CLICK... 312
CHANGING THE CASE OF A TEXT... 312
FORMING A TEXT WITH & 312
HOW TO MAKE EXCEL SHOW LEADING ZERO 313
EXTENDING FORMULA DOWN 313
CHANGING HOW ENTER WORKS 314
QUICK SELECT FORMULAS.. 314
DISABLING THE EXCEL START SCREEN.. 315
ACTIVATING CURRENT DATE AND TIME 315
CUSTOMIZING THE STATUS BAR 316
DELETING ERRORS CELLS.. 316
STRIKING THROUGH TEXTS IN EXCEL 317
HOW TO CLEAR FORMATTING 317
SHARING DATA ONLINE ON EXCEL 317
CONCLUSION 319
ABOUT THE AUTHOR... 320

PREFACE

As you will be taking your time to go through this user guide for Excel 2020, there are lots of stuffs to learn. The truth is, you don't have to be a computer expert in other to make use of this user guide for Excel 2020.

Here in this book, you will be learning the fundamentals of Excel which entails what Excel is all about, its uses, and how it can be manipulated.

In the course of going through this book, you will be exposed to the basic operations on Excel which include understanding the worksheet, working with cells and also how to format the cells.

Not only that, you will be exposed to variety of formulas and functions used in Excel and the new functions added in Excel 2020. You will also get to learn how to insert formulas and functions while working on the Excel sheet and other formatting features available to the use of formulas and functions.

Features like creating of charts, changing of chart layouts and types, how to add title in charts, resizing the chart sizes and other formatting features associated with charts will be explicitly explained as you take your time to go through this guide.

Finally, there are tips and tricks to learn which will enhance your effectiveness in the use of this software. Some of the tricks and trips are shortcuts and some operations that seem very hard but in the real sense, they are very easy to perform.

Having stated what you get to gain by going through this user guide, I am sure you don't want to miss out of this golden opportunity.

See you in the next section!

INTRODUCTION

Microsoft Excel is one of the most used software applications in the world today and it comes together with some other applications found in the Microsoft office suite. This app replaced Lotus 1-2-3 as the industry standard for spreadsheets majorly because of its adaptive and flexible features.

The Microsoft Excel has become an application that is sought after in big organizations in the world today because of its features to carry out some mathematical, financial and statistical operations that could have become cumbersome when done manually and with the use of Microsoft Excel, time and energy are saved for more productive works.

Currently, with the way the world is evolving, business organizations are not just looking for a person who is computer literate rather a person who has vast knowledge on how to use Microsoft Excel and more of a reason as an individual, you can't afford to lose a job opportunity because of you lack the skills to use of Microsoft Excel.

With researches made so far, it has been discovered that Microsoft excel is one of those applications' executive heads and heads of departments must train their staff to get accustomed to ensure the smooth running of such organization and not only that, to boost the work efficiency of the organization within and outside the organizations.

Truth be told, Microsoft Excel is not an easy application to learn and use and most people find it difficult to use but guess what? In this user guide, Microsoft Excel will be taught in a way that you can easily comprehend and use.

I wish you a safe trip as you take a ride to exploring this book

CHAPTER ONE

INTRODUCTION TO MICROSOFT EXCEL 2020

Excel 2020 is one of the latest applications developed by Microsoft Corporation itself with some features that have made it stand out from every other version that has been developed so far. In case you are a novice, let's quickly take a tour to what Excel is all about before diving into Excel 2020 and its basic operations.

WHAT IS EXCEL?

Excel is an application software that provides worksheets with rows and columns that helps to organize data. Space where the rows and columns intersect is known to be the cell. The Excel software was created by Microsoft Corporation and comes with the Microsoft Office Suite.

This tool is used for organizing and performing calculations and data, calculate statistics, generate pivot tables and display data in form of line graphs, histograms, and charts with a very limited three-dimension graphical display. With the Excel software, you can calculate monthly budgets, prepare payroll, track associated expenses and sort out data based on their categories or criteria.

This software is widely used these days by almost everyone because of its capacity to save time and energy and this application gives room for the updating of its features as well as introducing new features through Office 365 from time to time in a year. Researchers have proven so far that big organization in the world are ardent users of this application.

Initially, Excel was code named to be Odyssey while it was being developed before it was released on September 30, 1985.

USES OF EXCEL

Excel is one of the apps in the Microsoft Office Suite has a lot of advantages which cannot be overemphasized and here we will be talking about a few of them.

Analyzing and storing data: One of the uses of MS Excel is that it allows you to analyze data and break them down in such a way that they are displayed in form of graphs and charts in a well-organized and understood manner for its end purpose. Also, the organized data are stored systematically.

Data recovery: With the way this software is configured, it helps to recover lost or damaged file data with less or no stress.

Mathematical formulas: MS Excel allows one to tackle complex mathematical problems in a simpler and well-understood manner with less or little effort. Not only that, but MS Excel also contains a lot of mathematical formulas needed to perform the basic mathematical operation.

Security: With MS Excel, you can keep your files secure and also password them using visual basic programming or by directly securing them within the Excel file.

Online storage and access: MS excel being an outshoot of Office 365, gives the users the ability to access their files online and by implication, it means that they don't have to go around with their computers rather, they can access their files anytime anywhere using any device compatible with the use of MS excel.

Financial data: You can create your financial data like checking account, information, budgets, taxes, transactions, payrolls, invoices, receipts, forecast and the likes with the use of Excel

Forms: You can as well create form templates for handling inventory, evaluations, performance, reviews, questionnaires, timesheet, etc.

School grade or result: With Excel, teachers can create a grade sheet that helps calculate the students' grades as well as monitoring their academic performance.

Bringing of data together: This software helps to bring together different kinds of Files and documents in one location. Also, texts and images can be imported from other locations into one location with the other files and documents.

WHAT'S NEW IN EXCEL 2020?

It's no doubt that some new features have been added to the Microsoft Excel 2020 and for this study, we will be discussing the features that have made it different from other previous versions of Excel.

Automate data analyses with Excel's ideas: Ideas is one of the newly added features in Excel 2020 that helps to analyze data quickly and provides the insight needed for the data analyses. To locate Ideas in Excel, go to the Home tab of the Ribbon. Keep this in mind; you need to be actively connected to the internet to use this feature.

XLOOKUP in replacement of VLOOKUP: The XLOOKUP feature is a replacement of VLOOKUP. The XLOOKUP feature is a function used when you need to find things in a table or a range by row. Unlike the VLOOKUO that gives an appropriate match of what is being searched, the XLOOKUP gives the exact match of what is being searched for. It also allows you to search for data anywhere in the data entry.

The following syntax comes with the XLOOKUP function,

=XLOOKUP (lookup value, lookup array, return array).

Dynamic arrays: This is another feature of Excel that allows you to write a single formula that affects multiples cells simultaneously without the need to copy the formula one by one to all the cells.

In this feature, the following are made available; Filter, Sort, Sequence, Sort By, Randary and Unique.

MICROSOFT EXCEL TERMINOLOGIES

Workbook

The workbook refers to an Excel spreadsheet file. The workbook stores all of the data that you have entered and allows you to sort or calculate the results. A workbook that is accessible to be viewed and modified by multiple users on a network is called a Shared Workbook.

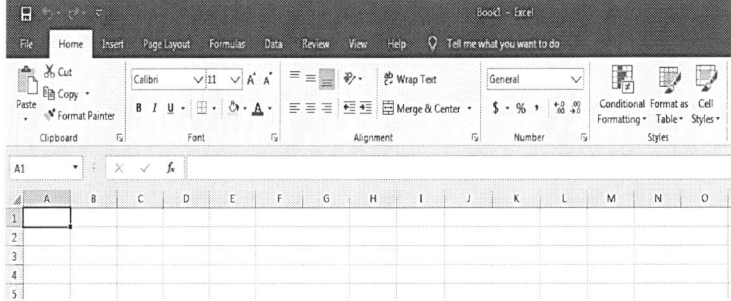

Worksheet

A worksheet is a sub-component document of a workbook. It is also called spreadsheets; you can have multiple sheets nestled in a workbook.

Tabs at the bottommost of the screen will indicate which of your worksheets you are presently working on; this is also known as an active sheet or active worksheet.

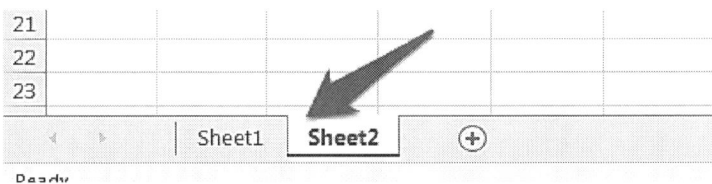

Cell

A cell is an intersection between a column and a row on a spreadsheet. Each cell in a spreadsheet can encompass any value that can be called using a virtual cell reference or called upon using a formula. Any data that you want to enter into your worksheet must be put in a cell. An Active Cell is one that is currently opened for editing.

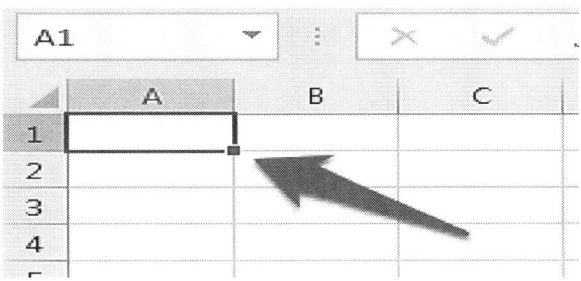

Columns and Rows

Columns and Rows refer to how your cells are aligned. Rows are aligned horizontally while columns are aligned vertically.

Column and Row Headings

These headings are the lettered and numbered gray areas located just outside of columns and rows. Clicking on a heading will select the entire row or column. You can also modify the row height or column width using the headings.

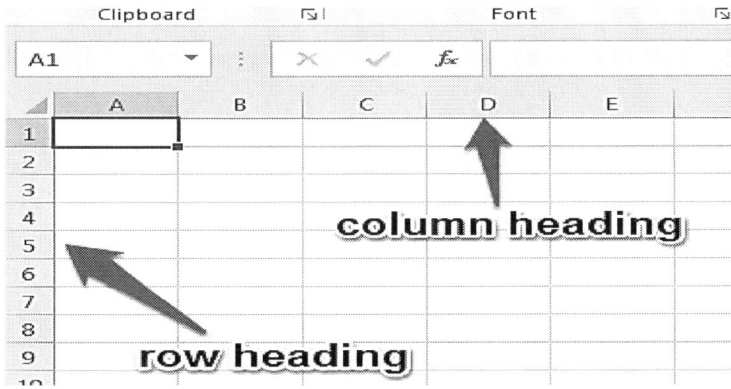

Workspace

Just like worksheets in a workbook, a workspace allows you to simultaneously open numerous files.

Ribbon

Above the workbook is a segment of command tabs known as the ribbon. A multitude of options is found behind each tab of the ribbon.

Cell Reference

A cell reference is a set of coordinates that classifies a specific cell. It's a combination of letters and numbers. For example, B3 would point to the cell situated where column B and row 3 intersect.

Cell Range

A Cell range is a cluster of cells that have been identified as a group based on a variety of criteria. By using a colon (:) between cell references. Excel can determine the range, also called an array. A range in a row, for example, could look like A3: D3, telling the formula to look at the cells in a row between A3 and D3, while C4: F9 would tell the formula to look at all cells in a box bounded by columns C and F and rows 4 and 9. A 3-D reference refers to a range that encompasses more than one worksheet in the same workbook.

Merged Cell

When two or more cells are united, it becomes what is known as a *merged cell.*

Template

A template is a formatted workbook or worksheet intended to help users fulfill a specific need in Excel. Examples of this include stock analysis, process map and calendar.

Operator

Operators are signs or symbols that specify which calculation must be made in an expression. Operators do not necessarily refer to simple mathematical types; comparison, concatenation, text or reference operators also exist.

Formula

A sequence inside a cell that is used to produce value is called formula. It must begin with an

equality sign (=). This could be a mathematical equation, functions, cell references, or operator. A formula is also known as an expression.

Formula Bar

Nestled between the workbook and ribbon, the Formula Bar will display the contents of an active cell. In the case of formulas, the formula bar will display all components of the formula.

Function

Functions are formulas that are pre-built into Excel. They are intended to help simplify hypothetically complex formulas in a worksheet.

Cell Formatting

This is the act of changing how a cell or its contents are displayed in the spreadsheet. When you format cells, only the visual appearance of the cells is altered; the value within the cells remains the same.

Error Code

Error Codes appear if Excel finds a problem with a formula provided.

Filter

Filters are guidelines that you can employ to choose which rows in a worksheet to display. These filters can use data such as conditions or values.

AutoFill

This enables you to copy data to more than one cell easily.

AutoSum

This feature will add up the numbers you have entered

in your sheet and displays the total in a cell of your choice.

AutoFormat

This is an automatic format application to cells that match pre-determined conditions. This could be as simple as size.

Data Validation

This feature helps to avert inappropriate data from being entered into your worksheet. Data validation promotes accuracy and consistency in the data to be entered.

Pivot Table

This is a data summarization tool most commonly used to sort, average, to sum up, data automatically. The information is heaved from one table while the results are presented in another.

Pivot Chart

This type of chart provides a visual aid for pivot tables by providing graphical illustrations of the pivot table data; the user can offer a level of interactivity with the data.

Pivot Area

The pivot area is a point on the worksheet where you would drag a Pivot Table field to rearrange how a report is displayed.

Source Data

This is the information used to create your pivot table. It can either exist within the worksheet or from an external database.

Values Area

In a pivot table, Value areas are recognized as the cells that contain the instantaneous information.

Item

These are sub-categories of fields in the pivot table. If you have an area that is marked Country, the items could be the United States of America, Italy and so on.

EXCEL TOOLS

There are certain tools found in Excel, that has made the use of Excel more convenient and productive, briefly, we shall be talking about them.

Excel add-in: These are mini software that are installed into Excel to provide additional features that are not available in Excel itself. When these add-ins are added, they are located among the ribbon tools. These add-ins are developed by a third party. Examples of Excel add-ins are Filter Mate, PivotPal, Tab Hound, Paste Buddy, etc.

EXCEL FILE TYPES

The file types or extensions in Excel are very important because they provide you with information about the files before opening and allows you to save your files weather as macro-enabled files, binary files, templates, etc.

Excel workbook (.xlsx): This is the default XML-based file format for Excel 2010 and Excel 2010. This cannot save Microsoft Visual Basic for Applications (VBA) macro code or Microsoft Office Excel 4.0 macro sheet (.xlm), Xlsx files organize data in cells which are stored in worksheets and are later stored in the workbook.

- **Excel macro-enabled workbook (.xlsm):** The XML file is a macro-enabled spreadsheet for Excel 2020, Excel 365, Excel 2019, Excel 2016, Excel 2013, Excel 2010, and Excel 2007. This also contains embedded macro programmed in the Visual Basic for Application (VBA) language.
- **Excel binary worksheet (.xlsb):** This is the binary format for Excel 2010 and Excel 2007. This file format is used to create and edit a spreadsheet and it is used more than the XLSX format because it compressed to save space and it is also easier to share among users.
- **Template (.xltx):** This is a template also used for creating spreadsheets and it contains default settings and layout information used to create XLSX files. This file format cannot store Microsoft Visual Basic for Applications (VBA) macro code or Microsoft Office Excel 4.0 macro sheet. It is used to create multiple spreadsheets with common formatting and properties. With the XLTX file format, you can create documents like budgets, calendars, inventories, etc.
- **Template (.xltm):** This file format contains default settings and layout for creating micro- enabled sheets that are used in turn to create a macro-enabled workbook in Excel 2007 and Excel 2010. This Excel's file format also stores Visual Basic Application or Excel 4.0 macro sheets.

- **Excel 97- Excel 2003 workbook (.xls):** This is the default file format for Excel 2003 and it is also known as Binary Interchange File Format (BIFF).
- **Excel 97- Excel 2003 template (.xlt):** This is a template also used for creating spreadsheets and it contains default settings and layout information used to create new.XLT files and the files are saved in Excel Binary File Format.

The following are other types of Excel Files:

- Microsoft Excel 5.0/95 Workbook (.xls)
- XML Spreadsheet 2003 (.xml)
- XML Data (.xml)
- Excel Add-in (.xlam)
- Excel 4.0 (.xlw)
- Works 6.0-9.0 spreadsheet

WHERE CAN I GET MICROSOFT EXCEL?

You might have been wondering where and how you can get Microsoft Excel installed on your computer. Your days of worries are finally over. To get Microsoft Excel, there are just three ways to go about it:

- **Web Version:** You can access Microsoft Excel and any other related Office programs free on the web, and to do this, all you need is to have a Microsoft account and head to **https://www.office.com** to sign up for the free version of the app. Provided you have done this, you will be presented with the screen below to choose any app you wish to run
- **Mobile Version:** You can also get Microsoft Excel on your Android, Windows, and Apple mobile devices. To get the app on your Android devices, visit the Google Play store. For Windows devices, visit Microsoft Store and for Apple devices, visit the Apple Store.
- **Desktop Version:** You can also get Microsoft Excel and any other related Office programs on your computer. To access it, visit **https://www.office.com** on your web browser and then go to **Get**

Office to see the versions of Microsoft Excel available. You will have to pay for the apps before you can use them. However, the Home version is just a trial version of 30 days and when it expires, you will have to upgrade it by paying

CHAPTER TWO

THE BASIC OPERATIONS ON EXCEL 2020

LAUNCHING AND QUITTING EXCEL 2020 FROM THE WINDOW

Before you launching Excel 2020 on your computer, it is expedient to understand the recommended Windows version that is permitted for it to run on is Windows 10. So, if you are using a computer with Windows 7 and 8 on it, you will need to upgrade your computer Window to Windows 10 before you can successfully install this app on it. To do this, you can visit your computer technician or go to Microsoft Office Centre to get your computer updated to the current Window.

STARTING YOUR EXCEL FROM WINDOW 10

There are different ways of starting Excel on your computer with Window 10 and we will be discussing them now.

Start button

You can launch your Excel by using the Start button using the procedure below:

- Click on the Windows icon on the screen
- Scroll downward on the alphabetical lists of apps until you locate Excel.

Search text box

Instead of opening the Window 10 Start menu, you can launch the Excel 2020 by:

- Locating the Search text box beside the Window button and type in the keyword
- Then click on enter and the app will display for launching.

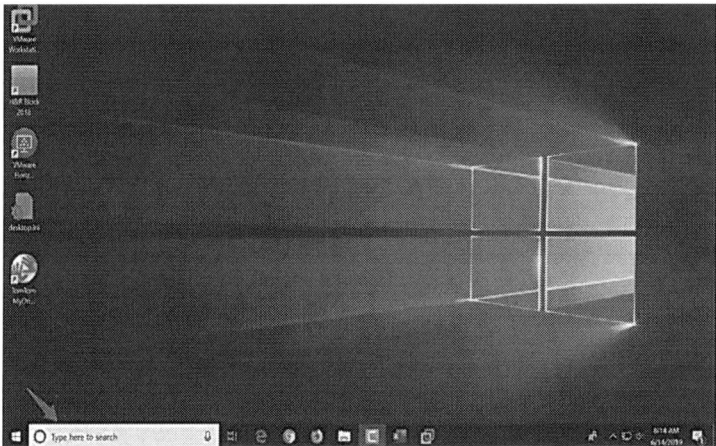

NOTE: You can also pin the app to the taskbar for easy location and to do this, right-click on the Excel program in the Start menu and then click on Pin to the Start item.

QUITTING EXCEL

In case you are done using your Excel and you wish to quit or close your Excel program, follow these simple procedures:

Press *Alt+F4* Or

Click on the Close button in the upper-right corner of the Excel Program Window.

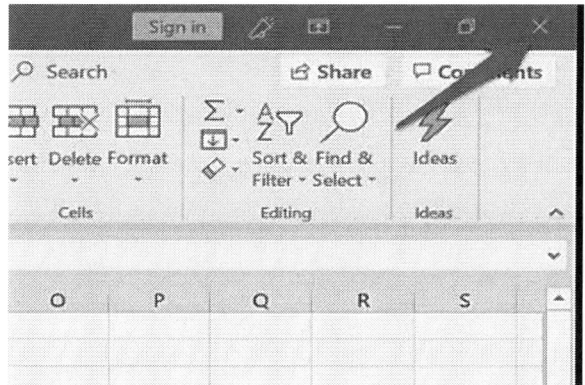

EXCEL'S START SCREEN

When you launch the Excel program, what displays on the screen is called the Start screen. This screen is divided into two; the right panel and the left panel.

The left panel has a green color with the Home icon selected which contains New Open items at the top, an Account, Feedback and options at the bottom.

The right panel shows a list of thumbnails that contains varieties of templates that can be used. Most importantly is the on the right panel is the Blank workbook which is used to open a new blank Excel workbook file.

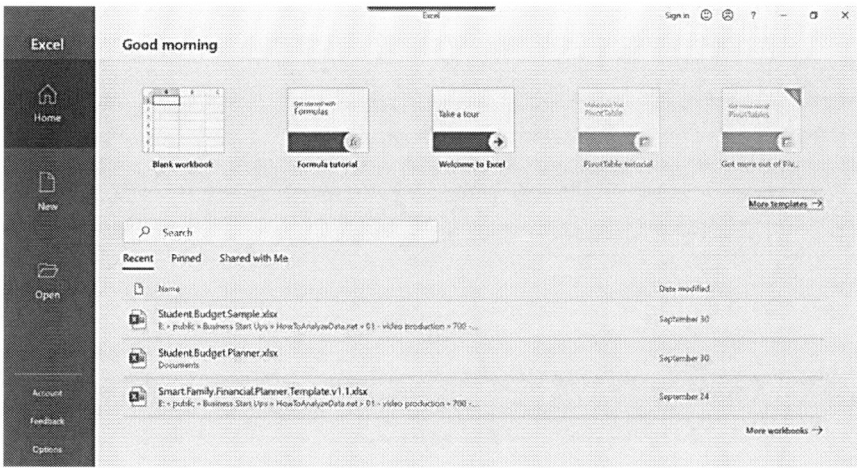

EXCEL'S RIBBON USER INTERFACE

When you open a new blank workbook, there are some features on the workbook which are necessary to work with on the blank page and these features are Excel's Ribbon interface and they are listed below into four categories:

File menu button: When you open this feature, what displays here are New, Open, Save As, Share, Export, Publish, Close and Account, and other options that allow you change the Excel's default settings

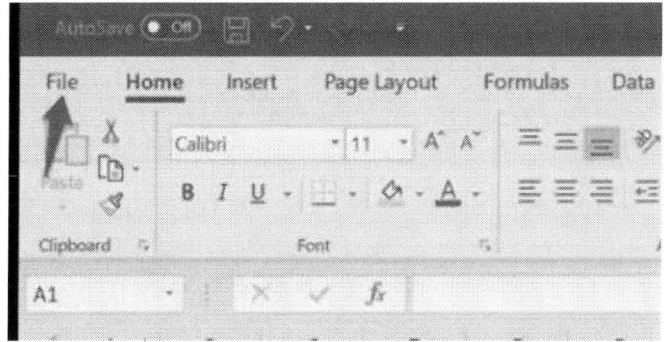

Quick Access toolbar: This is where features like AutoSave, Save, Undo and Redo are found

Ribbon: Most commands needed in Excel are found in the ribbon. They are arranged in the form of tabs from the Home through View.

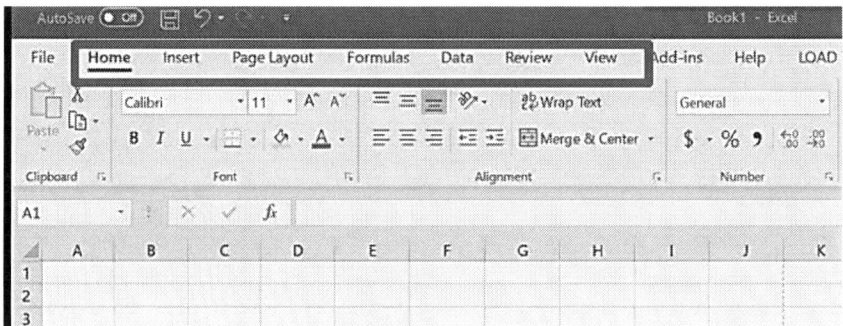

Formula bar: This shows the address of the cell being worked on alongside the content of the cell.

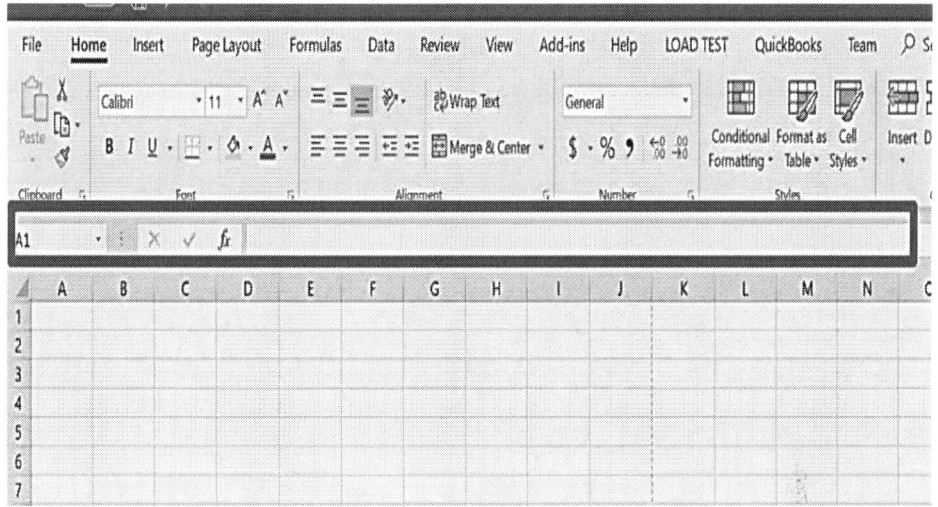

Worksheet area: This is where all the cells currently worked on are displayed for all to see with a column heading which uses letters and a row heading with numbers.

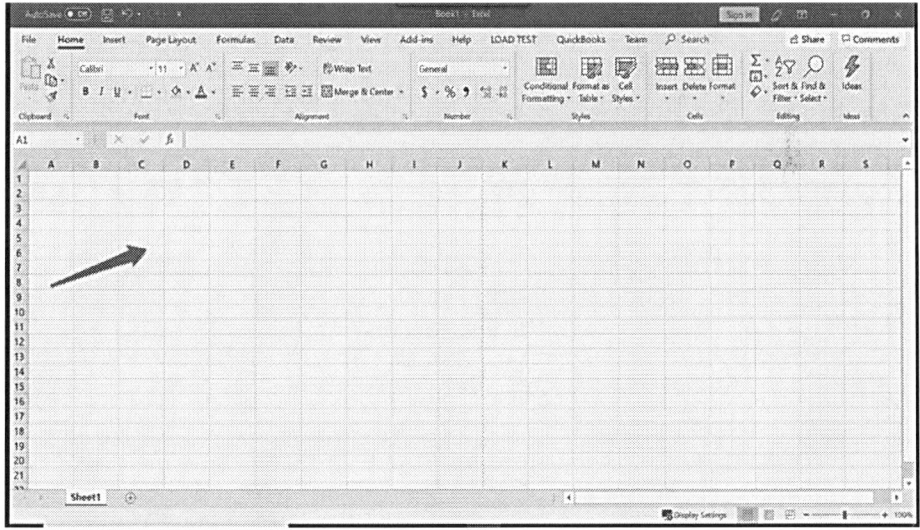

Status bar: This displays the current mode of the program and allows you to perform special operations on the worksheet. You can open a new blank worksheet with this tool as well as zooming in and zooming out.

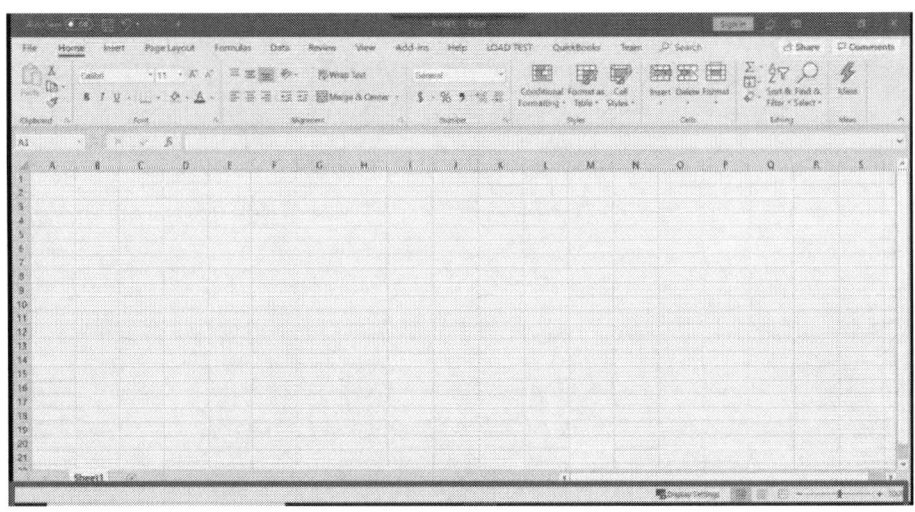

UNDERSTANDING THE WORKBOOK

We will be taking a tour on how to work on a workbook. Keep this in mind, every operation carried out on the Excel program is done right on the workbook.

The data inputted such as letters, numbers or formulas are stored on the workbook and the workbook there lies the worksheet.

A worksheet is found in a workbook and it contains 16,384 columns that are labeled by the letters of the alphabet and also contains 1,048,576 are labeled by number 1 to 1,048,576.

CREATING A NEW WORKSHEET

To create a new workbook on your Excel:

- Launch your Excel program to display the Excel start screen.
- Then click on New.

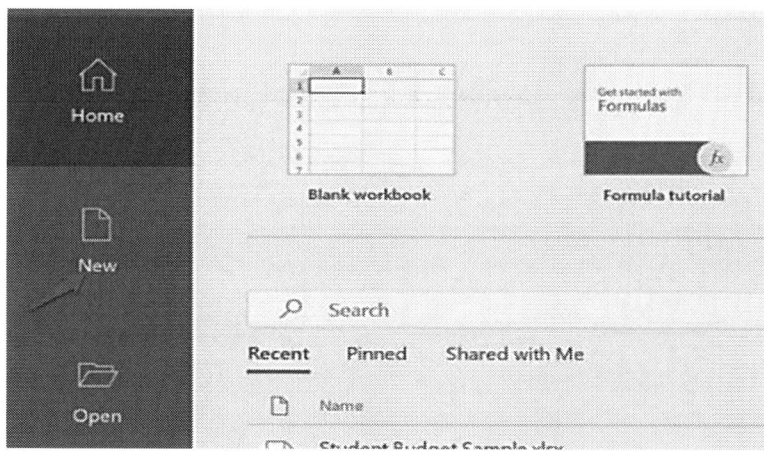

RENAMING A WORKSHEET

When you open a new Excel workbook, the default name given to it is Sheet1. You can however change the name to the one you desire and to do this,

- Right-click on the worksheet you want to rename

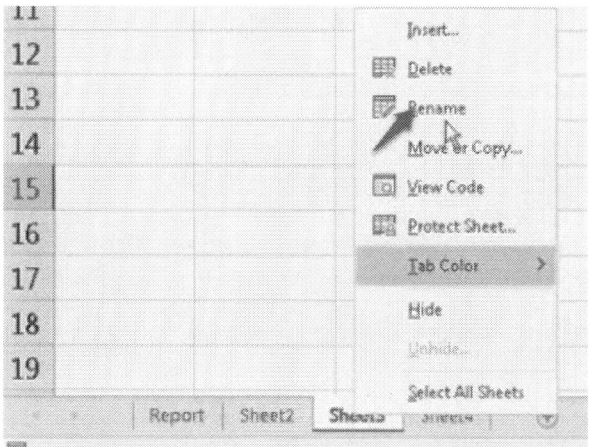

- Select the Rename option and type in the name you wish to change to and then click on enter

INSERTING A NEW WORKSHEET

To insert a new worksheet all you have to do is click on the + icon beside the worksheet.

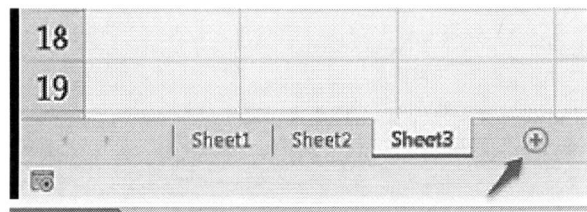

Now you can see that the new sheet has been added below in the picture

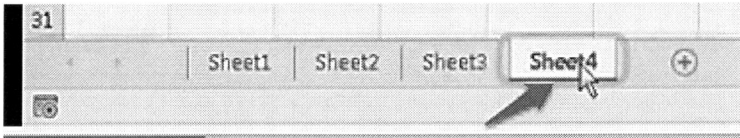

DELETING A WORKSHEET

To delete a worksheet, all you have to do is:

- Right-click on the worksheet you intend to delete

- Select the Delete option and the worksheet will be deleted from the workbook

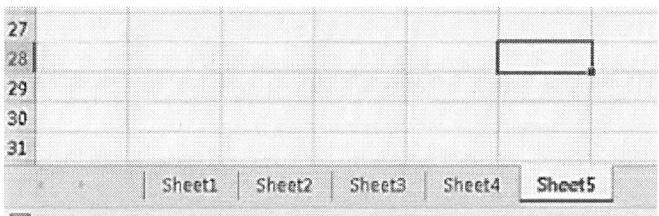

COPYING OR MOVING A WORKSHEET

You can move or copy a worksheet with a workbook. To do this, simply follow these simple instructions:

- Right-click on the worksheet you desire to move or copy
- Click on the Copy or Move option and the location will be changed

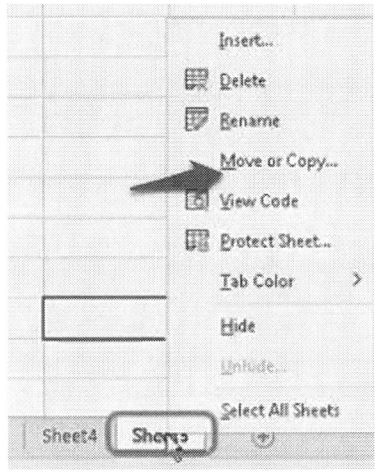

NOTE: *In case you only wish to move and not copy, all you have to do is drag the worksheet to the location you.*

CHANGING THE WORKSHEET COLOUR

You can change the colour of your worksheet by following this instruction:

- Right-click on the worksheet you desire to change its colour

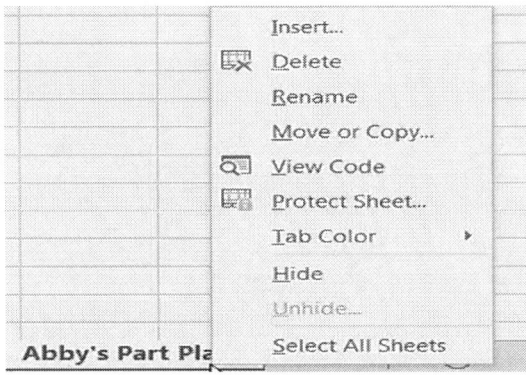

- Click on Tab colour and select the colour you want and press enter.

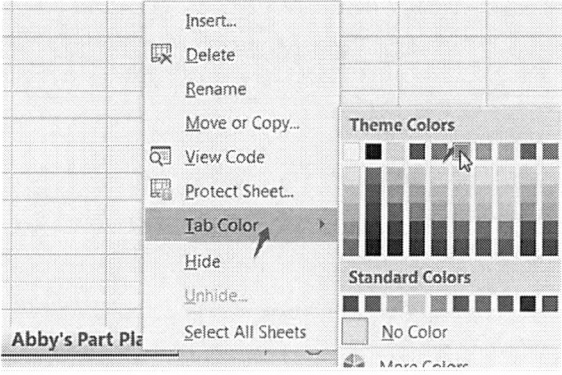

SAVING YOUR DOCUMENT

There are two different ways of saving a document in the Excel program after working on a workbook and briefly, we will explain both.

- **Save:** The save option is used when you edit a workbook that has already been on your computer. This option allows you to save the new changes made on your document. Here you don't need to create a file name and location to save.
- **Save As:** This option is used when a new document is created. Here you will need to create the file name and the location of the file. You can as well use this command to make a copy of a document but you will still need to choose a different name and location for the copied version to avoid overriding the old copied version.

To save using these commands

- Go to the Quick Access Toolbar and select the Save command.

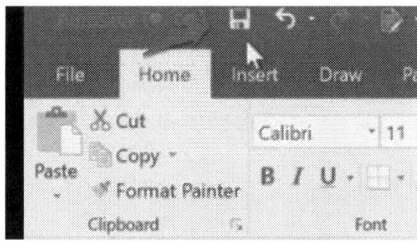

- If you are saving for the first time, click on Save As (here you will be required to create a file name and location) and if not click on Save

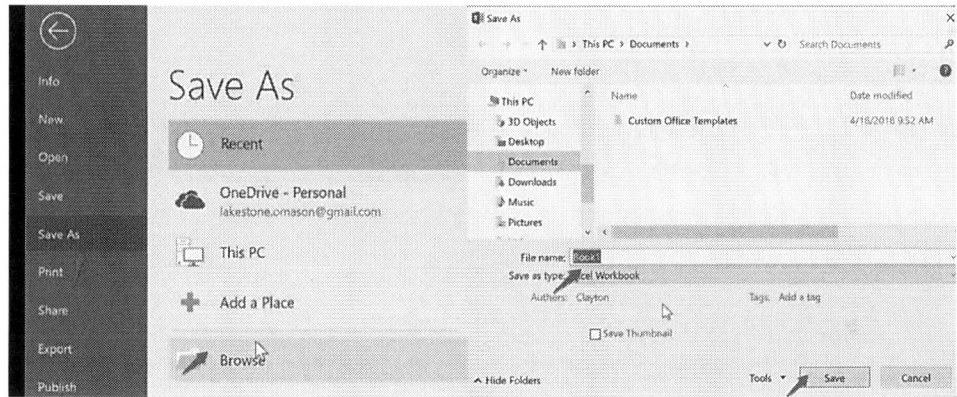

NOTE: *You can as well save your document on your OneDrive provided you sign in into Excel with your Microsoft account.*

HOW TO RECOVER YOUR DOCUMENT USING AUTOSAVE

Let's assume you lost a document and you are on how to get it, there are features made available in the Excel program that allows you to recover any lost document. All you need to do is follow the steps below:

- Relaunch your Excel program
- At the left-hand side of your workbook, click on the recovered version of the document you want.

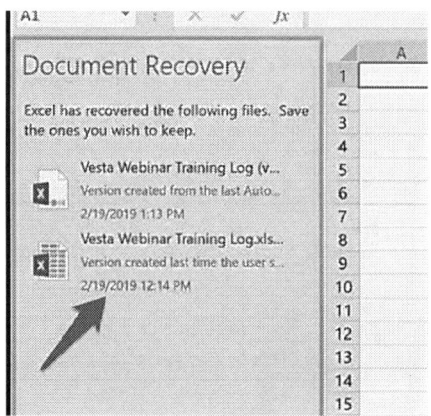

NOTE: *The Excel program autosaves your documents every 10 minutes and if your computer crashes before that time, the documents may be completely lost.*

EXPORTING WORKBOOKS

By default, the Excel workbooks are saved in the file format .xlsx. However, there are times there will be the need to use another file type or probably to a lesser version of the Excel program. Do not fret, all you need is to follow these simple steps:

- Open the backstage view of the Excel program and click on Export
- Then go to Create Pdf/XPS Document.

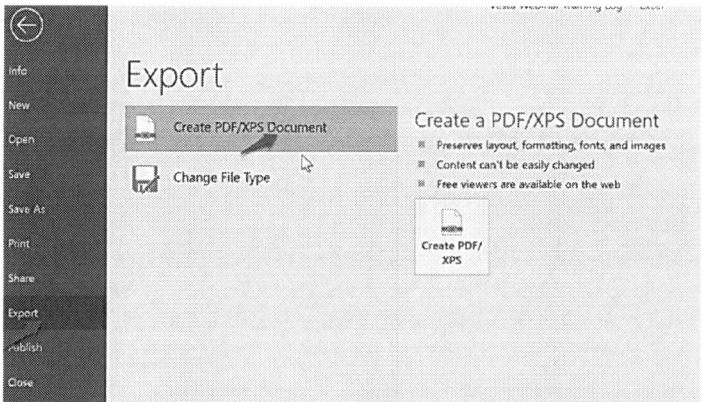

- In case you want to change the file type, go to Change File Type.

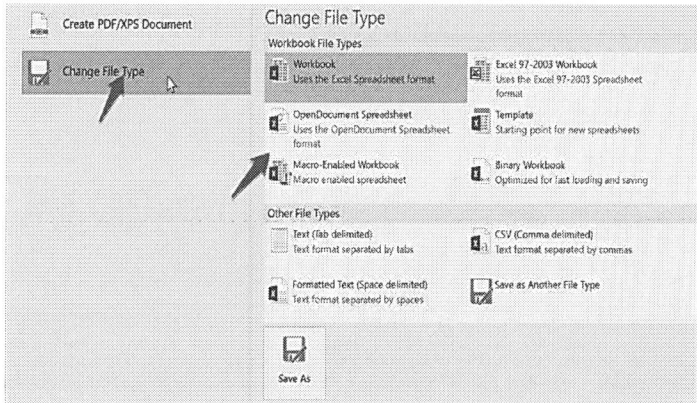

HOW TO SHARE EXCEL WORKBOOK

In case you need to share your Excel workbook to another user, all you have to do is:

- Click on the Share button on the top right corner of the Excel worksheet

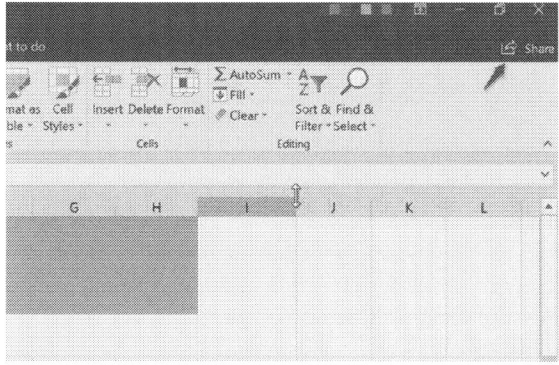

- Upload your file to OneDrive

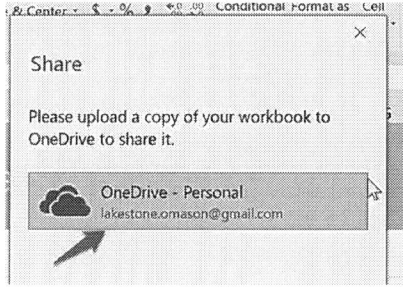

- Once it is uploaded, you can email an invitation link to your contacts to view or edit the documents.

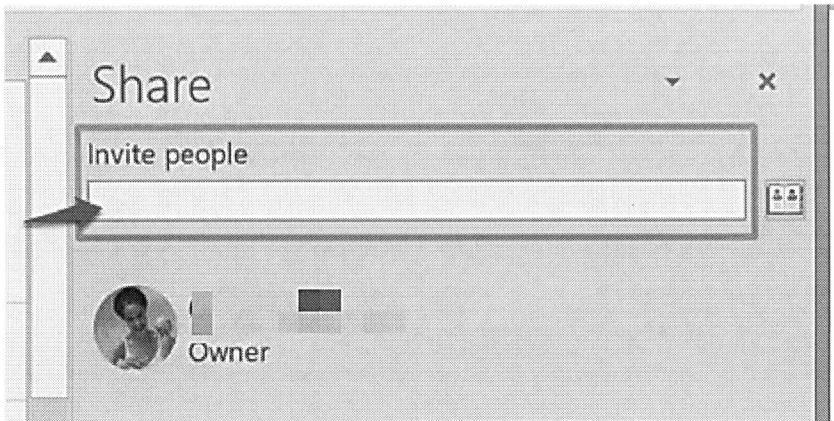

NOTE: *You can as well share files by sending the files as an attachment or sending a sharing link to access the files. Just move downward on the page where you sent the invite link to get the image below*

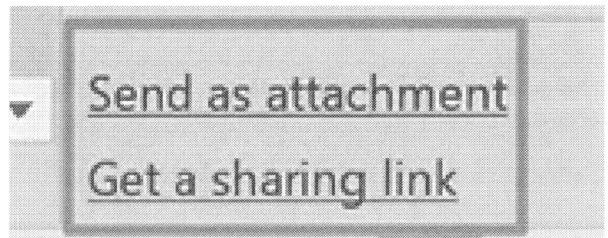

UNDERSTANDING THE CELL

The cell is where the information on the worksheet is entered. The worksheet contains thousands of rectangles that are known to be the cells. The cell, on the other hand, is an intersection of a row and a column. The Columns are tagged with letter of the alphabet (A, B, C, etc.) while the rows are tagged with numerical values (1, 2, 3, etc.)

Whenever you work with Excel, you'll enter information or content into cells. Cells are the basic building blocks of a worksheet. You'll need to learn the basics of cells and cell content to calculate, analyze and organize data in Excel.

WHAT'S A CELL?

Every worksheet is made up of thousands of rectangles which are called cells. A cell is the intersection of a row and a column. Columns are identified by letters (A, B, C), while rows are identified by numbers (1, 2, 3)

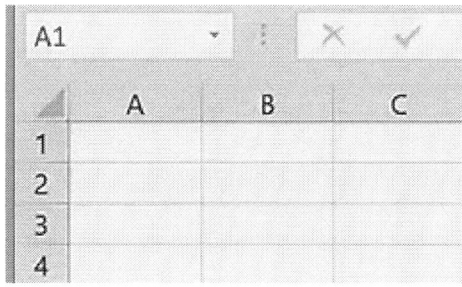

Every cell on the worksheet has its name or cell address and this is displayed at the top left corner of the worksheet

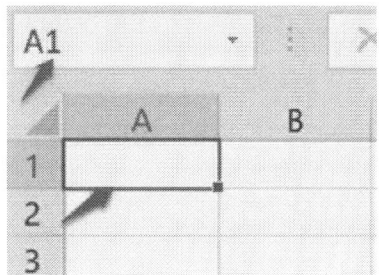

A group of cells is known as cell range; the cell range is the combination of more than two cells and for example, the cell range is written in this manner **A1: A5** or **B1: B5**

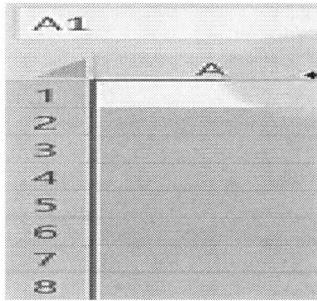

To select a cell range,

- Click, hold and drag the mouse to the cells you wish to highlight
- Release the mouse and select the cell range you desire.

INSERTING CONTENTS IN A CELL

To insert a content be it letter or numbers, all you need to do is:

- Click on the cell you wish to type into

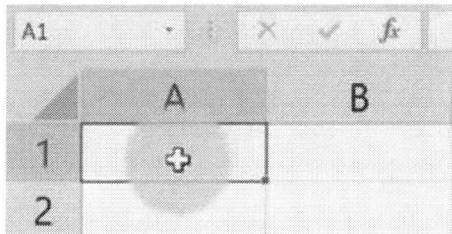

- Type the content into the cell and press Enter and the content will appear in the cell and also on the formula bar

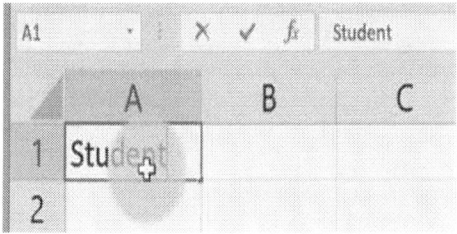

NOTE: You can delete the content of the cell by:

- *Selecting the cell content to be delete*
- *Press the Delete or Backspace to delete*

HOW TO DELETE A CELL

To delete a cell from the worksheet:

- Select the cell you wish to delete

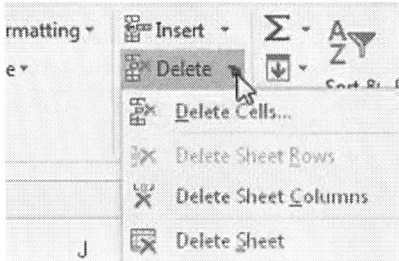

- Select the Delete command from the Home tab from the Ribbon and follow the option that suits you

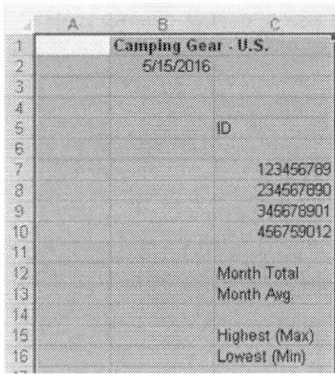

- After doing this, the cell will automatically shift up by itself.

COPYING AND PASTING CELL CONTENT

To perform this operation;

- Select the cell content you wish to copy

- Go to Copy command on the Home tab (you can use ctrl+C for this operation)

- Then select the area you wish to paste the content and then click on Paste on the Home tab. Keep this in mind that the copied cell will have a dashed box around them for identification (you can also use ctrl+ V to paste).

DRAGGING AND DROPPING THE CELL

To save you the stress of cutting, copying and pasting of the cells, you use the dragging and dropping method to move your contents from one cell to the other. To do this, all you need to do is:

- Select the cells you desire to move
- Move the mouse on the border of the cells you have selected and drop the cells to get their contents moved
- Click, hold and drag the cells to the desired location
- Release the mouse and the cells will be moved to the desired location.

USING THE FILL HANDLE IN A CELL

The fill handle in Excel helps save the stress of copying the content from a cell to other cells in a worksheet. With the fill handle, you can quickly copy and paste the content of a cell to adjacent cells within the same row or column.

To use the fill handle:

- Select the cell you wish to duplicate its content and the fill handle appears as a small square in the bottom right corner of the selected cell

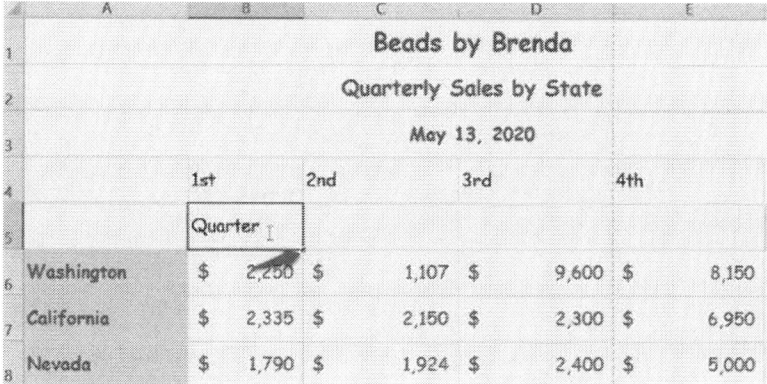

- Click, hold and drag the fill handle until all the cells you wish to fill are duplicated

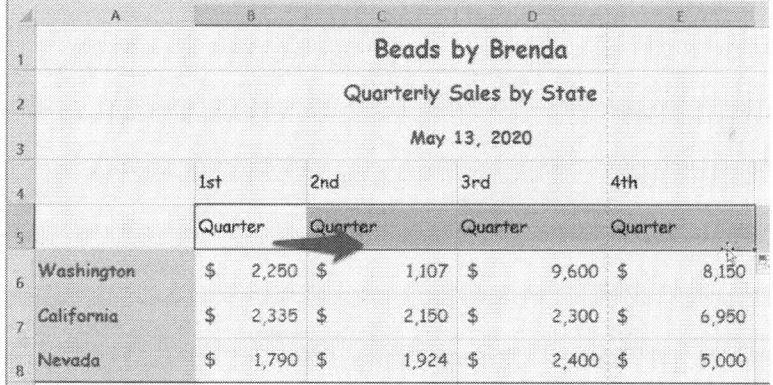

- Then release the mouse to fill the selected cell

You can as well use the fill handle to continue a series in the form of numbers (1,2,3) or days (Monday, Tuesday, Wednesday). In most cases, you will need to select more than one cell before this fill handle can work.

The pictures below will give us a clearer illustration of how to continue a series with the fill handle

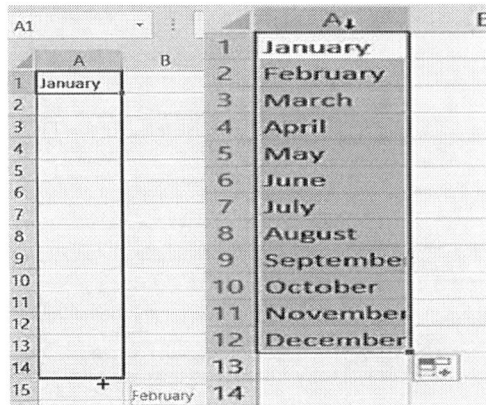

FORMATTING THE CELL

There are a lot of features available for formatting the cells and here we will be discussing on how to apply these features with simple guidelines.

CHANGING THE FONT

When the Excel program is launched, the default font that displays is the Calibri. This font is what shows when you begin to input words, numbers and the likes into the cells on the Excel worksheet. You can, however, change the font to anyone you like in the Home tab that allows for the changing of the font

To do this:

- Select the cell you wish to change its font

- Go to the Home tab, click on the Font command and change it to the desired font

CHANGING THE FONT SIZE

To change the font size, all you have to do is:

- Select the cell you wish to change its font size

- Go to the Home tab, click on the Font command and change the font size to the one you desire.

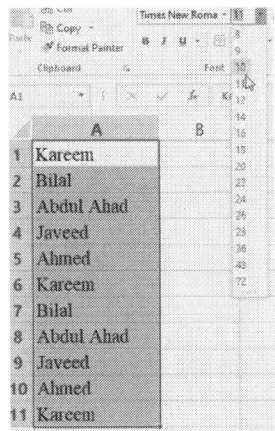

CHANGING THE FONT COLOR

To change the font color of your cell, all you need to do is;

- Select the cell you wish to change its font colour

- Go to the Home tab, click on the Font Colour command and change the font size to the one you desire

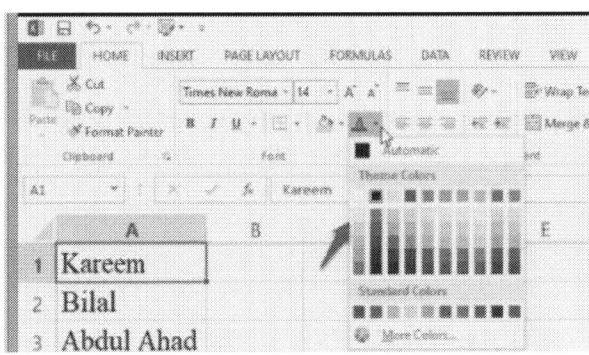

- After you must have done this, the font colour will change.

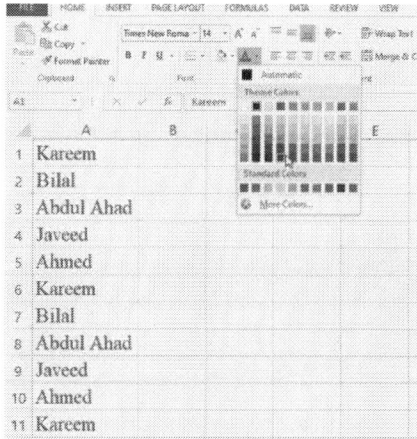

USING THE BOLD, ITALICS, AND UNDERLINED COMMANDS

- Select the cell you wish to change its font colour
- Go to the Home tab, click on bold, italics or underlined command to make the desired changes.

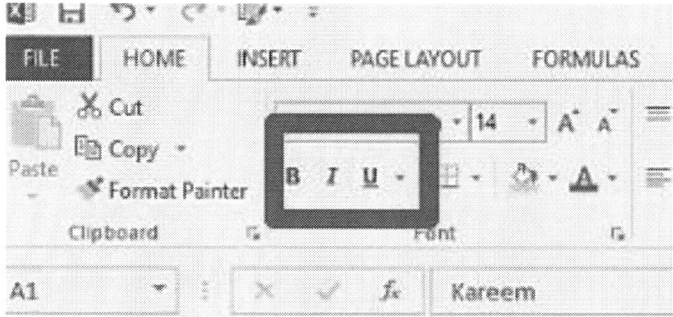

ADDING BACKGROUND COLOR USING THE FILL COLOR

The fill color allows you to add a background color to your cells making them stand out from every other part of the worksheet. You can add any color of your choice to the cell background.

To do this;

- Select the cell you wish to apply the fill colour to

- Go to the Home tab, click on the Fill colour and select the colour you want.

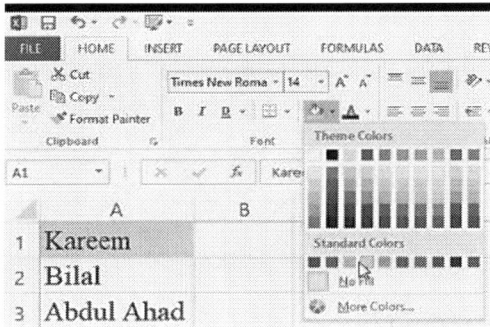

ADDING BORDERS TO CELLS

Creating a border in a worksheet helps to distinguish the cells from other cells in the worksheet. To add a border:

- Select the cell you wish to modify

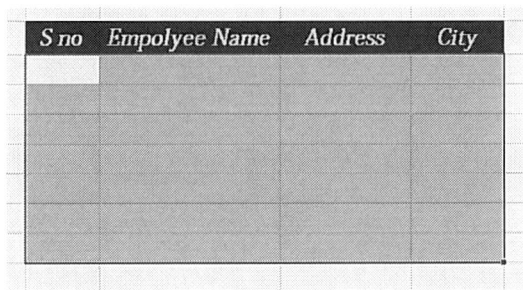

- Go to the Home tab, click on the Border command and select the border style you want

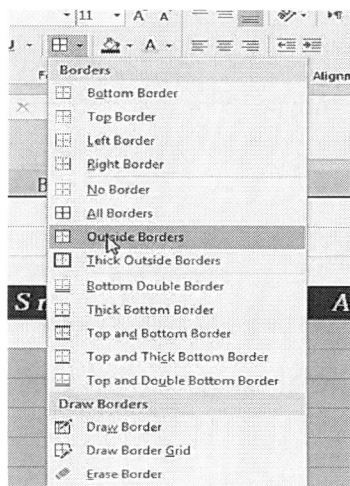

- Here on this page, the selected border will appear

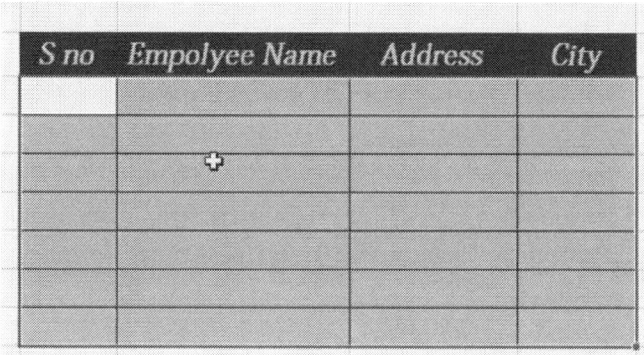

NOTE: You can also draw the border by yourself and also add colours to the border with the Draw tools at the bottom of the Borders drop-down menu.

CHANGING THE TEXT ALIGNMENT OF YOUR BORDER

By default, the text entered into the worksheet is always at the bottom of the cell. You can change the way your cell content is displayed in such a way that makes it easy to read. To change the alignment, all you have to do is:

- Select the cell you wish to change
- From the Home tab, select the Alignment command to choose the one you prefer.

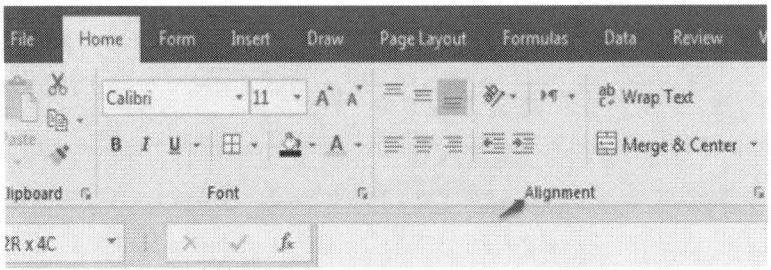

MODIFYING THE COLUMNS, ROWS, AND CELL IN A WORKSHEET

Modifying the columns, rows and cell allows you to change the height and width to different sizes you desire.

MODIFYING THE COLUMN WIDTH

To change the width of the column, all you have to do is:

- Place the mouse over the column line in the column heading and ensure that the white cross becomes a double arrow

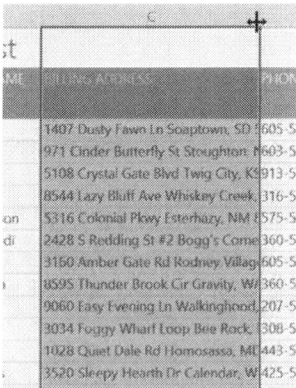

- Click, hold and drag the mouse to increase or decrease the column width.

- Release the mouse. The column width will be changed.

MODIFYING THE ROW HEIGHT

To change the height of the row, all you have to do is:

- Place the mouse over the column line in the row heading and ensure that the white cross becomes a double arrow.
- Click, hold, and drag the mouse to increase or decrease the row height.
- Release the mouse and the row height will be changed.

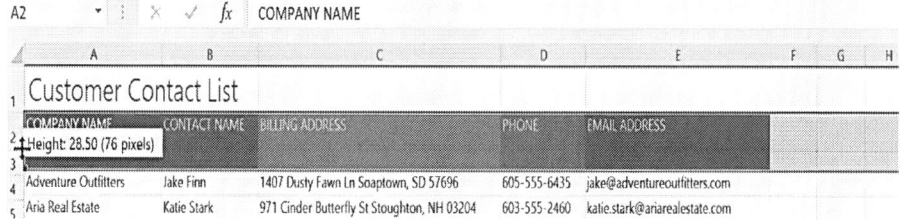

INSERTING NEW ROW

- Choose the row heading below where you desire the new row to display.
- Go to the home tab, select the insert command and click on Insert sheet rows and the new row will be seen.

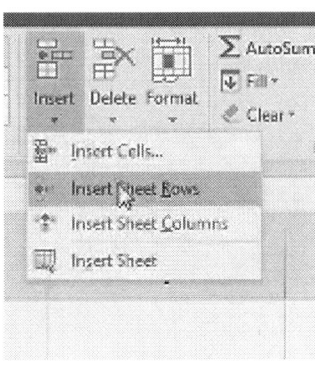

INSERTING NEW COLUMN

- Choose the column heading to the right where you desire the new column to display.
- Go to the home tab, select the insert command and click on Insert sheet columns and the new sheet will be seen.

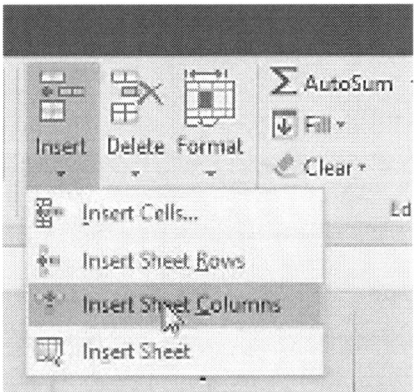

DELETING OF ROWS AND COLUMNS

In case you want to delete a row or column you don't find useful; all you need to do is:

- Select the rows and columns to be deleted.
- From the Home tab, click on the Delete command and the selected rows and columns will be deleted.

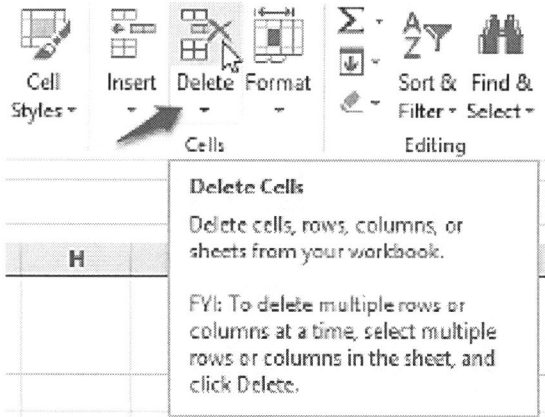

HOW TO HIDE AND UNHIDE ROWS OR COLUMNS

You can certainly hide some of your rows and columns on your worksheet while working on it and to do this:

- Select the column or row you intend to hide.
- Right-click on it and select Hide from the formatting menu.

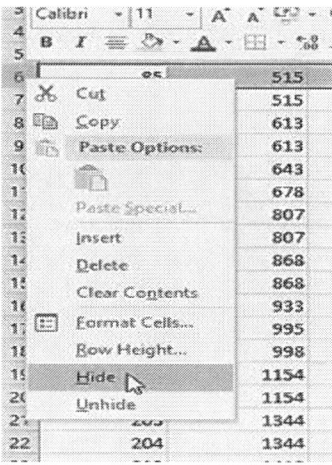

- The column or row is hidden with an indication of a green line on it.

- To unhide a column, select the columns on both sides of the hidden column.
- Right-click the mouse and select Unhide from the formatting menu and the hidden columns will appear.

WRAPPING TEXT AND MERGING CELLS

In the course of working on the worksheet, a cell may have too much content on it and you may need to wrap or merge the cell rather than increasing the size of the cell. With the use of wrapping, the texts are modified in such a way that they fit into the cell thereby adjusting the cell and displaying the content on multiple lines. Merging on its own allows you to combine or join a cell close to it by creating a large cell.

To merge cells

- Select the cell you want to merge.

- From the Home tab, go to Merge and Centre to choose the option you desire in the listed options.

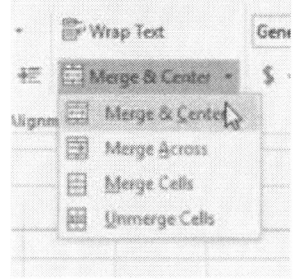

- Then the cell will be adjusted to the option chosen.

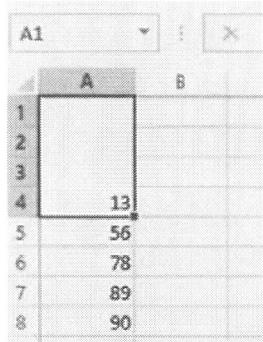

To wrap texts

- Select the cell you wish to wrap.

- From the Home tab, go to the Select Text command and the texts in the cells will be wrapped.

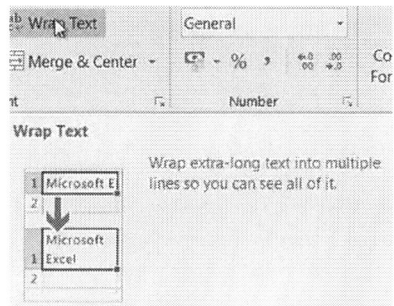

- The texts in the cells will be wrapped.

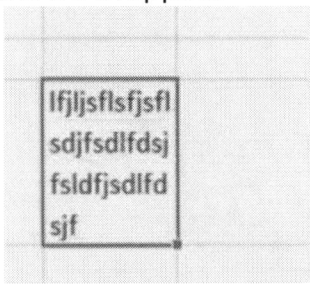

CUSTOMIZING THE DEFAULT WORKBOOK

Working on the Excel default workbook can be boring at times due to the interface of the workbook. However, you can make your Excel workbook look more captivating and exciting to work on by changing some features like the font size, font style, column width and heights, etc. which have been explained in Excel 1 under formatting the cells. To continue from there, we will be learning some other ways to customize the default workbook to suit your taste.

HOW TO CHANGE THE WORKSHEET THEME

From the Page **layout**, click on Themes to select anyone that suits your taste

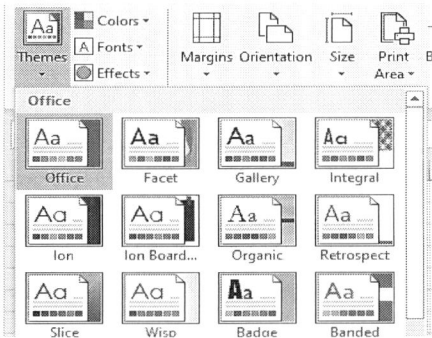

HOW TO CHANGE THE WORKSHEET THEME COLOUR

- Go to the **Page layout** and click on **Colours** to select anyone that suits your taste

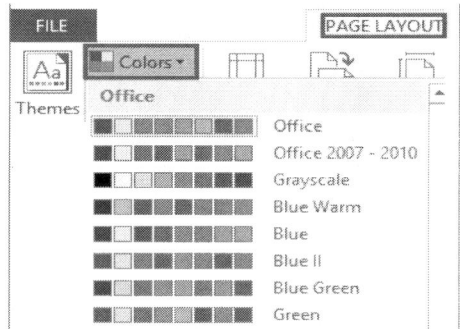

HOW TO CHANGE THE WORKSHEET THEME EFFECTS

- Go to the **Page layout** and click on **Effects** to select any that suits your taste

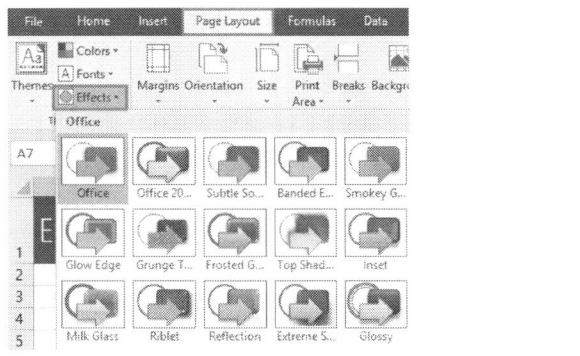

Go to the **Page layout** and click on **Fonts** to select any that suits your taste

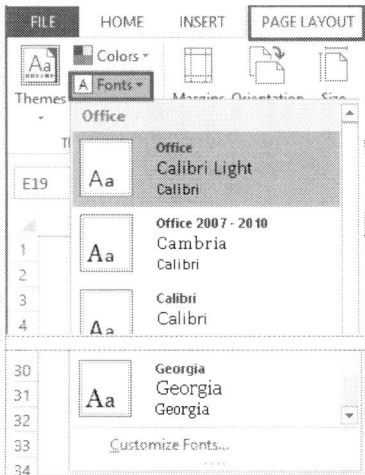

ZOOMING IN OR OUT OF THE SPREADSHEET

You can adjust the view of your default worksheet by zooming in or out. To do this, follow the steps below:

- To view 100%, go to the **View tab** and from the **Zoom group** click on **Zoom 100**
- To maximize the view of the spreadsheet, go to the **View tab** and from **the Zoom group** click **on Zoom to Selection**
- To enter a percentage or any other settings, go to the **View tab** and from **the Zoom group** click **on Zoom to Selection**

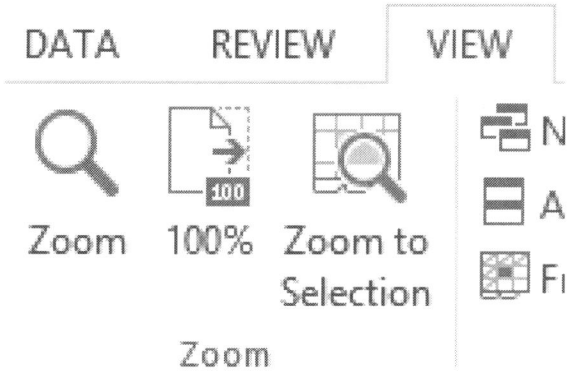

NOTE: You can use the **Zoom slider** on the status bar to zoom in or out.

ADDING MORE WORKSHEETS TO THE WORKBOOK

You can also customize your default workbook by adding more worksheets to the already existed worksheets. To do this, follow the steps below:

- Go to the **Home tab** and click on Insert
- From the **Insert drop-down arrow**, click on **Insert Sheet**

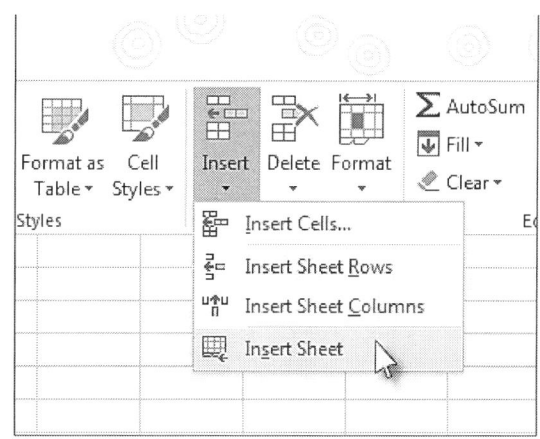

- You can also add a new worksheet by selecting the plus icon at the bottom of the worksheet

CHAPTER THREE

EXCEL TABLES AND CHARTS

WHAT IS AN EXCEL TABLE?

Excel Tables are containers for your input data. Tables tell excel that all the input data are related. Without a table, the only thing relating the data is proximity to each other.

Creating tables in Excel helps you to analyse your data. You can use table command to change a list of data into a formatted Excel table. With the Excel Table, you can use features like sorting and filtering that will give your data an organized and structured look. You can also conveniently insert formulas in the tables.

Before creating a formatted Excel Table for your data, follow the guidelines below to organize your data.

- The data must be organized and arranged in rows and columns.
- In the first row, each column must have a heading.
- Each column must contain one set of data.
- The list must have no blank rows and columns.

CREATING A TABLE

- Select all the lists of data in the worksheet to be inserted in a table

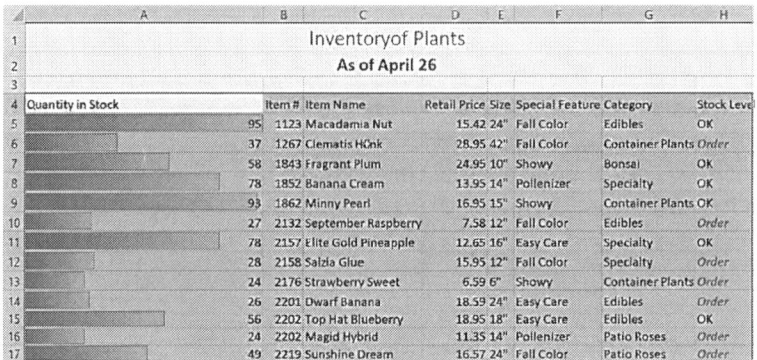

- From the **Insert tab**, go to the **Tables group** and click on **Table**

- In the **Create Table dialog box**, the range of your data automatically appears and you can make adjustments to the data range. Then check **My table has header** and click on **Ok**

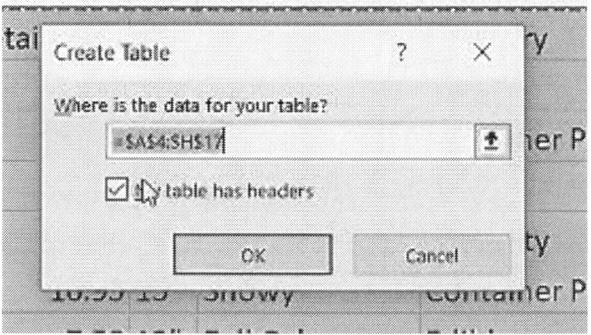

- Then the data are formatted in the Excel tables

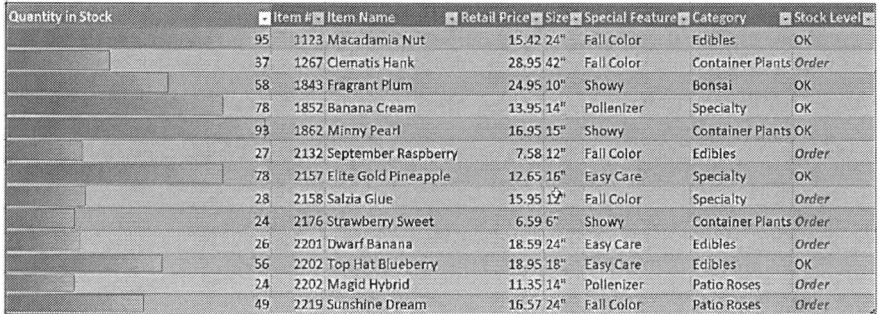

SORTING A TABLE

You can sort the data in a table by following these simple steps:

- Click on the arrow next to the **Item name** and select **Sort A to Z**
- Then click on **Ok**.

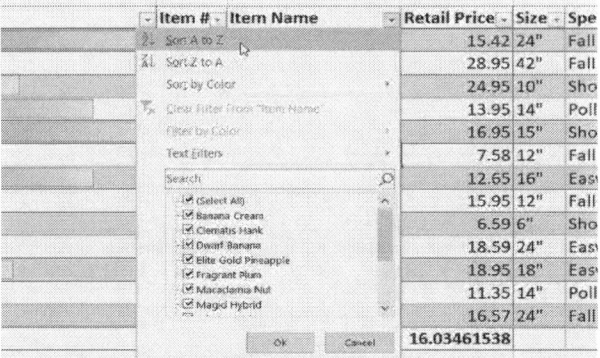

FILTERING A TABLE

You can choose to filter i.e.; select the data you wish to have displayed on your table by following these simple steps:

- Click on the arrow next to **Category** and select **Specialty**
- Then click on **Ok**.

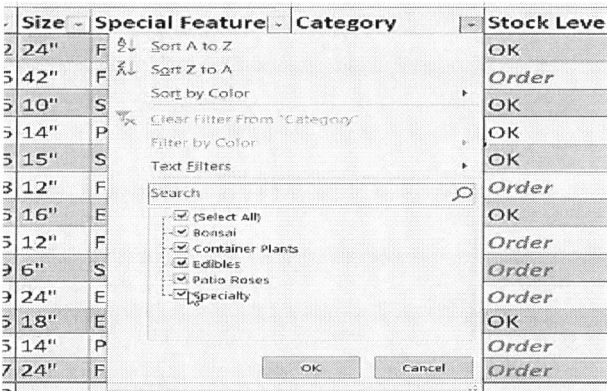

CREATING PIVOT TABLE AND CHARTS IN EXCEL

THE PIVOTTABLE

The Pivot Table is a powerful tool that is used to summarize, organize, sort, and analyze data stored in a table.

The following are the procedures on how to create a pivot table:

- Select the cell you wish to create a Pivot Table for
- From **Insert tab**, go to **Pivot Table**

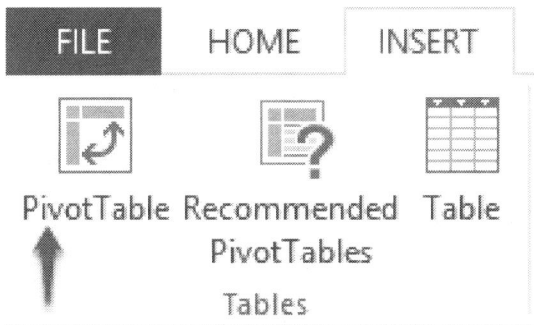

- From **Choose the data that you want to analyse**, choose either **table** or **range**.
- Under **Choose where you want the Pivot Table report to be placed,** you can select **New worksheet** or **Existing worksheet**.
- Then click on **Ok**.

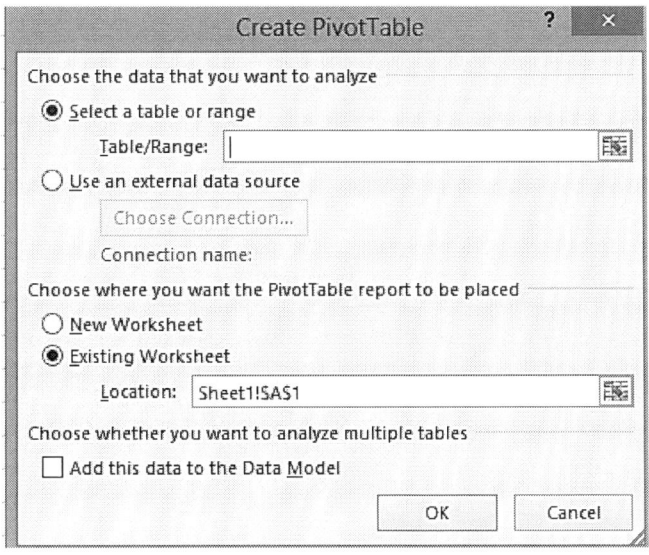

- To add a field to the Pivot table, go to the **Pivot tables Field pane and** select the field name checkbox.

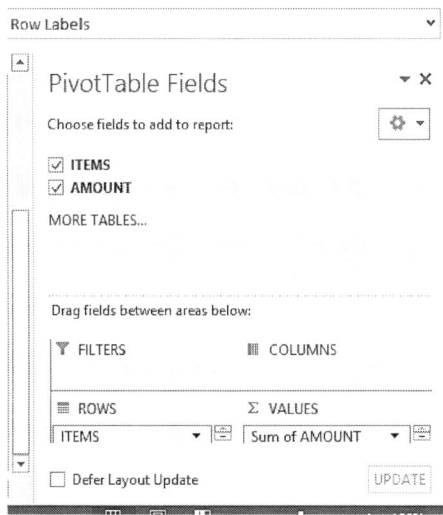

- Drag the field to the desired location with your mouse if you wish to move the field from one area to another

If you have followed the instructions above, your table will look like the image below

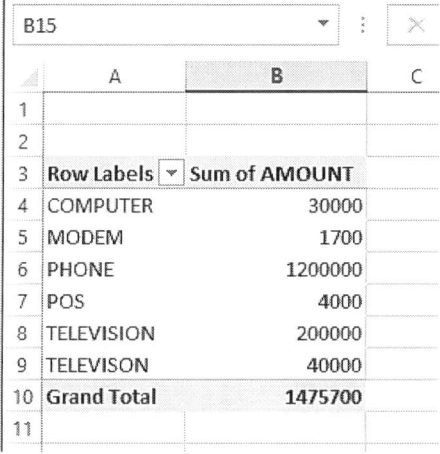

THE PIVOT CHART

The pivot chart is a visual representation of the data on the pivot table. To create a pivot chart from the pivot table, follow the instructions below:

- Select a cell in the pivot table.
- Go to Insert and click on pivot Chart.
- Then click on Ok.

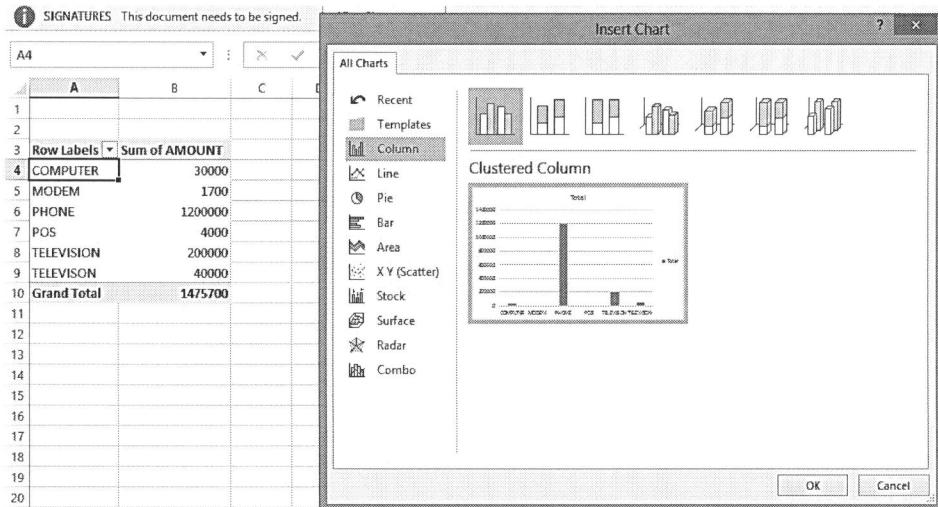

If you have followed the instructions above, your pivot table and chart will look like the image below;

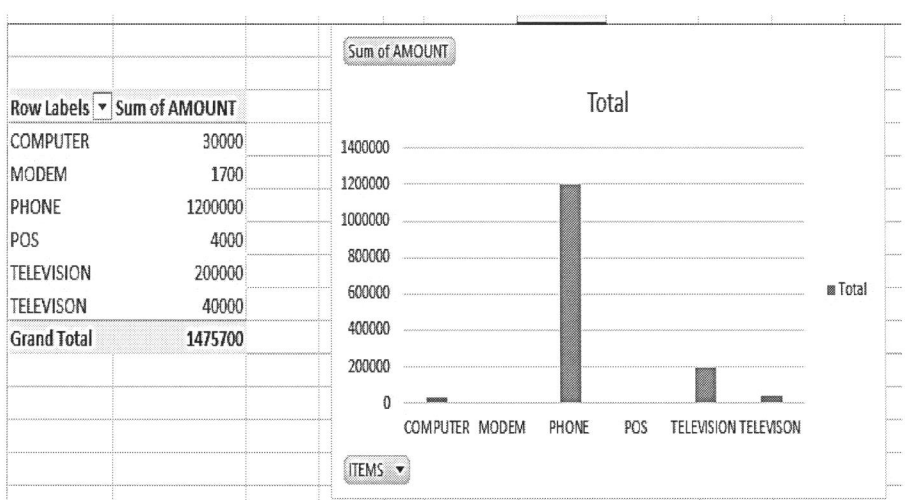

USING SLICER ON TABLES OR PIVOT TABLES

The slicer feature is used to filter data on tables or Pivot tables. It appears like a form of a button on the Excel worksheet to filter data.

To use the slicer;

- Select any cell on the table or the Pivot table
- From the **Home tab,** go to **Insert** and click on **Slicer**
- In the **Insert Slicers dialog box, select the field you want to display from the checks box**
- Then click on **Ok**

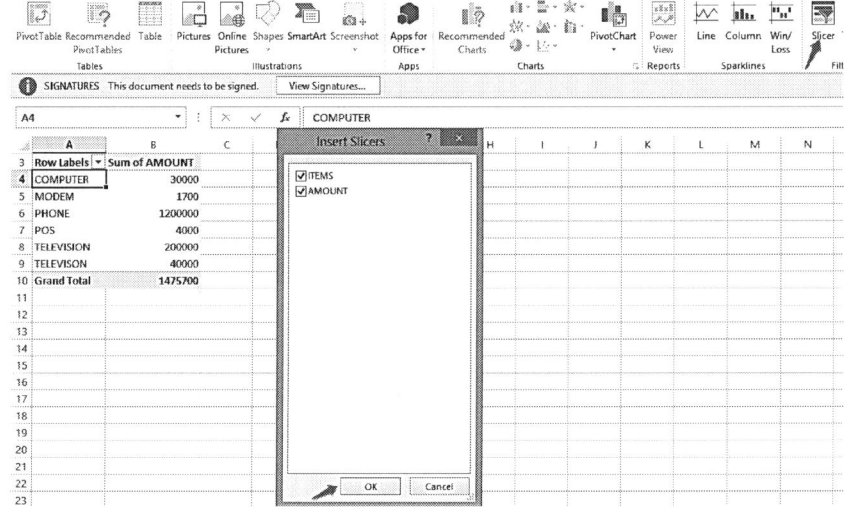

The picture below shows how the slicer looks like when used to filter data on table or Pivot table

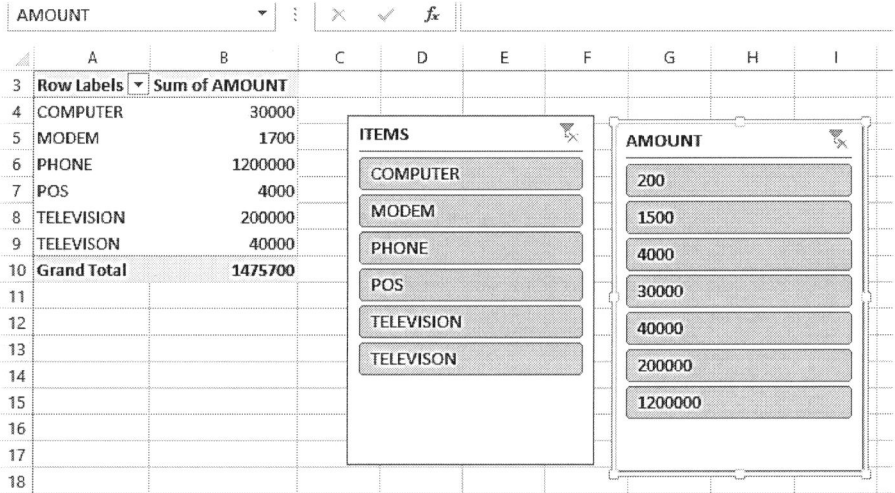

WORKING WITH CHARTS

Charts in Excel help to present data on your worksheet in a visual form thereby displaying the data which are in form of rows and columns as bars on a chart. These are varieties of charts that can be applied or used to display data. To mention a few, Excel provides charts like Pie chart, Line chart, Bar chart, Column chart, etc.

Data shown in charts are more interesting, clearer, and easier to read and understand. With the use of charts, you can evaluate your data and make comparisons between different values.

TYPES OF EXCEL CHART

There are different types of chart in Excel but briefly, we will be talking about just a few out of it.

Column Chart: This is a chart that compares values along the vertical axis and categories along the horizontal axis. There are different types of column charts such as clustered column, stacked column, 3-D stacked column, etc.

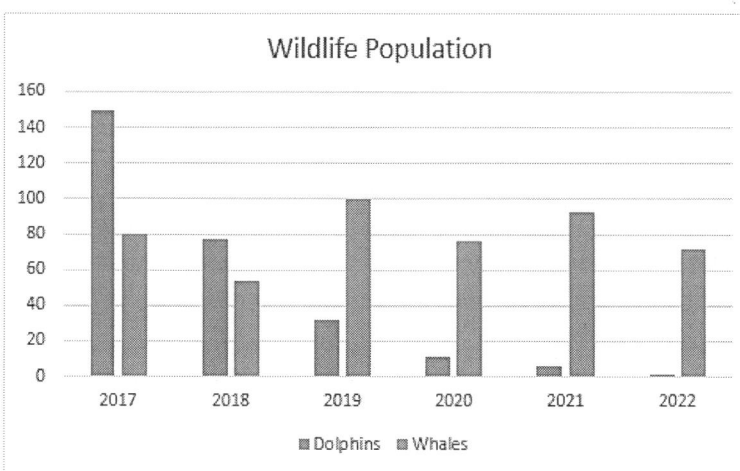

Line Chart: This is a chart that is used for showing trends in data at equal intervals e.g., months, years, days, etc. Examples of line chart are line, stacked line with markers, 100% stacked line, etc.

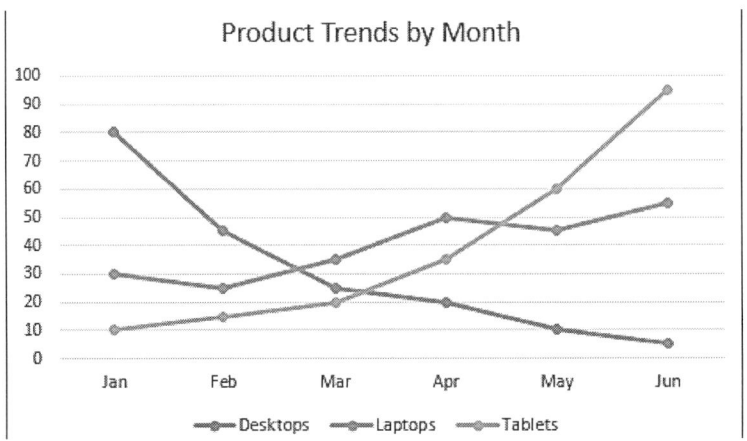

Bar Chart: Just like the column chart, the bar chart compares values along the vertical axis and categories along the horizontal axis. There are different types. The bar chart is used with large label texts. Examples of bar charts are clustered bar, stacked bar, 3-D stacked bar, etc.

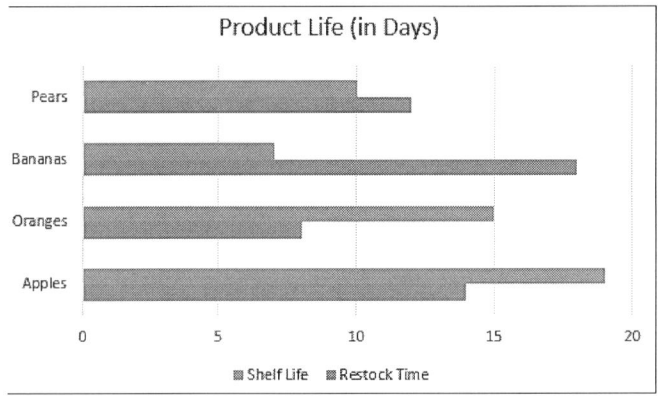

Pie Chart: This is a graph that presents or displays data in a circular graph. This chart displays information and information using a pie slice format.

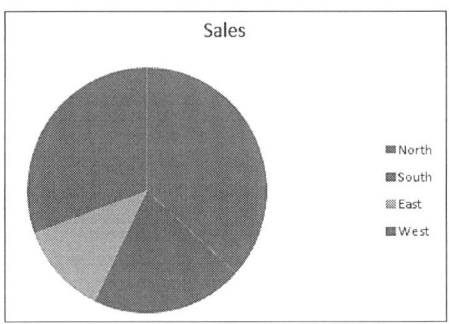

Doughnut Chart: This is a chart that shows the relationship of parts to a whole and when all pieces brought together will still amount to 100% percent just like the pie chart. The difference between the doughnut pie chart and the pie chart is that the doughnut chart can contain more than one series of data while the pie chart can only contain one data series.

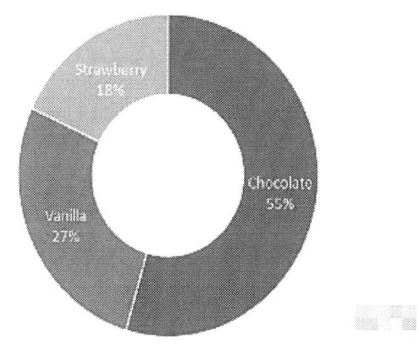

HOW TO INSERT A CHART IN EXCEL

- Select data for the chart

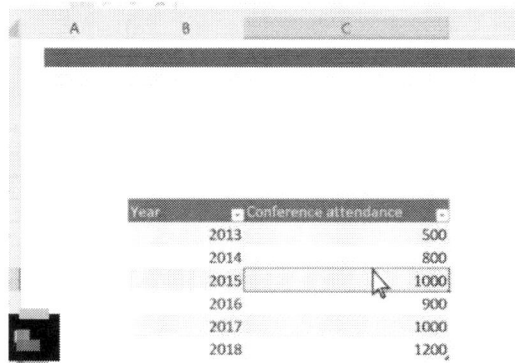

- Select Insert and go to Recommended Charts

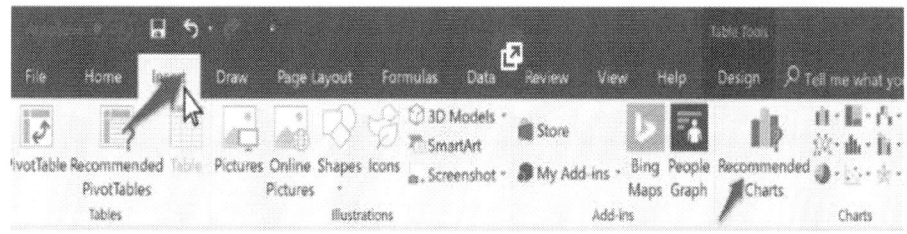

- Choose a chart on the Recommended charts tab and preview the chart

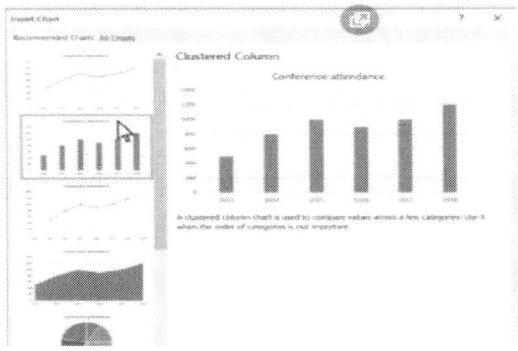

- Select the chart and click on Ok.

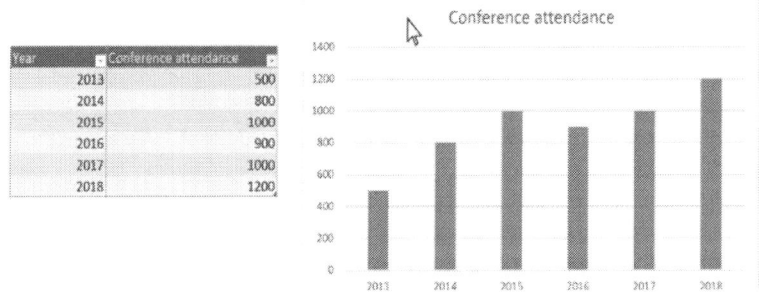

HOW TO ADD TITLE TO A CHART

When you add a title to your chart, it gives your chart a sense of purpose, and people going through your work on the Excel worksheet will be able to identify or recognize the purpose of the chart. To add a title to your chat, all you need is to do is:

- Click anywhere within the chart area

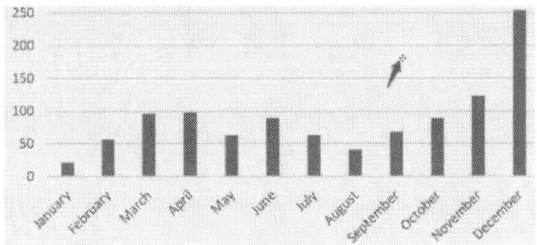

- Click on the plus sign at the upper part of the chart

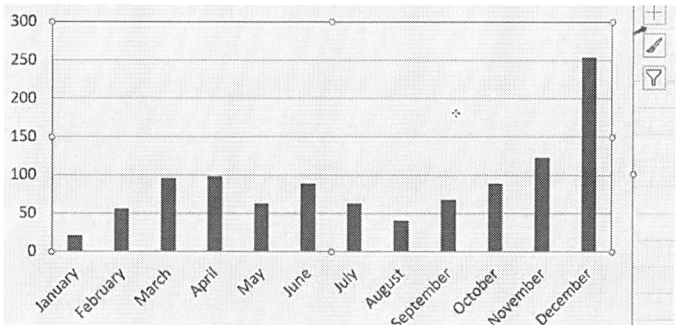

- Then click on Chart title among every other option listed

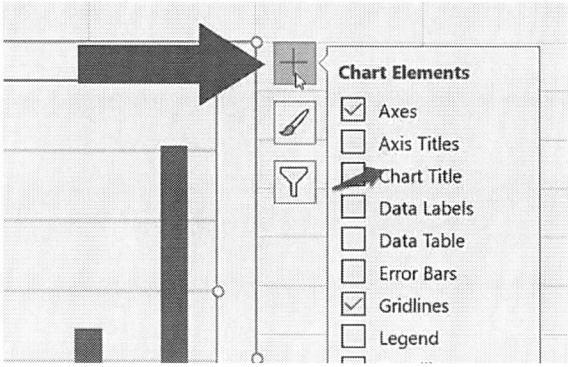

- And to change it from Chart Title, just click into the textbox to any title of your choice

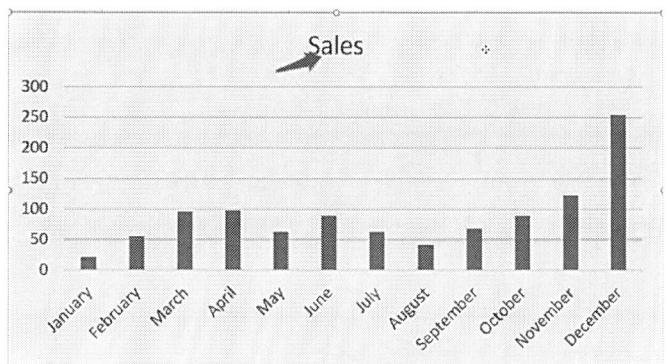

NOTE: *To change the color, font size, and the font type, just right-click on the Chart title.*

HOW TO CHANGE CHART TYPE IN EXCEL

There are different types of charts used in the presentation of data. In case the chart type you used in presenting your data is not suiting or appropriate, you can switch to another chart that best explained your data.

To get this done:

- Click on the chart you wish to modify

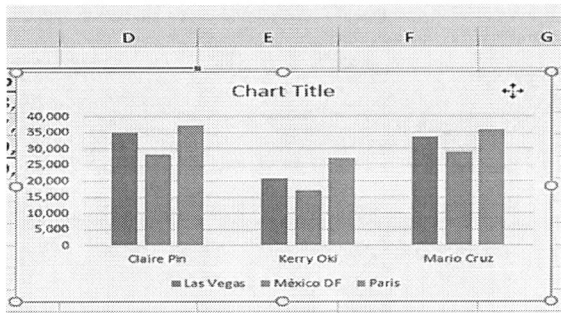

- Go to the Design tab and select Change Chart Type

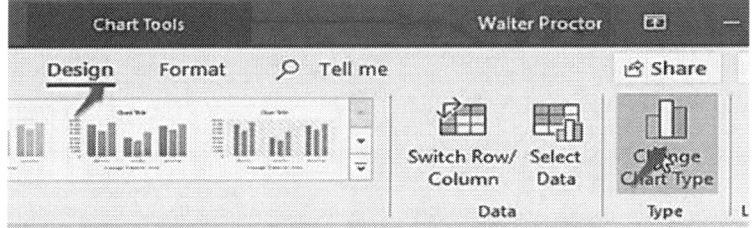

- From the Change Chart Type, a popup window will be displayed where you will have to pick your charts from Recommended charts or All charts

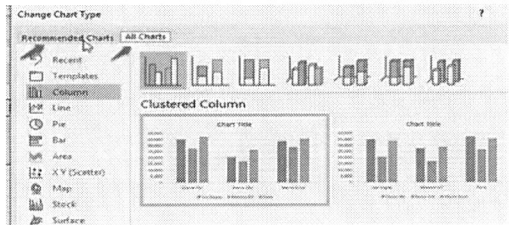

- Choose any chart you want and preview it

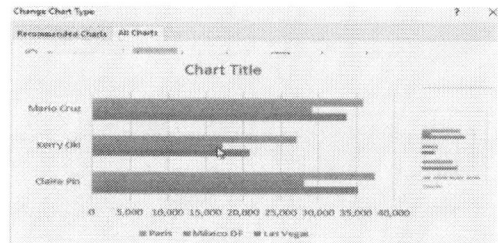

- Then click on Ok and the chart will be displayed in the worksheet.

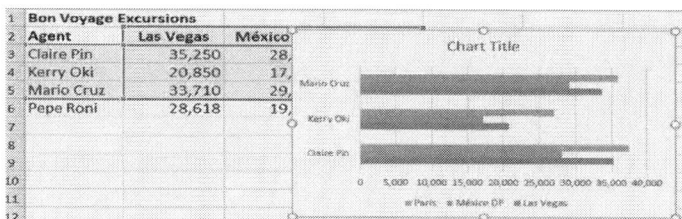

HOW TO CHANGE CHART STYLE IN EXCEL

To change the chart style in your Excel worksheet:

- Click on the chart you wish to modify

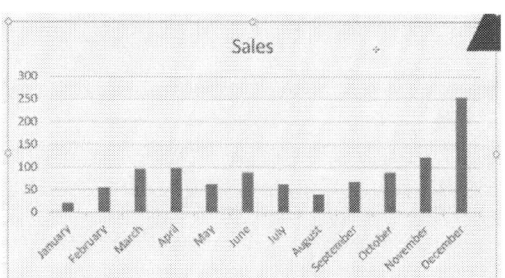

- Go to the Design tab and select Change Chart Style

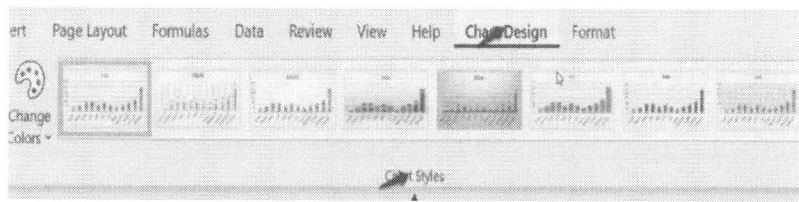

- Here on this page, the chart style will be changed.

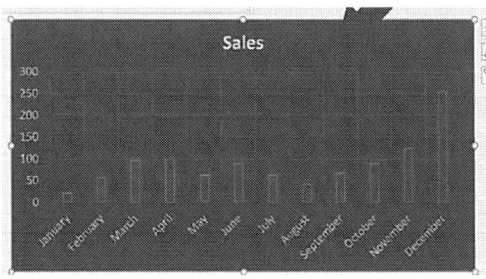

HOW TO CHANGE CHART LAYOUT IN EXCEL

- Click on the chart you wish to modify

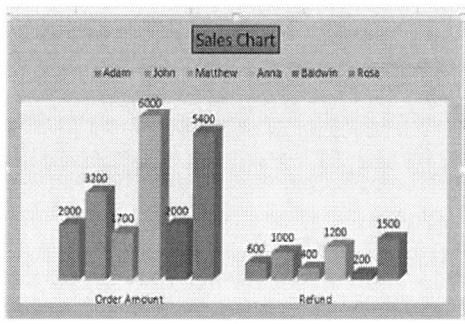

- Go to the Design tab and select Quick Layout

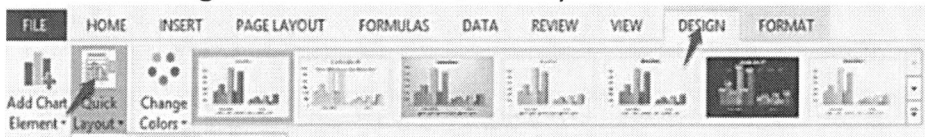

- Select the Chart layout you want and the changes will be effected on the Chart

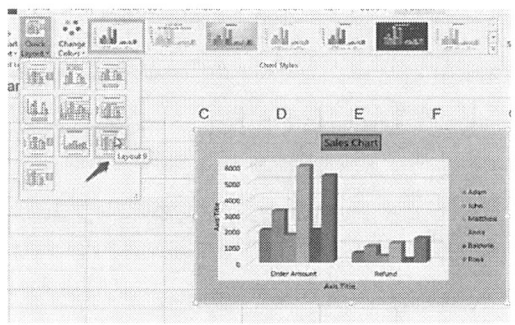

HOW TO SWITCH ROWS AND COLUMNS OF DATA IN A CHART

You can change the way charts arranges your rows and columns of your data to suit your interest. To get this done,

- Click on the chart you wish to modify

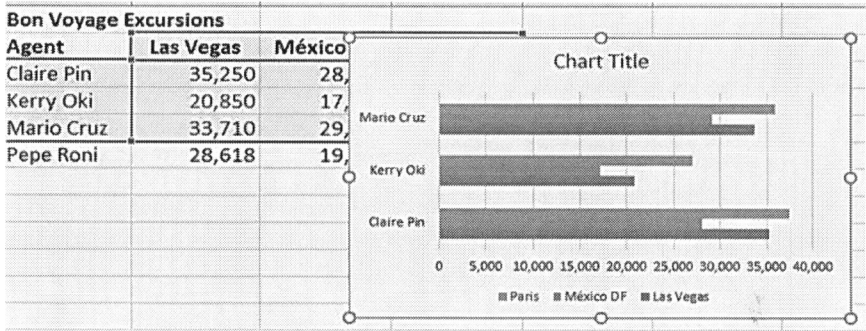

- Go to the Design tab and select Switch Row/Column

- Here on this page, the rows and columns of the data will be switched

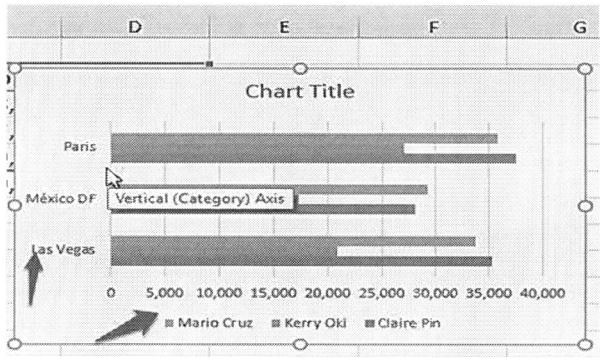

HOW TO MOVE A CHART

You can move a chart from any location on a worksheet or to a new or existing worksheet.

To move a chart within a worksheet with the mouse, drag it to the location you want but to move it to another worksheet,

- Click on the chart you wish to modify

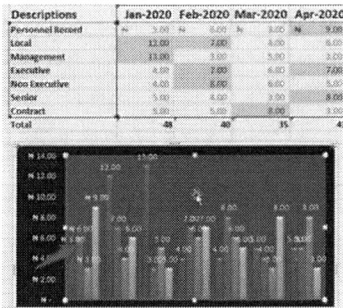

- Go to the Design tab and select Move Chart location

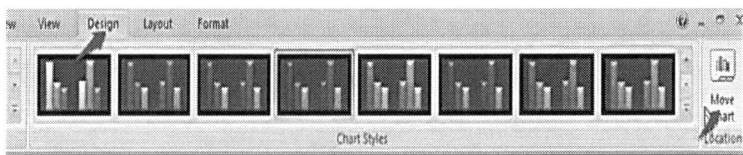

- After clicking on Move Chart Location, a window will pop up where you will need to choose where you want the chart to be placed

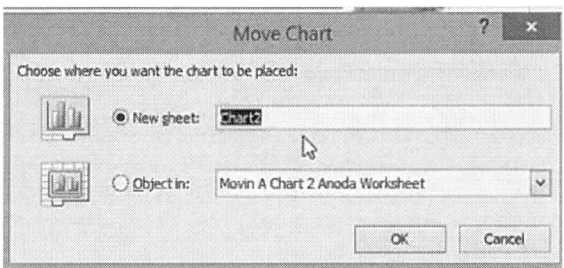

- Then click on Ok and the chart will be moved to another worksheet.

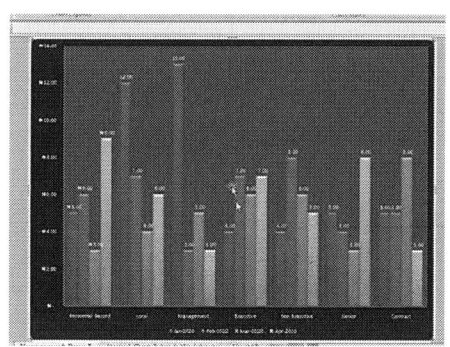

HOW TO RESIZE A CHART ON YOUR WORKSHEET

You can adjust the size of a chart to either small or big depending on what you want. To carry out this operation,

- Click on the chart to modify and at the edges of the chart, some loop handles will appear
- The loop handles allow you to change the horizontal and vertical arrangement of the chart

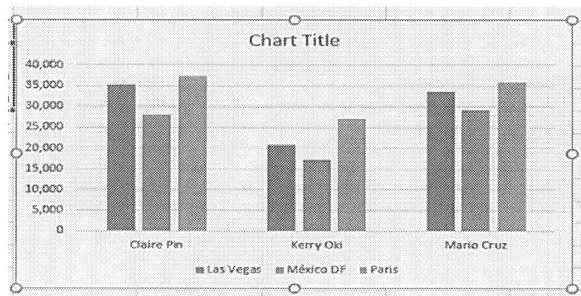

- Click on the loop handles to increase or decrease the size of the chart.

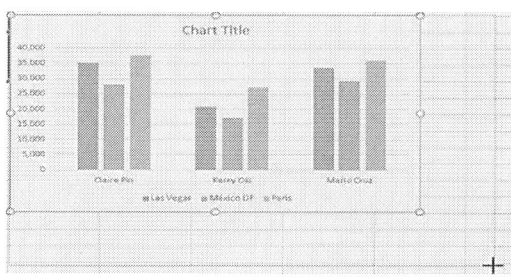

CHAPTER FOUR

CELL REFERENCING IN EXCEL

MEANING OF CELLS REFERENCING

A cell reference is an alphanumeric value or data that is used to locate or identify a cell in a worksheet. The cell reference contains one or more letters for the column and a number for the rows (A1). With the cell reference, you can locate the data you want the formula to calculate for you. Another name for cell reference is the **cell address**.

TYPES OF CELL REFERENCING

To understand the concept of cell reference better, there is a need to get familiar with the types of cell references. Therefore, we will be discussing the three types of cell references and how they can be used:

RELATIVE REFERENCES

All cell references by default are relative references. When you copy multiple cells, they change based on their relative positions of rows and columns. For example, when you multiply B4*C4 in cell D4. When you copy into cell D5, it will become B5*C5.

To create and copy a formula using relative references, follow the steps below:

- Select the cell that will contain the formula **(D4)** and put in the formula to calculate the desired values **(B4*C4)**

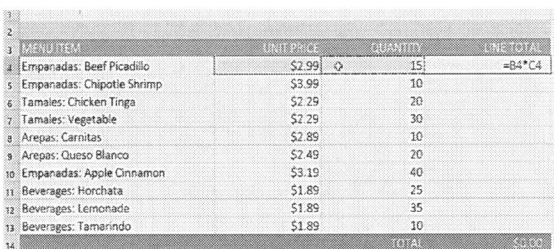

- Press **Enter** and the formula will be calculated with the result displayed in the cell.

MENU ITEM	UNIT PRICE	QUANTITY	LINE TOTAL
Empanadas: Beef Picadillo	$2.99	15	$44.85
Empanadas: Chipotle Shrimp	$3.99	10	
Tamales: Chicken Tinga	$2.29	20	
Tamales: Vegetable	$2.29	30	
Arepas: Carnitas	$2.89	10	
Arepas: Queso Blanco	$2.49	20	
Empanadas: Apple Cinnamon	$3.19	40	
Beverages: Horchata	$1.89	25	
Beverages: Lemonade	$1.89	35	
Beverages: Tamarindo	$1.89	10	
		TOTAL	$44.85

- Locate the **Fill handle** in the lower part of cell D4 and then click, hold and drag down to cell D13.

MENU ITEM	UNIT PRICE	QUANTITY	LINE TOTAL
Empanadas: Beef Picadillo	$2.99	15	$44.85
Empanadas: Chipotle Shrimp	$3.99	10	
Tamales: Chicken Tinga	$2.29	20	
Tamales: Vegetable	$2.29	30	
Arepas: Carnitas	$2.89	10	
Arepas: Queso Blanco	$2.49	20	
Empanadas: Apple Cinnamon	$3.19	40	
Beverages: Horchata	$1.89	25	
Beverages: Lemonade	$1.89	35	
Beverages: Tamarindo	$1.89	10	
		TOTAL	$44.85

- Release the mouse and the formula will be to the cells selected and values in each cell will be calculated.

MENU ITEM	UNIT PRICE	QUANTITY	SALES TAX	LINE TOTAL
Empanadas: Beef Picadillo	$2.99	15		$44.85
Empanadas: Chipotle Shrimp	$3.99	10		$39.90
Tamales: Chicken Tinga	$2.29	20		$45.80
Tamales: Vegetable	$2.29	30		$68.70
Arepas: Carnitas	$2.89	10		$28.90
Arepas: Queso Blanco	$2.49	20		$49.80
Empanadas: Apple Cinnamon	$3.19	40		$127.60
Beverages: Horchata	$1.89	25		$47.25
Beverages: Lemonade	$1.89	35		$66.15
Beverages: Tamarindo	$1.89	10		$18.90
			TOTAL	$537.85

ABSOLUTE AND MULTIPLE CELL REFERENCE

An absolute cell reference is a cell reference that uses the dollar sign ($) both row and column constant when copying a formula from one cell to the other in a worksheet.

A multiple cell reference is a cell reference that uses the dollar sign to keep either the row or column constant. In most cases, the relative and absolute are commonly used.

A3	The column and the row will not change when copied
A$2	The row will not change when copied
$A2	The column will not change when copied

HOW TO CREATE AND COPY A FORMULA USING THE ABSOLUTE REFERENCE

In the example below, we will use 7.5% sales tax rate in cell E1 to calculate the sales tax for all data in column D. There will be a need to use absolute reference £1$E in the formula so that each reference remains constant when the formula is copied and fill to other cells in column D.

If the absolute reference is not used in a case like this, the picture below will be the outcome of what the Excel workbook will look like.

	MENU ITEM	UNIT PRICE	QUANTITY	SALES TAX	LINE TOTAL
2				TAX RATE:	7.5%
3	MENU ITEM	UNIT PRICE	QUANTITY	SALES TAX	LINE TOTAL
4	Empanadas: Beef Picadillo	$2.99	15	=(B4*C4)*E2	$48.21
5	Empanadas: Chipotle Shrimp	$3.99	10	#VALUE!	#VALUE!
6	Tamales: Chicken Tinga	$2.29	20	$2,208.19	$2,253.99
7	Tamales: Vegetable	$2.29	30	#VALUE!	#VALUE!
8	Arepas: Carnitas	$2.89	10	$65,140.30	$65,169.20
9	Arepas: Queso Blanco	$2.49	20	#VALUE!	#VALUE!
10	Empanadas: Apple Cinnamon	$3.19	40	$8,315,590.40	$8,315,718.00
11	Beverages: Horchata	$1.89	25	#VALUE!	#VALUE!
12	Beverages: Lemonade	$1.89	35	############	############
13	Beverages: Tamarindo	$1.89	10	#VALUE!	#VALUE!
14				TOTAL	#VALUE!

To ensure this does not occur, follow the steps below:

- Select the cell that will contain the formula **(D4)** and put in the formula to calculate the desired values **(B4*C4)*£1$E**

MENU ITEM	UNIT PRICE	QUANTITY	TAX RATE:	7.5%
			SALES TAX	LINE TOTAL
Empanadas: Beef Picadillo	$2.99	15	=(B4*C4)*E2	$48.21
Empanadas: Chipotle Shrimp	$3.99	10	#VALUE!	#VALUE!
Tamales: Chicken Tinga	$2.29	20	$2,208.19	$2,253.99
Tamales: Vegetable	$2.29	30	#VALUE!	#VALUE!
Arepas: Carnitas	$2.89	10	$65,140.30	$65,169.20
Arepas: Queso Blanco	$2.49	20	#VALUE!	#VALUE!
Empanadas: Apple Cinnamon	$3.19	40	$8,315,590.40	$8,315,718.00
Beverages: Horchata	$1.89	25	#VALUE!	#VALUE!
Beverages: Lemonade	$1.89	35	#############	#############
Beverages: Tamarindo	$1.89	10	#VALUE!	#VALUE!
			TOTAL	#VALUE!

- Press **Enter** and the formula will be calculated with the result displayed in the cell.

	MENU ITEM	UNIT PRICE	QUANTITY	TAX RATE:	7.5%
2				SALES TAX	LINE TOTAL
3	MENU ITEM	UNIT PRICE	QUANTITY	SALES TAX	LINE TOTAL
4	Empanadas: Beef Picadillo	$2.99	15	$3.36	$48.21
5	Empanadas: Chipotle Shrimp	$3.99	10	#VALUE!	#VALUE!
6	Tamales: Chicken Tinga	$2.29	20	$2,208.19	$2,253.99
7	Tamales: Vegetable	$2.29	30	#VALUE!	#VALUE!
8	Arepas: Carnitas	$2.89	10	$65,140.30	$65,169.20
9	Arepas: Queso Blanco	$2.49	20	#VALUE!	#VALUE!
10	Empanadas: Apple Cinnamon	$3.19	40	$8,315,590.40	$8,315,718.00
11	Beverages: Horchata	$1.89	25	#VALUE!	#VALUE!
12	Beverages: Lemonade	$1.89	35	#############	#############
13	Beverages: Tamarindo	$1.89	10	#VALUE!	#VALUE!
14				TOTAL	#VALUE!

- Locate the **Fill handle** in the lower part of cell D4 and then click, hold and drag down to cell D13.

	MENU ITEM	UNIT PRICE	QUANTITY	TAX RATE:	7.5%
2				SALES TAX	LINE TOTAL
3	MENU ITEM	UNIT PRICE	QUANTITY	SALES TAX	LINE TOTAL
4	Empanadas: Beef Picadillo	$2.99	15	$3.36	$48.21
5	Empanadas: Chipotle Shrimp	$3.99	10	#VALUE!	#VALUE!
6	Tamales: Chicken Tinga	$2.29	20	$2,208.19	$2,253.99
7	Tamales: Vegetable	$2.29	30	#VALUE!	#VALUE!
8	Arepas: Carnitas	$2.89	10	$65,140.30	$65,169.20
9	Arepas: Queso Blanco	$2.49	20	#VALUE!	#VALUE!
10	Empanadas: Apple Cinnamon	$3.19	40	$8,315,590.40	$8,315,718.00
11	Beverages: Horchata	$1.89	25	#VALUE!	#VALUE!
12	Beverages: Lemonade	$1.89	35	#############	#############
13	Beverages: Tamarindo	$1.89	10	#VALUE!	#VALUE!
14				TOTAL	#VALUE!

- Release the mouse and the formula will be to the cells selected and values in each cell will be calculated.

	MENU ITEM	UNIT PRICE	QUANTITY	SALES TAX	LINE TOTAL
2				TAX RATE:	7.5%
3	MENU ITEM	UNIT PRICE	QUANTITY	SALES TAX	LINE TOTAL
4	Empanadas: Beef Picadillo	$2.99	15	$3.36	$48.21
5	Empanadas: Chipotle Shrimp	$3.99	10	$2.99	$42.89
6	Tamales: Chicken Tinga	$2.29	20	$3.44	$49.24
7	Tamales: Vegetable	$2.29	30	$5.15	$73.85
8	Arepas: Carnitas	$2.89	10	$2.17	$31.07
9	Arepas: Queso Blanco	$2.49	20	$3.74	$53.54
10	Empanadas: Apple Cinnamon	$3.19	40	$9.57	$137.17
11	Beverages: Horchata	$1.89	25	$3.54	$50.79
12	Beverages: Lemonade	$1.89	35	$4.96	$71.11
13	Beverages: Tamarindo	$1.89	10	$1.42	$20.32
14				TOTAL	$578.19

REFERENCES TO OTHER WORKSHEET

You can use the same value on one or more worksheet without the need to write or copy the formula again.

- Identify the cell you wish to reference **(D14)**, take note of the name of the worksheet **(Menu Order)**
- Open the worksheet **(Catering Invoice)** you intend to use

	MENU ITEM	UNIT PRICE	QUANTITY	SALES TAX	LINE TOTAL
3	MENU ITEM	UNIT PRICE	QUANTITY	SALES TAX	LINE TOTAL
4	Empanadas: Beef Picadillo	$2.99	15	$3.36	$48.21
5	Empanadas: Chipotle Shrimp	$3.99	10	$2.99	$42.89
6	Tamales: Chicken Tinga	$2.29	20	$3.44	$49.24
7	Tamales: Vegetable	$2.29	30	$5.15	$73.85
8	Arepas: Carnitas	$2.89	10	$2.17	$31.07
9	Arepas: Queso Blanco	$2.49	20	$3.74	$53.54
10	Empanadas: Apple Cinnamon	$3.19	40	$9.57	$137.17
11	Beverages: Horchata	$1.89	25	$3.54	$50.79
12	Beverages: Lemonade	$1.89	35	$4.96	$71.11
13	Beverages: Tamarindo	$1.89	10	$1.42	$20.32
14				TOTAL	$578.19
15					

Catering Invoice | Menu Order

- Select the cell where you wish for the value to appear**(C4)**. Type the **equal sign (=)**, the **sheet name**, an **exclamation mark (!)**, and the **cell address (='Menu Order'!E14)**

MENU ITEM	UNIT PRICE	LINE TOTAL
Menu Order	Food & beverage	<u>I</u>='Menu Order'!E14
Paper Goods	Plates, utensils, cups	$110.87
Rental Equipment	Tables, chairs, linens	$249.95
Service Fee	18% of food & beverage	$0.00
	TOTAL	$360.82

- Press **Enter** and the value of the reference cell will be replicated in the new worksheet and if there is any change in the **Menu Order** worksheet, it will be automatically updated on the **Catering Invoice** worksheet.

MENU ITEM	UNIT PRICE	LINE TOTAL
Menu Order	Food & beverage	$578.19
Paper Goods	Plates, utensils, cups	$110.87
Rental Equipment	Tables, chairs, linens	$249.95
Service Fee	18% of food & beverage	$104.07
	TOTAL	$1,043.08

REFERENCES TO WORKSHEETS IN OTHER WORKBOOK

You can make reference to a worksheet on another workbook. In the example below, we want to calculate the difference between two months' expenses in different workbooks. To get this done, follow the procedures below:

- Open the worksheet for the current month **(Overview)**. Select the cell that will contain the formula **(C8)** and type **=C6-** inside the selected cell.

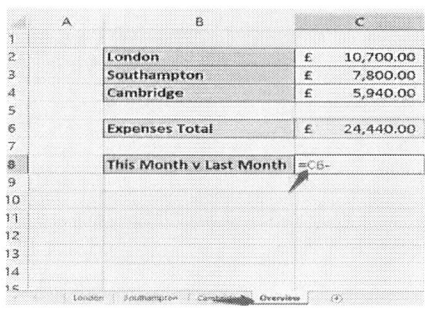

- On the View tab, click on Switch Windows and select the other workbook (**last month expenses**).

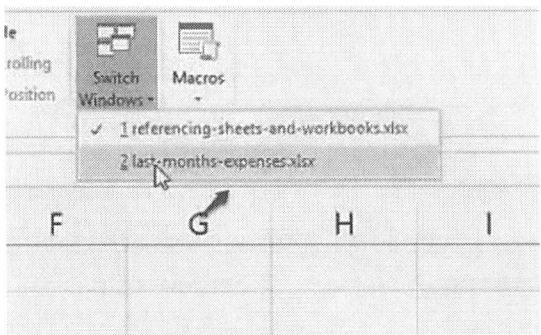

- Then click on worksheet **C6** and press **Enter**

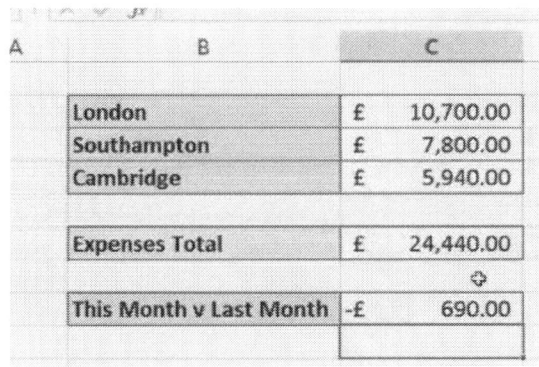

On the **Overview sheet**, the value of the reference cell will be replicated and if there is any change, it will be automatically updated on both the **Overview worksheet and Last month expenses workbook.**

CHAPTER FIVE

INTRODUCTION TO EXCEL FORMULAS & FUNCTIONS

WHAT'S A FORMULA?

Formulas in excel are statements written in the alphanumeric pattern which can perform a particular function on a cell or a range of cells based on the values from other cells or range of cells. For instance; {=Sum (A1+A2) adds up the value in cell A1 with the one in cell A2.}, {=Average (A1: A5) shows a simple average of the values from cell A1 to cell A5}.

Excel uses standard operators for formulas such as a plus sign for addition (+), a minus sign for subtraction (-), an asterisk for multiplication (*), a forward slash for division (/), and a caret (^) for exponents.

HOW TO INSERT FORMULAS IN EXCEL 2020

To create a formula, you must first understand what a cell reference is and the cell reference is what contains the cell address which is used to create a formula. With the cell reference, you can check if the formulas are accurate and you can as well change the value of the cell reference without having to change the formula. For example, the A1 and A2 in the table below is the cell reference.

=A1+A2	Adds cells A1 and A2
=C4-3	Subtracts 3 from C4
=E7/J4	Divide cell E7 by J4
=N10*1.05	Multiply cell N10 by 1.05
=R5^2	Finds the square of cell R5

To create a formula in Excel:

- Select the cell that will contain the formula.

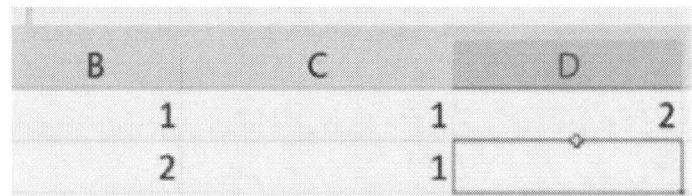

- Start typing in the formula with the equal sign preceded by the first cell address with the mathematical sign you wish to use and lastly followed by the other cell address.

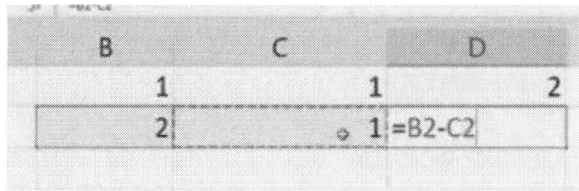

- Click the Enter key and the formula will be calculated with the value displayed in the cell.

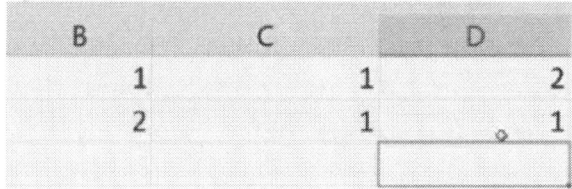

NOTE: let's assume you want to make some changes to a formula in the cell, all you have to do is just:

- Select the cell that contains the formula to be edited.

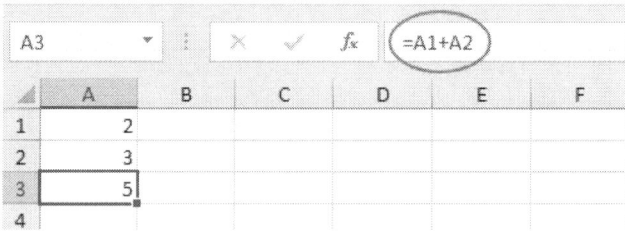

- Click on the Formula bar to make changes and a border will display on the reference cell.

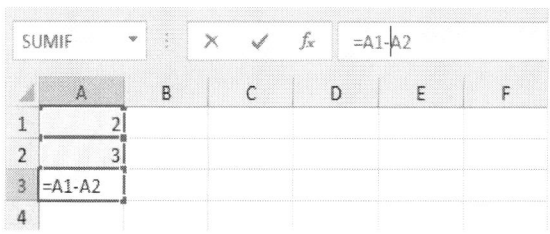

- After this, press the Enter key and automatically, the formula will be updated by itself.

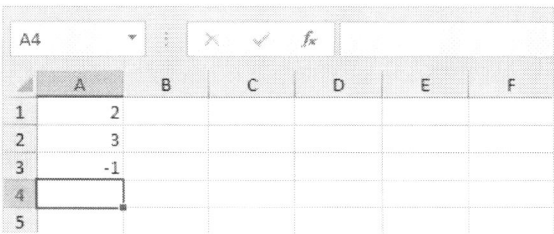

WHAT'S A FUNCTION?

Functions are pre-programmed formulas already available in Excel which makes it easier to perform calculations on topics like statistics, date and time arithmetic, financial calculations, engineering, and the likes. Just like the formula, you need to start the function with an equal sign before the function name.

To use a function, one must understand what an argument is. The argument is what contains what is to be calculated in form of cell addresses and they are contained or enclosed within parenthesis.

Examples of Functions are SUM, AVERAGE, COUNT, MAX, MIN, COUNTA, IF, TRIM, etc.

HOW TO INSERT A FUNCTION

Excel contains varieties of functions that can be created depending on what operation you want to carry out. To insert a function on your Excel program:

- Click on the cell that will contain the function.

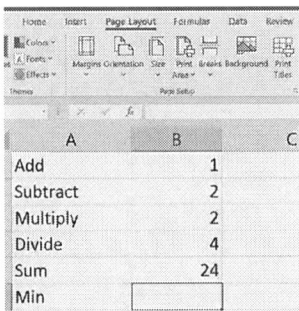

- Type in first the equal sign and then the function name.

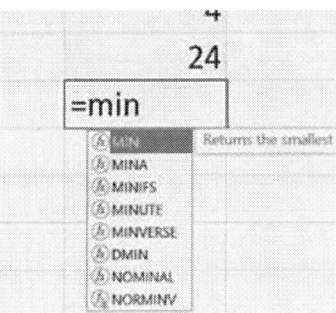

- Open the parenthesis and highlight the cells to affect the changes and then click on Enter and the final result will be displayed at the end of the cell.

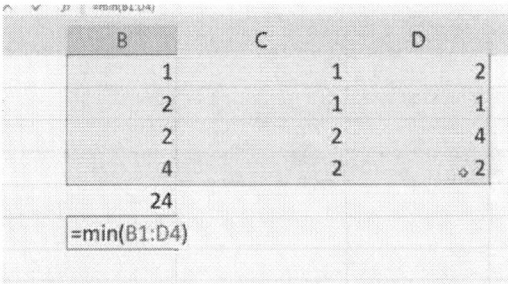

You can also insert a function by using the Function command by following the steps below:

- Select a cell and click on the Insert function button above the worksheet.

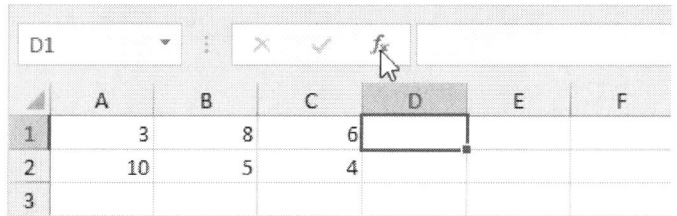

- Choose any out of the categories of functions that will be displayed then click on **Ok**.

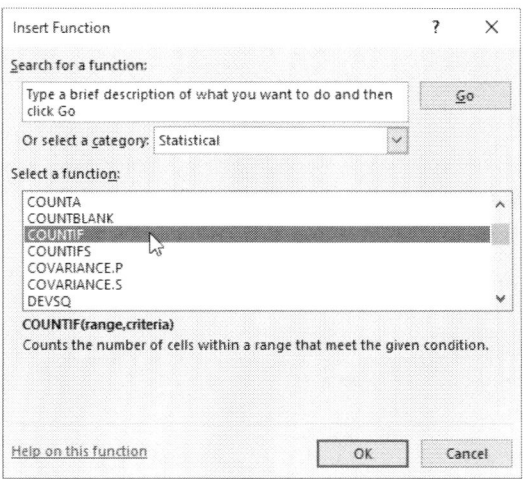

- In the next page, the Function Arguments dialogue box will appear.
- Select the range from the Range box and the criteria from the criteria box.

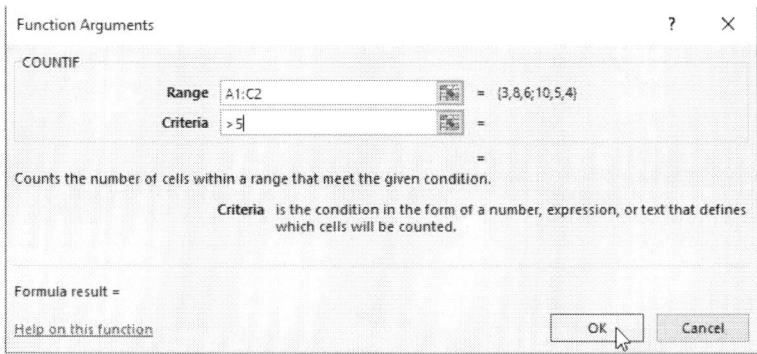

- Then click on Ok.

77

INTRODUCING THE FORMULAR TAB

The Excel ribbon which is located at the top of Excel contains a lot of tabs in which the formula tab is included. The Formula tab is used to insert functions, create a named range, review the formula, etc. The formula tab is divided into four groups, namely:

- *Function library*
- *Defined Names*
- *Formula Auditing*
- *Calculation*

Function Library: Excel contains 461 functions and these are located in the Function Library Group. With the Function Library, you can learn and find a new formula from the formula categories such as Logical, Financial, Text, Math & Trig, etc.

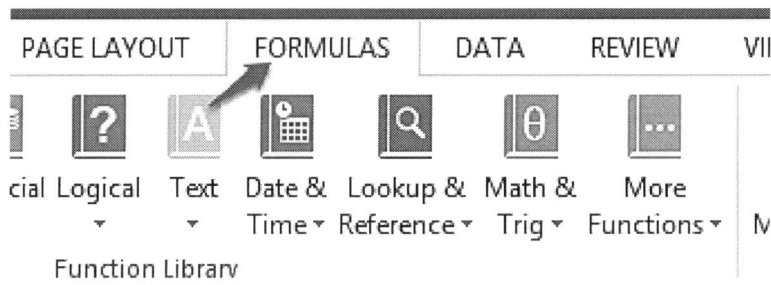

Defined Names: This option allows you to define the name of a cell. This feature allows you to view the named sections on the worksheet in the Name manager and also edit them to any desired defined name if you want

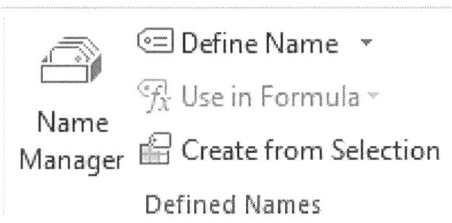

Formula Auditing: This option is used for checking and correcting formulas. This option has the following features;

- o **Trace Precedent:** This helps to know where the formula is based or located on the cell
- o **Trace Dependent:** This helps to check if the active cell is used by any formula
- o **Remove Arrow:** This is used to remove arrows from the cell
- o **Show Formula:** This shows the formula in the worksheet
- o **Error Checking:** This option checks the error in the formula on the worksheet
- o **Evaluate Formula**: This evaluates the formula step by step on the worksheet
- o **Watch Window:** This option allows you to monitor the values on all the cells within the window.

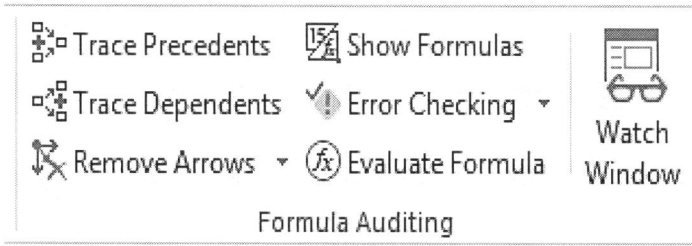

- **Calculation:** This is the option that allows you to switch calculation from automatic to manual

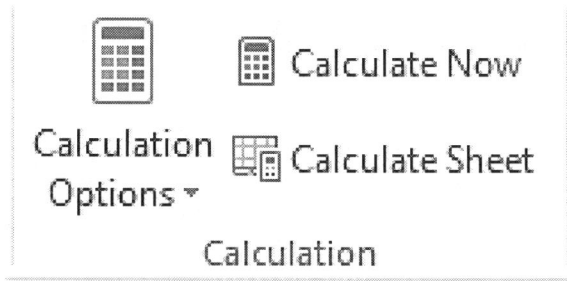

THE FORMULA BAR

The formula bar is a section in the Microsoft Excel worksheet where data or formulas entered into the worksheet appear in the active cell. With the formula bar, you can edit any data or formula typed into the active cell. Another name for the formula bar is the **Formula box.**

WHERE IS THE FORMULA BAR LOCATED IN MICROSOFT EXCEL?

The formula bar can be located above the spreadsheet. Check the picture below to see how the formula bar looks like and where it is located.

EXPANDING THE FORMULA BAR

There are two ways to expand the formula in Excel and they are:

Expanding the Formula Bar Horizontally: To expand the formula bar horizontally

- Move the mouse cursor in between the Name Box and the Formula Bar until the cursor becomes a horizontal double-ended arrow
- Left-click and drag the arrow to adjust the size

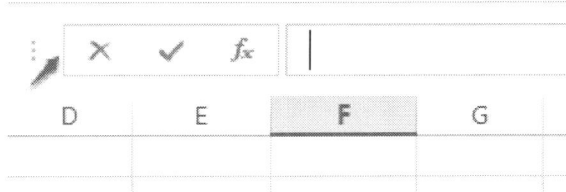

Expanding the Formula Bar Vertically: To expand the formula bar vertically,

- Move the mouse cursor to the bottom of the formula bar until the cursor becomes a horizontal double-ended arrow.
- Left-click and drag the arrow to adjust the size.

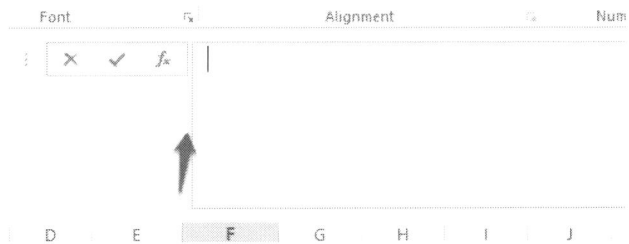

CONTRACTING THE FORMULA BAR

To contract the Formula bar, all you need is to locate the **Contract** or **Expand Toggle** at the right hand.

ENTERING AND EDITING DATA IN THE FORMULA BAR

To enter or edit any data into the formula bar:

- Select the cell you wish to input the data and start typing.
- As the data is being typed in the cell, automatically it appears in the formula bar.
- To accept any data entered, click the **Check Mark** on the formula bar or press **Enter**. To discard the data entered either click the **X** on the formula bar or press **Esc**

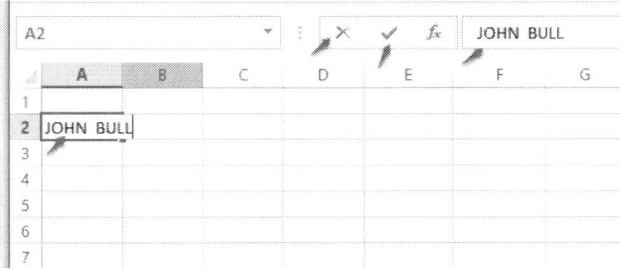

THE INSERT FUNCTION DIALOGUE BOX

This is a dialog box that is used to insert function to any data in a cell in the Excel worksheet. To use the Insert Function box

- Select the cell you wish to insert the function
- Click on the **Insert Function Dialog Box** and select a function
- Then press **Ok**

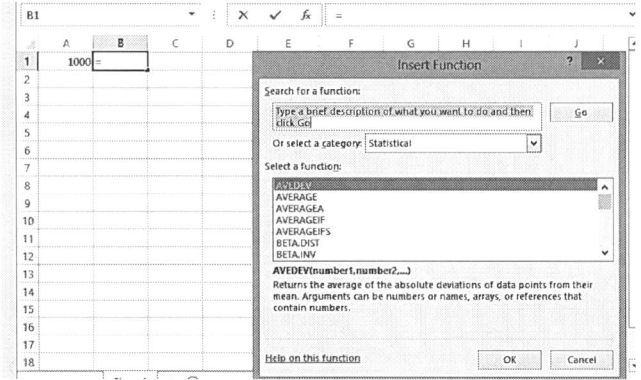

THE FUNCTION ARGUMENT DIALOG BOX

To use the **Function Argument Dialog Box,** you must have first used the **Insert Function Dialog Box.** The Function Argument shows the value that must be provided to get the function's result in the Excel worksheet.

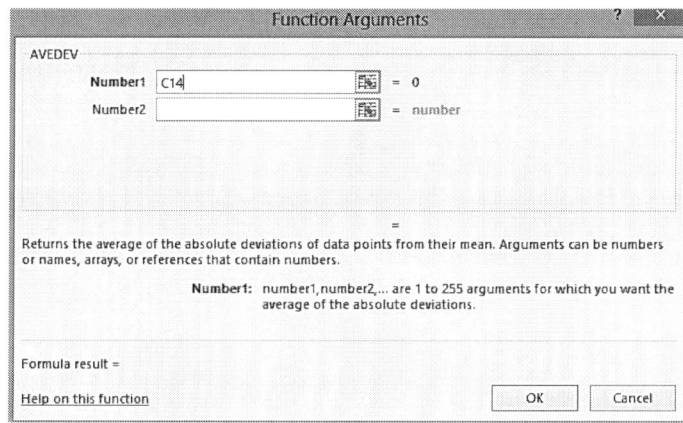

CONTROLLING THE DISPLAY OF THE FORMULA BAR

You can choose to control the display of the formula bar in your worksheet whether to make it visible or not. To do this, follow the steps below:

- From the **File tab**, go to **Option**
- At the left-hand side of the dialog box, click on **Advanced**
- Scroll downward to **Display** and select **Show formula bar**

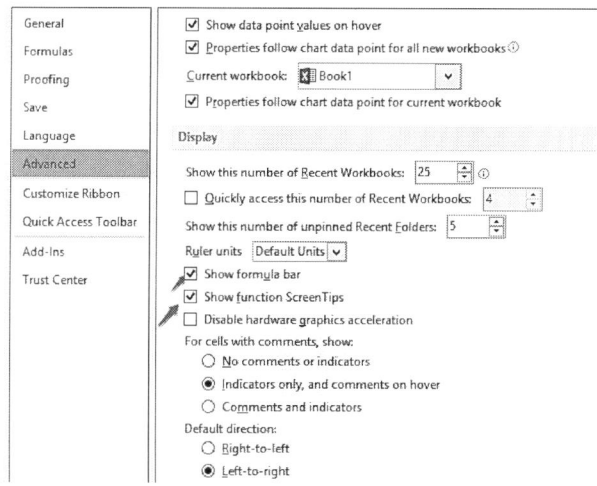

WHAT TYPE OF DATA DOES THE EXCEL FORMULA ACCEPT?

The Excel formula has certain data value it accepts and anything apart from all these may not work. Briefly, let's talk about these values

- **Constant:** These are numbers inputted directly into the formula. A good example is when you enter **=6+5** into a cell to get **11**

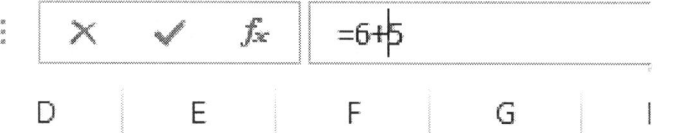

- **Operators:** These are symbols used to perform arithmetic operations (addition, subtraction, division, etc.), comparing values (greater than and less than) and joining values together (&) on Excel.

    For example, inputting **=6>4** into the formula returns the value to **TRUE** and this is because 6 is greater than 4

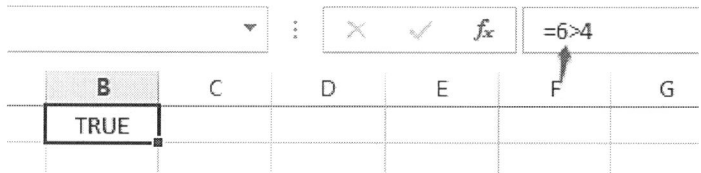

- **Cell References**: These are the values in a worksheet that refer you back to a single cell or range of cells. For Example, inputting A1+B1 in a cell shows that Excel adds the values in both cells in the formula

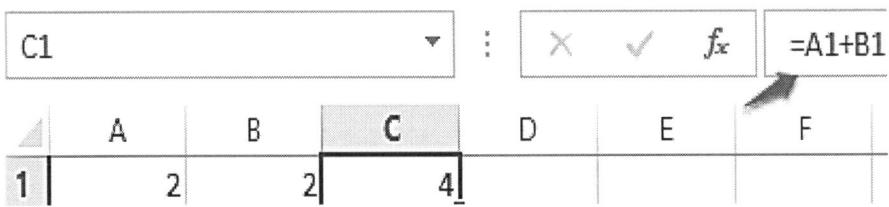

METHODS OF ENTERING AND EDITING OF FORMULAS

Here, we will be talking about how to enter formulas in Excel and also how to edit or make changes to any formulas.

METHODS OF ENTERING OR INSERTING FORMULAS

There are many ways to enter a formula into a cell and they include the following:

- **Simple Insertion:** This involves typing the formula into the cell or formula bar; the formula bar is located above the column headers. This always starts by typing an equality sign, accompanied by the name of the function, and then press **Enter**

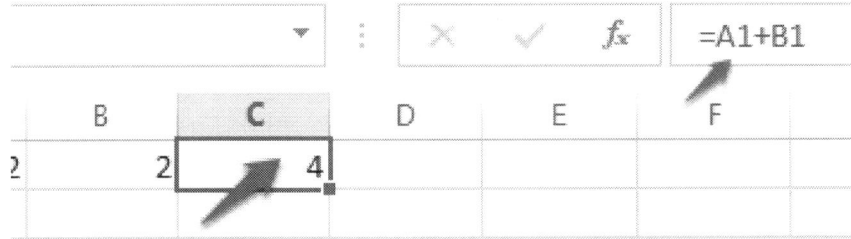

- **The Insert Function:** Another way of entering a formula in Excel is through the Excel Insert Function dialogue box. To use this, go to the **Formulas tab** and select the **Insert function**. The Insert Function contains all the functions you need to use on the worksheet

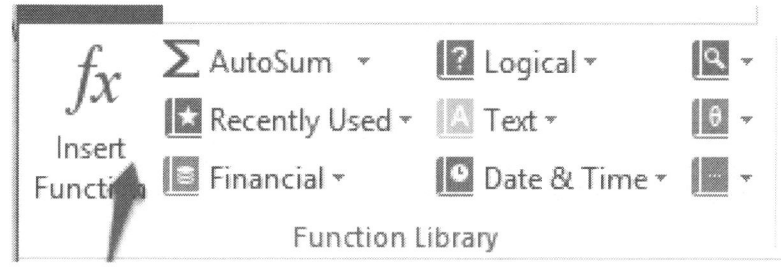

- **Selecting A Formula from One of The Groups in The Formula Tab:** You can enter formulas into your worksheet by selecting the formula from the groups of formula in the Formula tab. To locate a group of formula, move to the **Formula tab** and then select the preferred group from all other groups. In case you don't see your preference, you can click on **More function** options. These groups of the formula are found in the Formula Library

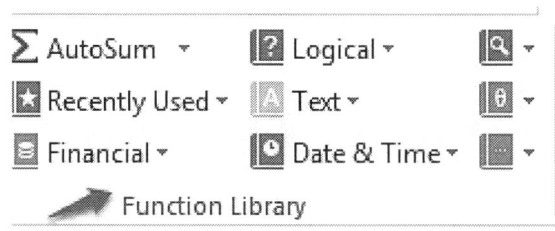

EDITING A FORMULA

Let's assume you need to edit a formula in your worksheet, there are three ways to go about it and they are listed below:

- **Editing Directly in The Formula Bar**: To edit any formula, go to the Formula to start the editing of the formula

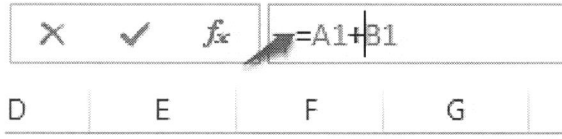

- **Double Clicking on The Formula Cell:** You can also edit any formula by clicking directly into the cell. By doing this, the cell is activated into an **Edit mode** where the formula can be edited

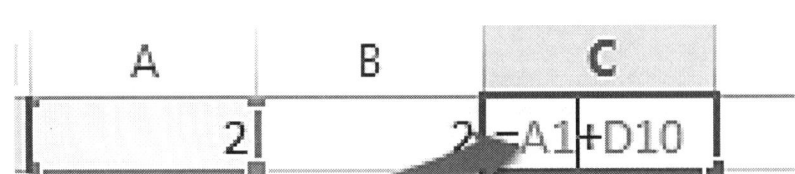

USING THE FORMULA OPERATORS

Formula operators are symbols that specify the operation to be carried out or accomplished in the Excel formula. The formula operators are divided into seven categories which are:

- Arithmetic
- Comparison
- Concatenation
- Logical
- Access
- the If
- the Alt operators.

Arithmetic Operators: These are operators that perform basic mathematical operations such as addition, subtraction, division or multiplication. These operators work with numbers. The different arithmetic operators are as follows in the table below:

ARITHMETIC OPERATOR	NUMBERS OF OPERANDS	ARITHMETIC FUNCTION	EXAMPLES
Plus sign +	2	Addition	3+5
Minus sign -	2	Subtraction	6-2
Minus sign -	1	Negation	-6
Asterisk *	2	Multiplication	3*7
Forward slash /	2	Division	4/2
Exponentiation ^	2	Raise the power of a value	4^2
Percent %	1	Divide by 100	45%

Comparison Operators: These operators compare two numbers with each other and they involve two input values and produce one output value. These operators involve greater than, less than, etc. They are listed in the table below:

COMPARISON OPERATOR	MEANING	EXAMPLE
Equal sign =	Equal to	5=5
Less than sign <	Less than	2<4
Greater than sign >	Greater than	5>3
Greater than or equal to sign >=	Greater than or equal to	67>=321
Less than or equal to sign =<	Less than or equal to	521=321
Not equal to sign <>	Not equal to	5<>7

Concatenation Operator: This operator joins or connects two or more texts or strings to produce a single text or string. The input values received by this operator are texts and if otherwise, they are automatically changed to texts.

OPERATOR	MEANING	EXAMPLE
Ampersand &	Connect or join two values to produce a single text	"In" & "put" to form "Input"

Logical Operators: There are three logical operations which are *And, Or, and Not*. They receive Boolean values as the values of their operands and they produce one Boolean value as their result or output. The logical operators are expressed in the table below:

LOGICAL OPERATOR	NUMBERS OF OPERANDS	MEANINGS	EXAMPLE
And	2	True if both input values are true	5<3 **and** amount <3
Or	2	True if one of the input value is true	7>5 **or** 4<7
Not	1	Reverses the value of its input value	**not** 5>6

Reference Operators: These operators join cells together for calculations and they are as follows:

REFERENCE OPERATOR	MEANING
(colon):	Range operator: This gives one reference to all the cells between two reference
comma '	Union operator: This joins multiple references into one reference
space	Intersection operator: This gives one reference to cells common to the two references.

- **Access Operators:** These consist of the Dot operator (.), the Index operator ([]), and the at operator (@).
- **The "Alt" Operator:** This operator is used to specify several alternative formulae that can be used in a cell
- **The "if" Operator:** The If operator is used to performing conditional calculations on the Excel worksheet.

ORDER OF FORMULA OPERATORS PRECEDENCE

Formula operator precedence can be defined as the order in which the numeric base executes or carry out the operation in the formula. In the Excel worksheet, the operators are evaluated to execute calculations or workings in a specific order. For instance, Excel executes division before subtraction. The order of operators' formula is as follows:

- The member access operator (. [] and @)
- Negation (-1)
- Multiplication and division (* and /)
- Addition and subtraction (+ and -)
- The comparison operators (= < > <= >= < and >)
- Concatenation operator (&)
- Logical operator (not and or)
- The If operator
- The Alt operator

THE NESTED PARENTHESES

Nested parentheses are parentheses inside other parentheses. When there is a set of parentheses inside another, Excel evaluates the innermost set of parentheses first before the outer parentheses; = ((A2+B2) +(C2/D2) *E2

Note that every open parenthesis must have a matching close parenthesis. In the course of adding parentheses to your formula, you can get confused and lost and that is why Excel helps to give the open parenthesis and matching close parentheses the same colour for easy and quick identification.

WORKING WITH FUNCTIONS

As earlier said, a function is a predefined or pre-set formula. Functions give a quick and easy way to accomplish or execute a common task. There are a lot of calculations that cannot be done with formula except with functions.

WHY SHOULD YOU USE FUNCTIONS?

There are several reasons why you should use or get yourself acquainted with the use of Excel function. The following are the reasons:
- One of the benefits of the Excel function is that it helps to simplify your formula. For instance, you can add the value of C1 to C3 by using =SUM (C1:C3) rather than using =(C1+C2+C3).
- Function helps to execute calculations that cannot be done using the standard formula. For instance, there is no way you can get the highest or lowest number using the formula but with the function, you can use the **MAX** or **MIN** function.
- Function also helps to save time and reduce the stress of having to accomplish what you would have naturally done with a formula for long hours to be done in just a short period. For instance, using the LEFT function to bring out the left 8 characters in a cell; =LEFT(A1,10).

THE FUNCTION ARGUMENTS

Function arguments are the inputs or values needed by functions to perform or carry out calculations on the worksheet. For functions to calculate correctly, some information is needed which are known as the arguments.

To construct a function, the function name and arguments are required. When you need to use a function, enter the name of the function, open the parenthesis, followed by the argument to use, and lastly the close parenthesis; e.g., **AVERAGE (B2:C5)**

USING FUNCTIONS WITH NO ARGUMENTS

Some functions do not require the use of arguments to carry out their operations. These functions include RAND, TODAY, and NOW function. **Note** that even though these functions do not require the use of arguments, they still need to be used with the open and close parentheses; **=RAND ()**

USING FUNCTION WITH ONE OR MORE ARGUMENTS

There are some functions that require more than one argument to execute their operations. To separate the arguments in the function, a

comma is used. A very good example is the LARGE function. The LARGE function returns the largest number within the range of a cell. For instance, to get the fourth largest value in a range from A1 to A50, just type in the LARGE function on the formula bar

=LAREGE (A1:A3, 4)

USING FUNCTIONS WITH BOTH REQUIRED AND OPTIONAL ARGUMENT

Some functions do not only use their required arguments, they also come with optional arguments to execute their operations of which the NETWORKDAYS function is included.

The NETWORKDAYS function gives or returns the number of workdays between the start date and the end date. To get this result, you will need to use the required arguments which are the start date and the end date. And by implication, the answer will be 260 workdays from January 1, 2015 to December 31, 2015.

=NETWORKDAYS ("1/1/2015","12/31/2015")

The optional arguments in the NETWORKDAYS Function allow you to exclude the range that contains the list of holiday dates. The function sees each date in the optional arguments as non-working days and thereby, returning the result to be 255 workdays from January 1, 2015, and December 31, 2015.

NETWORKDAYS ("1/1/2015","12/31/2015", A1:A5)

LOCATING A FUNCTION'S ARGUMENTS

There are two ways of finding the required arguments of a function in a worksheet. They include the following:

- *The Function Dialogue Box*
- *Tooltip Windows in Excel*

- **The Excel Function Dialogue Boxes**: Every function in Excel has a dialogue box that contains or shows the list of the required and optional arguments. To open a function dialogue box, all you need to do is;
    - Go to the Ribbon and click on the Formula tab
    - Click on Insert Function and the function argument box will be displayed

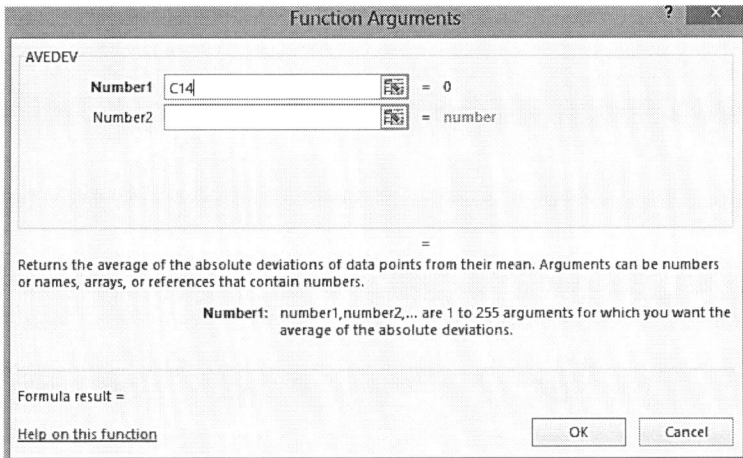

- **Tooltips**: Another way to find the function's arguments in Excel is through the Tooltips. To find the arguments;
    - Select a cell and type the equal sign to notify the program that a formula is inputted

- Type the function's name with the open parenthesis: by doing this, the function name and its arguments are listed in the tooltips

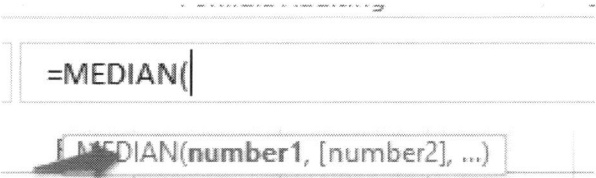

ERRORS IN FORMULAS AND FUNCTIONS

Of a truth, working with Excel functions and formulas can be difficult and time-consuming, especially when the formula or function returns an error in value instead of what you have in mind. Quickly, I will open your eyes to the seven errors that can occur while working with your functions and formulas and as well as the reason behind them.

#DIV/0! This error value implies that the formula is attempting to divide a value by zero. And mathematically, no number can be divided by zero. This can also occur when you are trying to divide an empty cell by zero.

#NAME? This error value means that the name used in a formula is not recognized by Excel as a valid object. This error can occur as a result of wrong spelling of function, sheet name, cell reference, or other syntax error.

#N/A: This error value means that the formula cannot give a valid or legitimate result. This error occurs when an inappropriate argument is used in a function. Also, this can happen when the lookup function does not a match.

#NULL! This error value implies that the formula uses an intersection of two ranges that do not relate or interact.

#NUM! This error value implies that there is a problem with a number in your formula most especially an invalid argument in math or trig function. For instance, when you are expected to give a positive number but you gave a negative number.

#REF! This error value connotes that the formula contains an invalid cell reference and this can be caused when a row or column to which the formula is referred is deleted or the formula uses a cell reference that does not exist.

#VALUE This error value implies that there is a wrong usage of data for operation by your formula.

DIFFERENCES BETWEEN AN EXCEL FORMULA AND FUNCTION

The Excel formulas and functions look-alike in so many ways and can be used interchangeably to perform the same operations. However, there is a lot of differences between them. Therefore, we will be stating some of the common differences:

- A **Formula** is a statement written by the users to calculate the value of data in a cell (A1*B2, C3*D4, etc. **WHILE** a **Function** is a piece of code already designed in the Excel worksheet to carry out a pre-defined operation on the Excel (SUM, AVERAGE, MIN, MAX, etc.).
- A **Formula** does not have a name **WHILE** every **Function** has a name.
- A **Formula** does not have a structure or syntax **WHILE Functions** have syntax.
- A **Formula** does not have a predefined parameter **WHILE** every **Function** has its predefined parameter for executing result.
- **Formulas** are mathematical equations WHILE **Function** uses words.

While using the Excel formula, keep the following in mind:

- Excel formulas must begin with an equal (=) sign. With this sign, Excel is able to identify it as a formula
- The answer to the formula is shown in the cell where the formula is entered.

USING CALCULATION OPERATORS IN EXCEL FORMULAS

Operators in Excel helps to identify or distinguish the type of calculation to be performed with the Formulas. There are four major types of calculation operators and they are as follows:

Arithmetic Operators: These are used to perform mathematical operations such as addition, subtraction, multiplication and division with numbers combined with them to produce a numeric result.

Arithmetic Operator	Meaning
+ (plus sign)	Addition
- (minus sign)	Subtraction
* (asterisk)	Multiplication
/ (forward slash)	Division
% (percent)	Percent
^ (caret)	Exponentiation

Comparison Operators: These are operators used to compare two values, therefore, giving a logical value. The following are the comparison operators

Comparison Operator	Meaning
=	Equal to
>	Greater than
<	Less than
>=	Greater than or equal to
<=	Less than or equal to
<>	Not equal to

Text Concatenation Operator: This uses the ampersand sign (&) to concatenate i.e., join one or more texts to form a single piece of text.

Reference Operators: These operators join cells together for calculations and they are as follows:

Reference Operator	Meaning
: (colon)	Range operator: This gives one reference to all the cells between two reference
, (comma)	Union operator: This joins multiple references into one reference
(space)	Intersection operator: This gives one reference to cells common to the two references.

MATHEMATICAL ORDER OF OPERATION IN EXCEL

There is an order of operation to follow when carrying out a mathematical calculation on Excel, especially arithmetic operation. Excel follows the general mathematical rules which are **Parenthesis, Exponents, Multiplication and Division**, and **Addition and Subtraction**. The following steps below show how they are applied;

- The values inside the parenthesis are calculated first.
- Secondly, the exponents are calculated.
- Then the multiplication or division is calculated.
- Lastly, the addition or subtraction is also calculated.

ARITHMETIC IN EXCEL

Here, we will be performing some basic arithmetic operations such as addition, subtraction, division, multiplication, etc.

The Plus Sign (+): This performs the addition of one or more cell

To add,

- Select the cell that will contain the formula
- Type in first, the equal to sign followed. by the first cell address with the **Plus sign** and lastly followed by the last cell address
- Then click on enter.

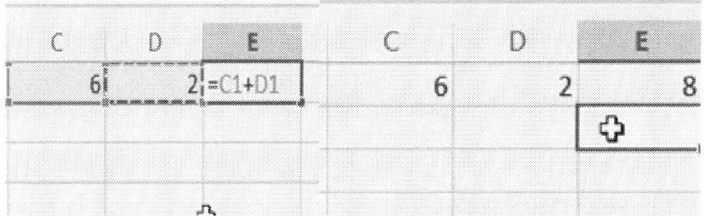

The Minus Sign (-): This is used for subtracting one cell from the other.

To subtract,

- Select the cell that will contain the formula
- Type in first, the equal to sign followed by the first cell address with the **Minus sign** and lastly followed by the last cell address
- Then click on enter.

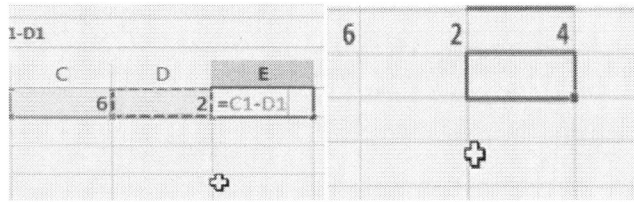

The Asterisk (*): This is used to perform multiplication between two or more cells.

To multiply,

- Select the cell that will contain the formula
- Type in first, the equal to sign followed by the first cell address with the **Asterisk sign** and lastly followed by the last cell address
- Then click on enter.

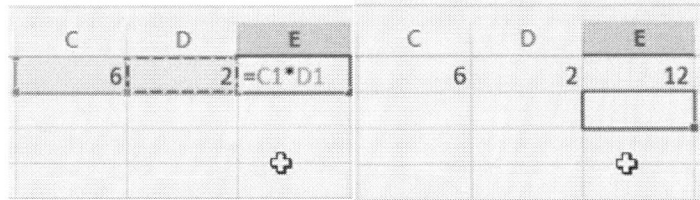

The Forward Slash (/): This is used for dividing

- Select the cell that will contain the formula
- Type in first, the equal to sign followed by the first cell address with the **Forward slash sign** and lastly followed by the last cell address
- Then click on enter.

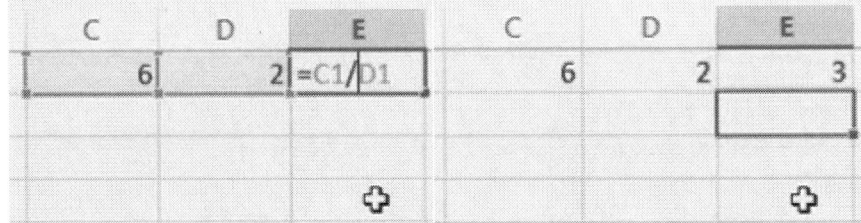

The Percent Sign (%): This divides numbers in the cell by 100

- Select the cell that will contain the formula
- Type in first, the equal to sign followed by the first cell address and followed by the **Percentage sign**
- Then click on enter.

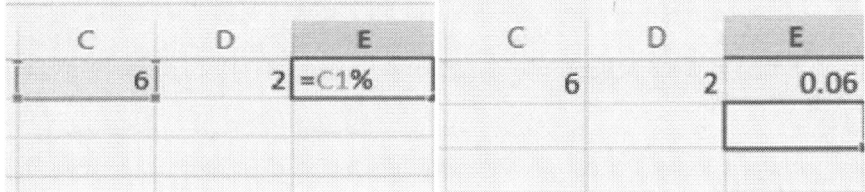

The Caret Sign (^): This is used to perform exponentiation

- Select the cell that will contain the formula
- Type in first, the equal to sign followed by the first cell address and followed by the **Caret sign**
- Then click on enter.

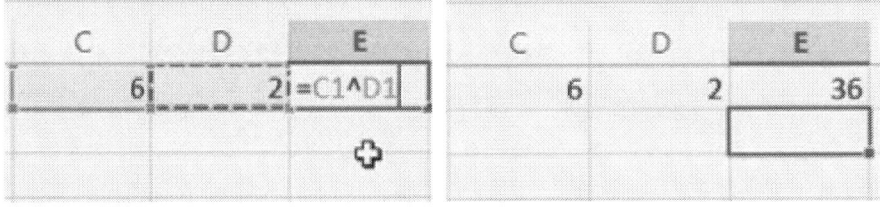

CHAPTER SIX

MUST KNOW EXCEL FORMULAS & FUNCTIONS

Since you have made it this far in this journey of learning more about Excel, there are certain formulas and functions in Excel you should be well acquainted with whether you are a pro or a rookie, it just doesn't matter. Therefore, we will be taking our time to discuss the basic formulas and functions that you need to know.

MATH FUNCTIONS

Math functions are functions that are used to perform arithmetic operations such as percentage of totals, addition, and basic business analysis.

THE SUM FUNCTION

The SUM function allows you to add or sum up the value of selected rows or columns.

=SUM (number1, [number2], ...)

For reference purpose

To insert the SUM function

- In the cell, type the SUM function
- Go to the Function argument to select the cells into the cell range box
- Then click on Enter.

The SUM function uses the following arguments

=SUM (number1, [number2], [number3]......)

- **Number1(Required Argument):** This is the first value to sum
- **Number2 (Optional Argument):** This is the second value to sum

- **Number3 (Optional Argument):** This is the third value to sum

USING THE SUM FUNCTION

With the table, let's calculate the sum of the sales made from Monday to Friday using the SUM function

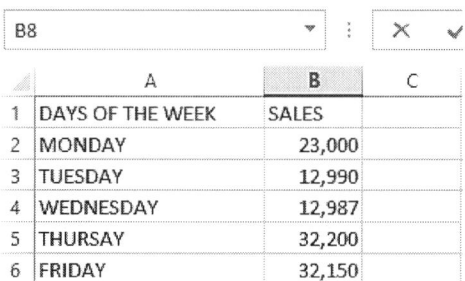

To calculate the sales from Monday to Friday using SUM, follow the steps below

- Select an empty cell and type in the function with the cell range to be summed up; **=SUM (A2:B6)**

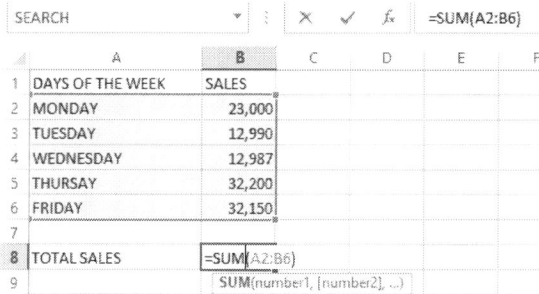

- If you have followed the steps above, the total sales from Monday to Friday will be **113327**

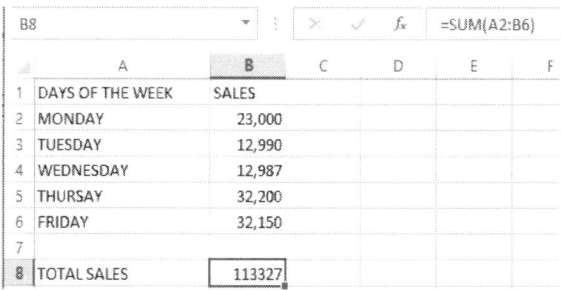

NOTE: Keep this in mind while using the SUM function

- #VALUE! error occurs when the criteria supplied is more than 255 characters long
- SUM function ignores empty cells and cells with text values automatically
- The arguments provided can be constants, ranges, named ranges, or cell references
- Any argument that contains errors is returned as an error by the SUM function

THE SUMIF FUNCTION

The SUM function is one that sums up cells based on the criteria or condition provided. The Criteria or conditions are based on dates, numbers, and texts. This function makes use of logical operators such as <, >, etc. and wildcats (*,?)

The SUMIF function uses the following arguments

=SUMIF (range, criteria, [sum_range]

- **Range (Required Argument):** This is the range of cell that the criteria are applied against
- **Criteria (Required Argument):** This is what determines the cells to be summed up. Criteria arguments can be supplied in
    - A numerical value such as integer, decimal, or time
    - A text string such as Monday, East, Price, etc.
    - An expression e.g. >11, <3 etc.
- **Sum_range (Optional Argument):** This is the cell to sum up if there are other cells to sum up apart from the ones specified in the range argument

USING THE SUMIF FUNCTION

To have a clear picture of how the SUMIF function is used, let's calculate the sales made in January and also in USA

First of all, let's calculate the total sales made in Jan by following the steps below

- Select an empty cell, type in the function with the cell range to be summed up; **=SUM (A2:A8**

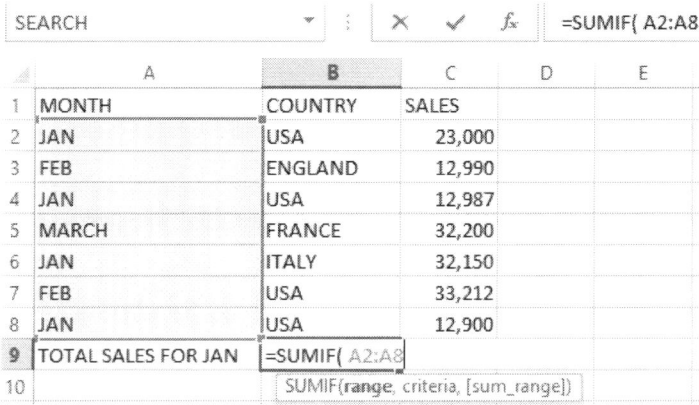

- Put in the criteria which is **Jan**; **SUM (A2:A8, "JAN",**

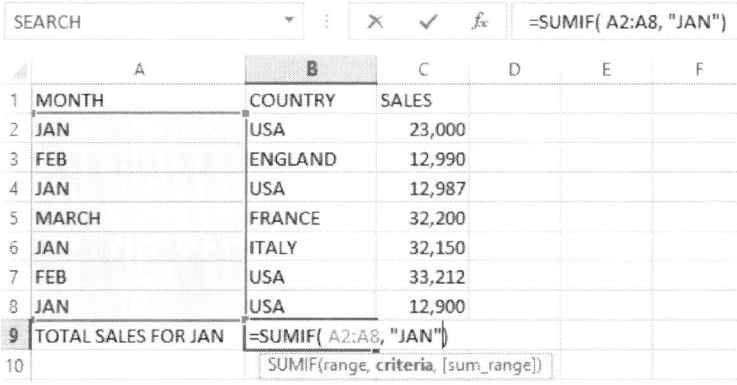

- Then put in the sum_range; **SUM (A2:A8, "JAN", C2;C8)**

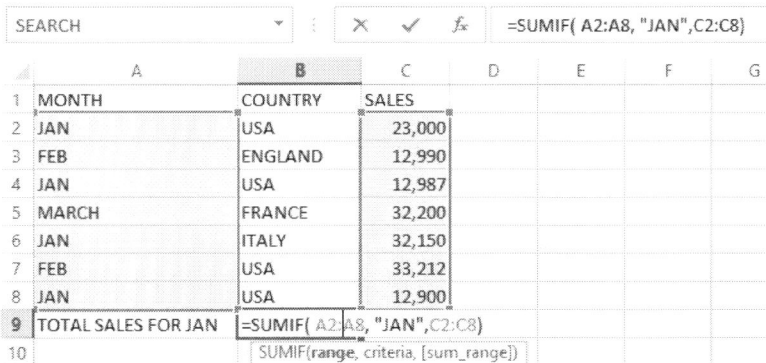

- The total sale of Jan is **81,037** and it is shown in the table below

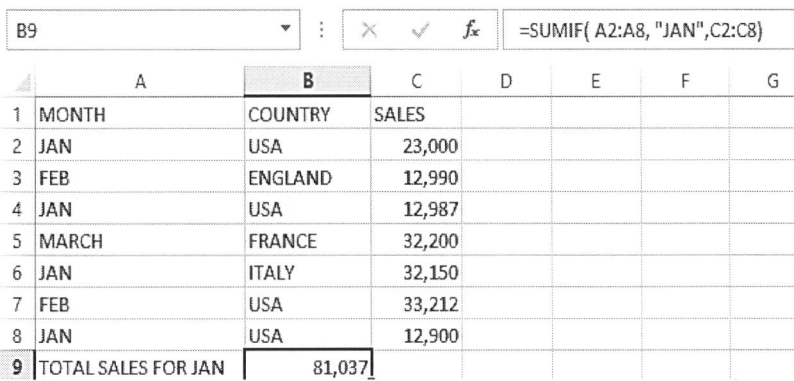

To get the total sales made in USA;

- Select an empty cell and type in the function with the cell range to be summed up; **=SUM(B2:B8**

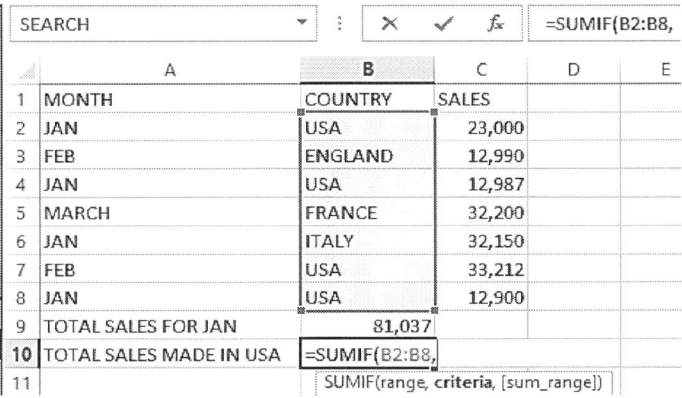

- Put in the criteria which are **USA**; **SUM(B2:B8 "USA"**

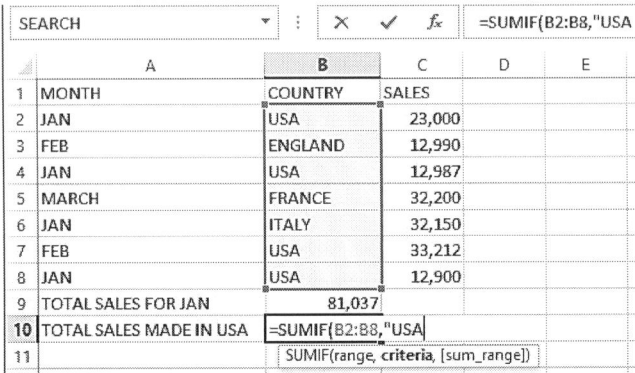

- Then put in the sum_range; **SUM(B2:B8, "USA", B2:B8)**

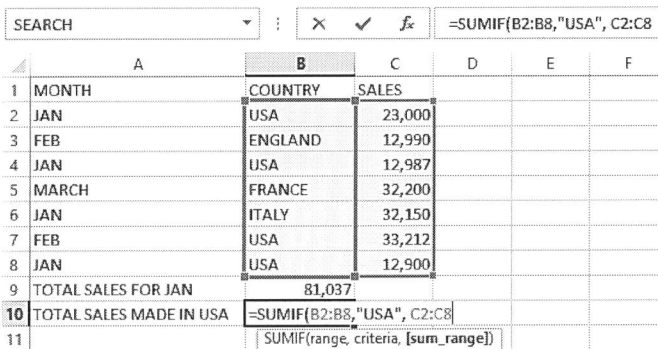

- The total sales made in USA is shown in the table below

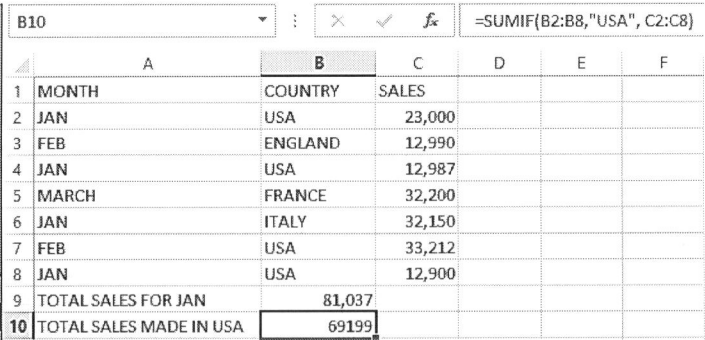

NOTE: Keep this in mind when using the SUMIF FUNCTION

- VALUE! error occurs when the criteria supplied is more than 255 characters long

- The cells in range will be summed automatically when the sum_range is omitted
- Text strings in criteria must be enclosed in double-quotes otherwise, it will not work
- The wildcards ? and * can be used in the SUMIF function

THE SUMIFS FUNCTION

The SUMIFS function is a function that is used to add cells that meet multiple criteria or conditions. The Criteria or conditions are based on dates, numbers, and texts. This function makes use of logical operators such as <, >, ≤ etc., and wildcards (*,?)

The SUMIFS FUNCTION uses the following arguments

SUMIFS (sum_range, criteria_range1, criteria1, [criteria_range2, criteria2] ...)

- **Sum_range:** This is the range to be summed up
- **Criteria_range1:** This is the range of cells that the criteria1 will be applied against
- **Criteria1:** This is used to determine the cells to be added
- **Criteria_range2:** This is the range of cells that the criteria2 will be applied against

USING THE SUMIFS FUNCTION

With the table below, let's calculate the total quantity of Apples supplied by Pete using the **SUMIFS** function

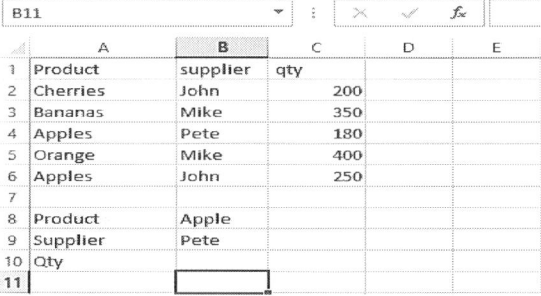

To calculate the total quantity of Apple that was supplied by Pete, follow the steps below

- Select an empty cell and type in the function with the cell range to be summed up; **=SUMIFS(C2:C6, A2:A6, "apples", B2:B6, "Pete")**

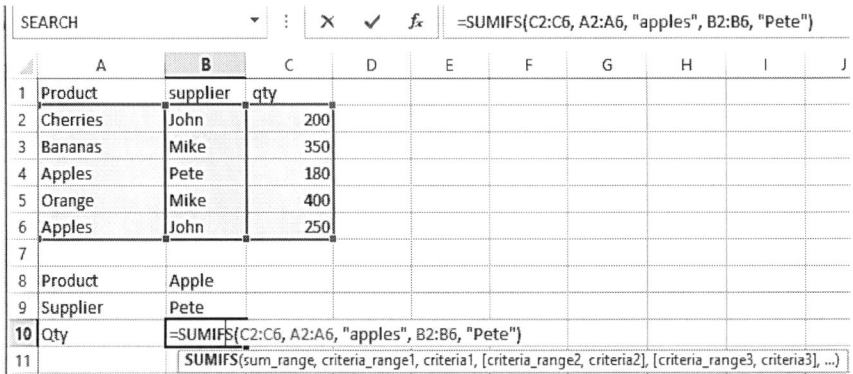

- After following the formula above, the total quantity of apples supplied will be **180**

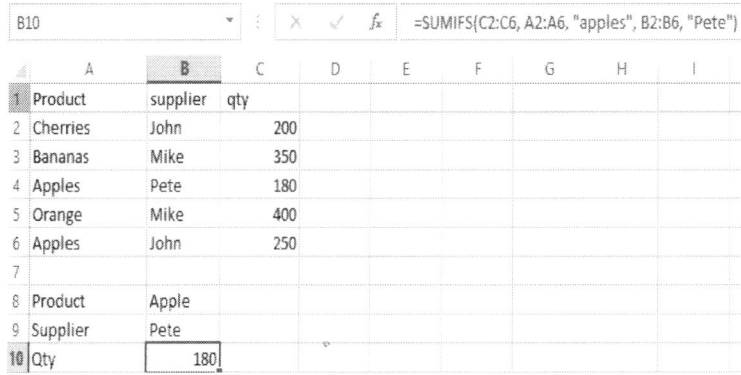

NOTE: Take note of the following when using the SUMIFS functions

- Text strings in criteria must be enclosed in double-quotes ("") e.g., "orange"
- The additional range must have the same number of rows and columns as sum_range.
- #VALUE error occurs when the supplied ranges do not match
- Cell references in criteria are not enclosed in quotes
- SUMIFS can be used on ranges and not on arrays

THE MOD FUNCTION

The MOD function is used to find the remainder of a number (dividend) that has been divided by another number (divisor).

The MOD function uses the following arguments:

- **Number (Required Argument):** This is the number you wish to find the remainder
- **Divisor (Required Argument):** This is the number by which we wish to divide the number

USING THE MOD FUNCTION

With the table below, find the remainder of cell A2 using the MOD function

	A	B	C	D
1	Number	Divisor	MOD FUNCTION	
2	23	2		
3	21	3		
4				
5				
6				

To find the remainder of A2, follow the steps below:

- Click on an empty cell, type in the function to be used, the number, and the divisor; **=MOD(A2, B2**

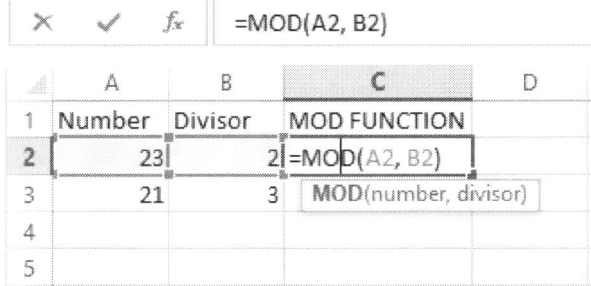

- The result of the above step is shown in the table below

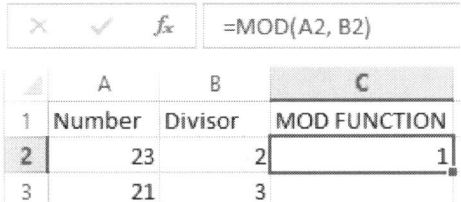

NOTE: Things to keep in mind while using the MOD function:

- #DID/0! Error occurs when the divisor value is zero
- The MOD function will return a result in the same sign as the divisor

RANDBETWEEN FUNCTION

The RANDBETWEEN function is a function that returns a random integer as the numbers provided. This function recalculates each time the worksheet is opened or changed.

The RANDBETWEEN function uses the following arguments

=RANDBETWEEN (bottom, top)

- **Bottom: (Required Function):** This is the smallest integer in which the function will return in the range
- **Top (Required Function):** This is the largest integer in which the function will return in the range

USING THE RANDBETWEEN FUNCTION

To understand how the RANDBETWEEN function is being used, let examine the table below

	A	B	C	D
1	Bottom	Top	Result	
2	2	3	3	
3	3	10	4	
4	120	300	205	
5	32	121	102	

Formula: =RANDBETWEEN(A2, B2)

The table above shows that the RANDBETWEEN function has been applied; =RANDBETWEEN (A2, B2).

- When the calculations on the table are executed again, the worksheet changes its result as shown in the table below

	A	B	C	D
1	Bottom	Top	Result	
2	2	3	2	
3	3	10	8	
4	120	300	181	
5	32	121	87	

NOTE: Few notes to keep in mind when using the RANDBETWEEN function

- RANDBETWEEN function returns a new value each time the worksheet is recalculated or changed.
- To stop the random number from changing when the worksheet is calculated, type the RANDBETWEEN function in the formula bar and then press F9 to change the formula into its result
- To generate a set of random numbers in multiple cells, select the cells, enter the RANDBETWEEN function and then press **Ctrl + Enter**

THE ROUND FUNCTION

The ROUND function is a function that rounds up a number to a specific number of digits. This function can either round up or down.

The ROUND function uses the following arguments

=ROUND(number, num_digits)

- **Number1 (Required Argument):** This is the number you want to round

- **Num_digits (Required Argument):** This is the number of digits to which you want to round the number

USING THE ROUND FUNCTION

Let's round 1844.123 to one decimal place, two decimal, nearest integer, nearest 10, nearest 100, and nearest 1000 using the ROUND function

- Round 1844.123 to one decimal place by entering **=ROUND(A1, 1)**

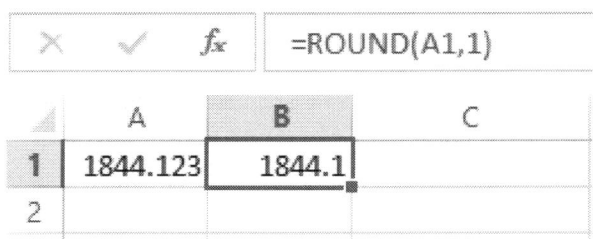

- Round 1844.123 to two decimal place by entering **=ROUND(A1, 2)**

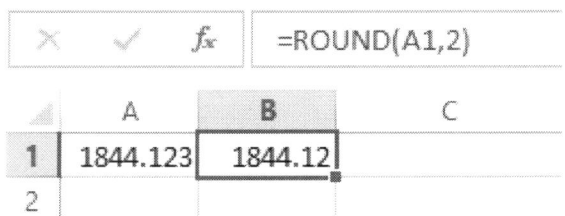

- Round 1844.123 to the nearest integer by entering **=ROUND(A1, 0)**

- Round 1844.123 to the nearest 10 by entering **=ROUND(A1, -1)**

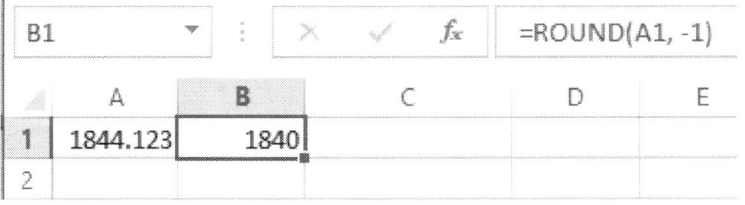

- Round 1844.123 to the nearest 100 by entering **=ROUND(A1,- 2)**

	A	B	C	D	E
1	1844.123	1800			
2					

- Round 1844.123 to the nearest 1000 by entering **=ROUND(A1, -3)**

	A	B	C	D	E
1	1844.123	2000			
2					

THE ROUNDUP FUNCTION

The ROUNDUP function is a function that allows you to round up numbers from a certain number of decimal points.

The ROUNDUP function uses the following arguments

=ROUNDUP(number, num_digits)

- **Number1 (Required Argument):** This is the number you want to round up
- **Num_digits (Required Argument):** This is the number of digits to which you want to round the number

USING THE ROUNDUP FUNCTION

Let's round up 1233.345 to one decimal place, two decimal, nearest integer, nearest 10, nearest 100, and nearest 1000 using the ROUNDUP function

- Round up 1233.345 to one decimal place by entering **=ROUNDUP(A1, 1)**

	A	B	C	D	E
1	1233.345	1233.4			
2					

- Round up 1233.345 to two decimal place by entering **=ROUNDUP(A1, 2)**

	A	B	C	D	E
1	1233.345	1233.35			
2					

- Round up 1233.345 to the nearest integer by entering **=ROUNDUP(A1, 0)**

	A	B	C	D	E
1	1233.345	1234			
2					

- Round up 1233.345 to the nearest 10 by entering **=ROUNDUP(A1, -1)**

	A	B	C	D	E
1	1233.345	1240			
2					

- Round up 1233.345 to the nearest 100 by entering =ROUNDUP(A1, -2)

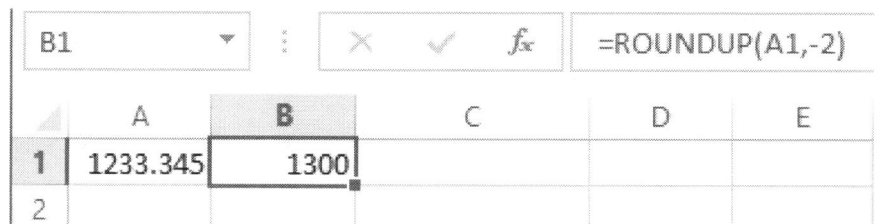

- Round up 1233.345 to the nearest 1000 by entering =ROUNDUP(A1, -3)

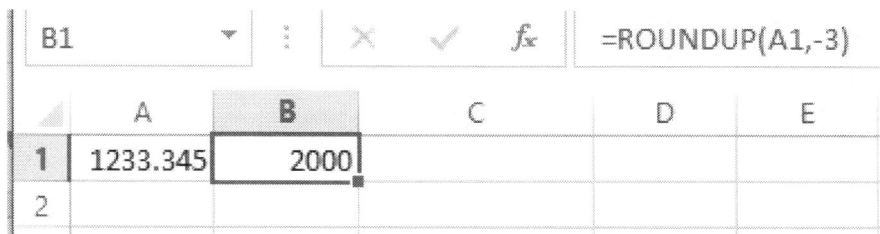

THE ROUNDDOWN FUNCTION

The ROUND DOWN function is a function that allows you to round down numbers from a certain number of decimal points.

The ROUND DOWN function uses the following arguments

=ROUNDUP(number, num_digits)

- **Number1 (Required Argument):** This is the number you want to round down
- **Num_digits (Required Argument):** This is the number of digits to which you want to round the number

USING THE ROUNDDOWN FUNCTION

Let's round up 1233.345 to one decimal place, two decimal, nearest integer, nearest 10, nearest 100, and nearest 1000 using the **ROUNDDOWN** function

- Round down 1233.345 to one decimal place by entering **=ROUNDDOWN(A1, 1)**

- Round down 1233.345 to two decimal place by entering **=ROUNDDOWN(A1, 2)**

- Round down 1233.345 to the nearest integer by entering **=ROUNDDOWN(A1, 0)**

- Round down 1233.345 to the nearest 10 by entering **=ROUNDDOWN(A1, -1)**

- Round down 1233.345 to the nearest 100 by entering =ROUNDDOWN(A1, -2)

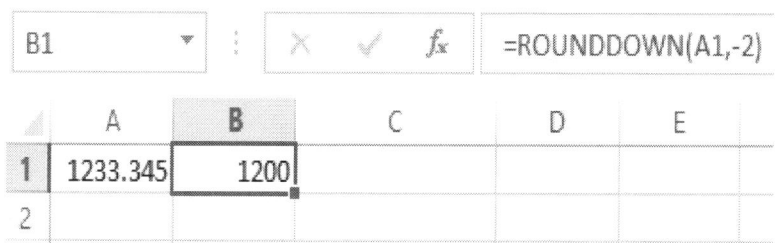

- Round up 1233.345 to the nearest 1000 by entering =ROUNDUP(A1, -3)

THE SORT FUNCTION

The Sort function is a function that is used to sort the content of a column in an ascending or descending order

The SORT function uses the following arguments

=SORT (array, [sort_index], [sort_order], [by col])

- **Array (Required argument)**: This is the range or array that contains the value to be sorted out
- **Sort_index (Optional Argument):** This specifies the row or column to sorted out
- **Sort _order (Optional Argument):** This is the number for sorting the cells; 1 for ascending and -1 for descending. If this part is omitted. It will sort automatically in ascending order
- **By_col (Optional Argument):** This specifies where the sorting is directed to; FALSE to sort by row and TRUE to sort by column.

USING THE SORT FUNCTION

Using the table below, arrange the cells in ascending order using the SORT formula

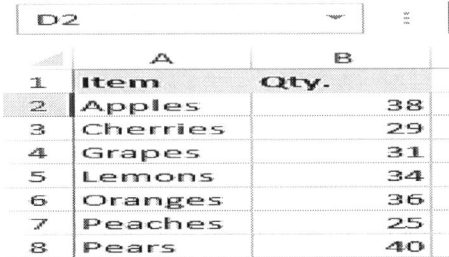

To sort in ascending order i.e., arranging from the smallest to the highest, follow the steps below

- Click into an empty cell and type in the function to be used (**=SORT**), the source array (**A2:B8**), the sort index **(2)**, and sort_order **(1)**. In summary, =SORT(A2:B8, 2, 1)

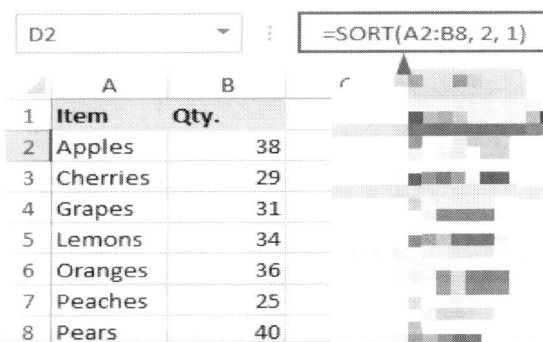

- Click on Enter, and the data will be arranged in ascending order

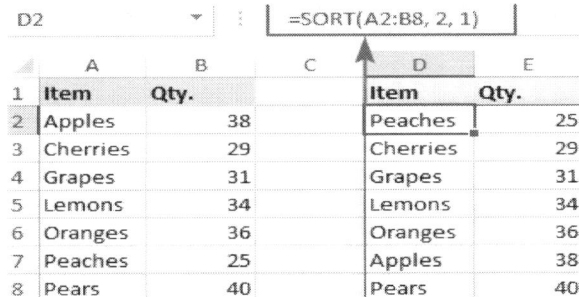

To sort in descending order, i.e., arranging from highest to the lowest

- Click into an empty cell and type in the function to be used (**=SORT**), the source array (**A2:B8**), the sort index **(2)**, and sort_order **(1)**. In summary =**SORT(A2:B8, 2,- 1)**

- Click on Enter, and the data will be arranged in descending order

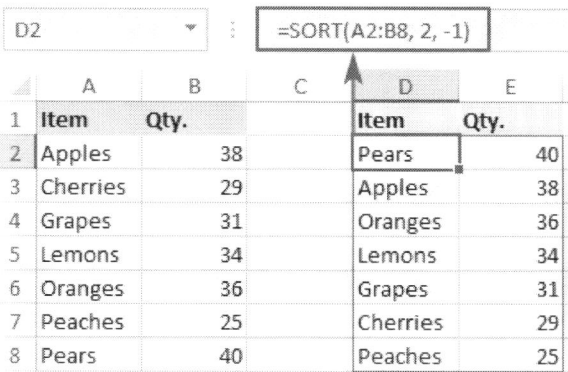

NOTE: Things to know about the SORT function

- By default, the SORT function sort values in ascending order using the first column
- The SORT function is only available in Microsoft 365 subscription
- The result is updated automatically as the source data is changing

CHAPTER SEVEN

STATISTICAL FUNCTIONS

The statistical functions are functions that apply mathematical processes or operations to a range of cells in a worksheet. The statistical functions were introduced from Excel 2013 and all later versions. Examples of statistical functions are COUNT, COUNTA, AVERAGE, etc.

THE COUNT FUNCTION

The COUNT function is a function that counts the number of cells that contain numbers and also counts the numbers of arguments that contain numbers.

The COUNT function uses the following arguments

=COUNT(value1, value2…)

- **Value1 (Required Argument)**: This is the cell range with which you wish to count the ones with numbers.
- **Value2, …(Optional Argument):** Here, you can add up to additional 255 items, cell references, or ranges within which you wish to count numbers

USING THE COUNT FUNCTION

Using the table below, let's count the number of cells that have numbers using the COUNT function

To know the cells that have numbers, using the COUNT function, follow the steps below

- Select an empty cell, type in the function name, and followed by the arguments; **=COUNT(A2:B5)**

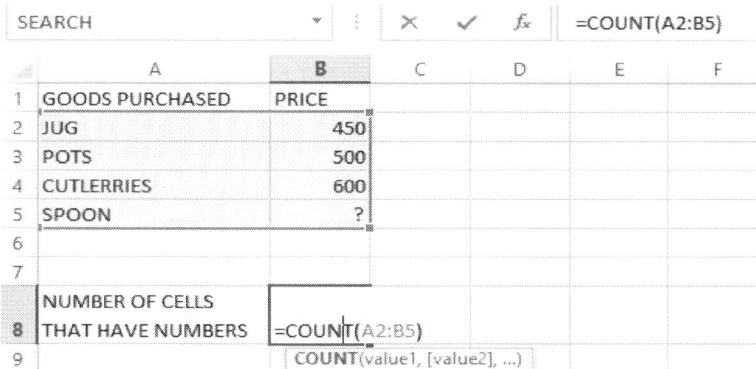

- Click on Enter and the result will be **3**

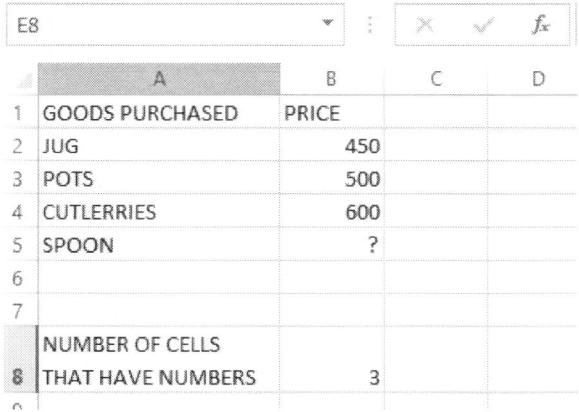

NOTE: Keep these in mind when using the COUNT function

- Argument with numbers, dates, or a text representing numbers are counted in the COUNT function
- Arguments with values or text errors are not counted by the COUNT function
- To count logical values, use the COUNTA function
- To count numbers based on criteria, use the COUNTAIF or IF function

- The COUNT function does not count logical value TRUE or FALSE
- When an argument is an array or reference, only the numbers in the reference or array are counted

THE COUNTIF FUNCTION

The COUNTIF function is used to count the number of cells that meet a certain criterion or condition. This can also be used to count cells that contain dates, numbers, and text. This function also supports the use of logical operators and wildcards.

The COUNTIF function has the following arguments

=COUNTIF(Range, criteria)

- **Range (Required Argument):** This indicates the range of cells that are to be counted.
- **Criteria (Required Argument):** This is the condition to be met by the cells provided in the worksheet. The criteria can be in the following:
    - A numerical value such as integer, decimal, time, or logical value
    - A text string such as Monday, East, Price and including wildcards such as asterisks and question mark

USING THE COUNTIF FUNCTION

With the table below, let's use the COUNTIF function to count how many times James' name appears on the list.

	A	B	C	D
1	YEAR	NAMES		
2	2001	James		
3	2002	James		
4	2003	Peter		
5	2004	Jasmine		
6	2006	Gregg		

To get the number of times James' name appear on the list, follow the steps below

- Select an empty cell, type in the function name and the arguments to be used; **=COUNTIF(B2:B6, "James")**

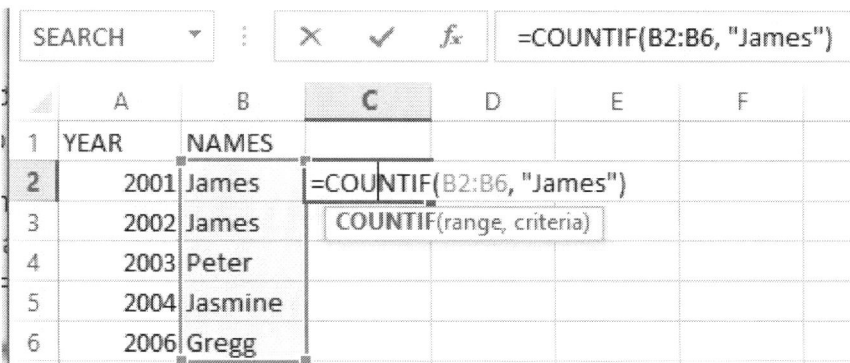

- Click on Enter and the result will be **2**

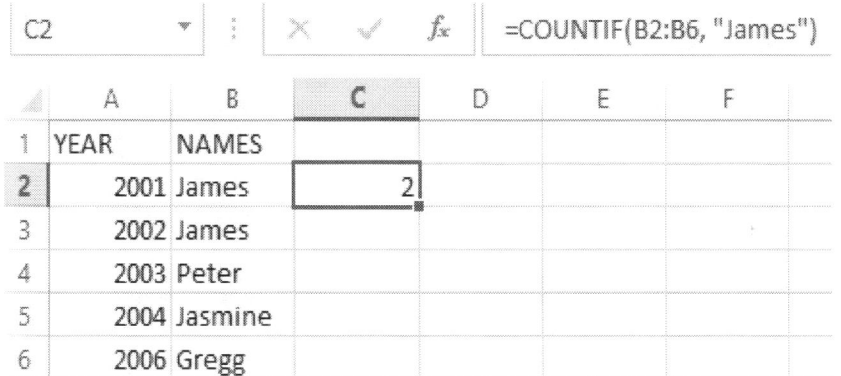

NOTE: Take note of the following points when using the COUNTIF function

- When using the COUNTIF function, make sure the criteria argument is enclosed in quotes e.g., "James"
- When the provided criteria argument is a text string that is more than 255 characters in length, #VALUE ERROR occurs
- #VALUE error occurs when the formula is referring to a cell or range of cells in a closed workbook

THE COUNTIFS FUNCTION

The COUNTIFS function is a function used for counting cells that meet single or multiple conditions or criteria. Just like the COUNT, COUNTIF functions, the COUNTIFS function is used with criteria or conditions relating to numbers, dates, text, logical operators, and wildcards.

The COUNTIFS function has the following arguments

=COUNTIFS(criteria_range1, criteria1, [criteria_range2, criteria2]...)

- **Criteria_range1 (Required Argument):** This is the first range that would be evaluated with the related criteria
- **Critteria1 (Required Argument):** This is the criteria to be used on criteria_range1 and it may come in form of expression, numbers, cell reference, or a text that specifies what cells are to be counted. For instance, criteria can be expressed as 43, >23, D2, etc.
- **Criteria_range2, criteria2 (Optional Argument):** This contains the additional ranges and their related criteria. This function permits up to 127 range or criteria pairs. The criteria can be in the following:
    - A numerical value such as integer, decimal, time, or logical value
    - A text string such as Monday, East, Price and including wildcards such as asterisks and question mark

USING THE COUNTIFS FUNCTION

Using the table below, let's count the numbers of shoes that have red color

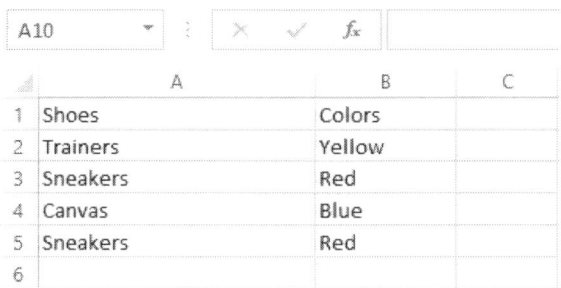

To get the number of shoes with red color on the list, follow the steps below:

- Select an empty cell, type in the function name and the arguments to be used; =**COUNTIFS(A2:A5, "sneakers", B2:B5, "red"**

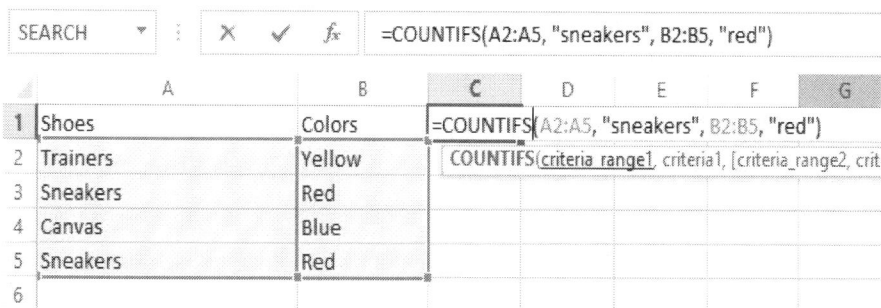

- Click on Enter and the result will be **2** as shown in the table below

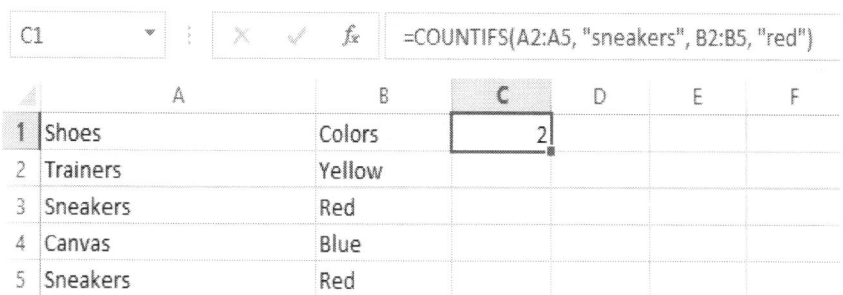

NOTE: Take note of the following when using the COUNTIFS FUNCTION

- The COUNTIFS function sees an empty cell as 0 when the criteria argument is a reference to an empty cell.
- #VALUE! error occurs when the criteria range arrays are not of the same length and also when the criteria arguments given are text strings that are greater than 255 characters long
- The use of the wildcard characters (question mark and asterisks) is made possible in criteria
- If the first cells meet their related criteria, the count is increased by 1 and if the second cells also meet their related criteria, the count is also increased by 1 and this continues until all the cells are evaluated

THE COUNTA FUNCTION

The COUNTA function is a function that returns the number of cells that are not empty within a range. The COUNTA function does not count empty cells. The COUNTA function can also be referred to as the **Excel COUNIF Not Blank** formula

The COUNTA function has the following arguments

=COUNTA(value1, [value2]

- **Value1 (Required Argument):** This is the argument indicating the values to be counted
- **Value2,…(Optional Argument):** This is the additional argument indicating the values to be counted with a maximum of 255 arguments

USING THE COUNTA FUNCTION

With the table below, let's count the number of cells that are not empty using the COUNTA function

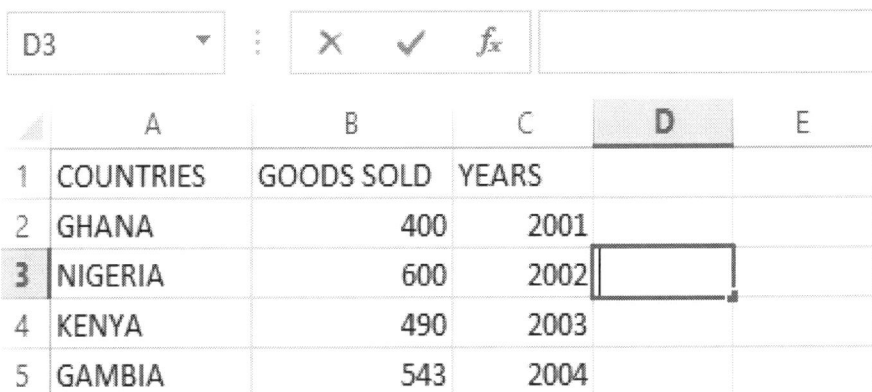

To get the number of cells that are not empty in the worksheet, follow the steps below

- Select an empty cell and type in the function name and its arguments; =COUNTA(A1:C5)

	A	B	C	D	E	F	G
1	COUNTRIES	GOODS SOLD	YEARS				
2	GHANA	400	2001				
3	NIGERIA	600	2002		=COUNTA(A1:C5)		
4	KENYA	490	2003		COUNTA(value1, [value2], ...)		
5	GAMBIA	543	2004				
6							

- Click on enter and the result will be 15 as shown in the table below

	A	B	C	D	E	F
1	COUNTRIES	GOODS SOLD	YEARS			
2	GHANA	400	2001			
3	NIGERIA	600	2002		15	
4	KENYA	490	2003			
5	GAMBIA	543	2004			

NOTE: Keep these in mind when using the COUNTA function

- The COUNTA function does not count empty cells
- In case you don't want to count logical values, text, or error values, the COUNT function is to be used
- To count cells that meet certain criteria, use the COUNTIF or COUNTIFS function

THE COUNTBLANK FUNCTION

The COUNTBLANK is a function that returns the numbers of empty cells within a range of cells in a workbook

The COUNTA function has just one argument

=CONNTBLANK(range)

Range (Required Argument): This is the range at which the blank cells will be counted

USING THE COUNTABLANK FUNCTION

Let's count the number of cells that are blank in the table below using the COUNTBLANK function

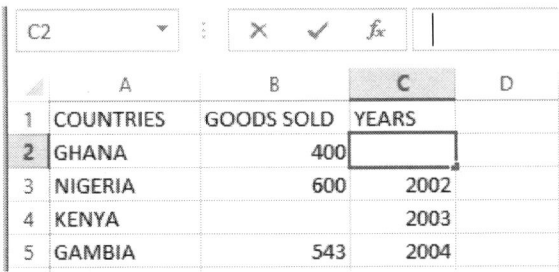

To count the blank cells using the COUNTBLANK function, follow the steps given below

- Select an empty cell, type in the function name and the arguments to be used; =COUNTBLANK(A1:C5)

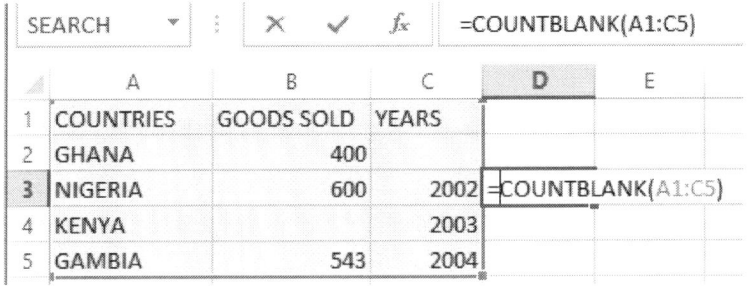

- Click on enter and the result will be 2 as shown in the table below

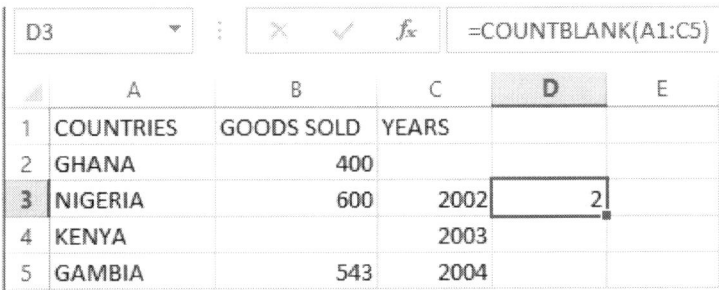

NOTE: Keep these in mind while using the COUNTA function

- The COUNTBLANK function does not count any cell that contains text, numbers, errors, etc.
- The COUNTBLANK function considers any formula blank when it returns an empty cell and thus, such a cell will be counted.
- Cells containing zero are not considered blank and will not be counted by the COUNTBLANK function

The AVERAGE Function

The AVERAGE function helps to calculate the arithmetic mean of a supplied set of arguments in a worksheet. The AVERAGE function can take up to 255 individual arguments which may include cell references, ranges, arrays, and constants.

The AVERAGE function uses the following arguments

- **Number1 (Required Argument):** This is the first number of a cell reference or range one wishes to find the average.
- **Number2 (Optional Argument):** These are additional numbers, cell references, or ranges one wishes to find the average with up to a maximum of 255 characters to be inputted.

USING THE AVERAGE FUNCTION

Find the arithmetic mean of the goods sold in the table given below, using the AVERAGE function

To find the average of the goods sold using the AVERAGE function, follow the steps given below

- Select an empty cell, type in the function name and its arguments; **=AVERAGE(B2:B5)**

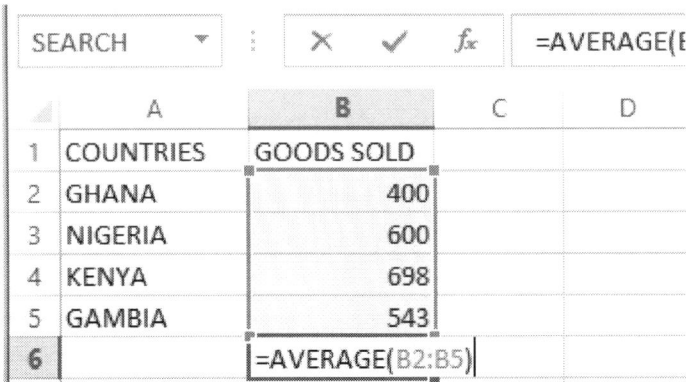

- Click on enter and the result will be 560.25 as shown in the table below

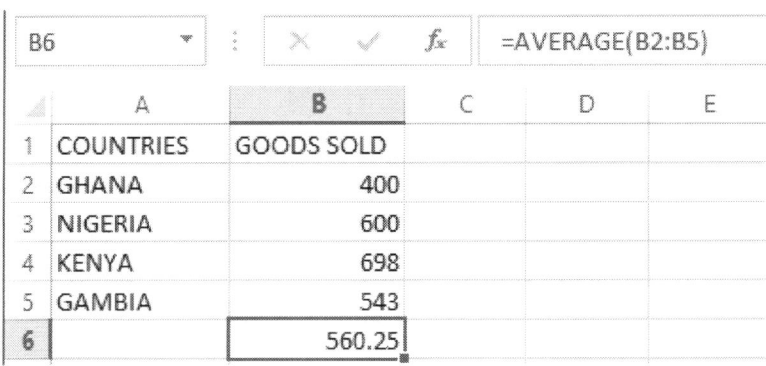

NOTE: Keep this in mind when using the AVERAGE function

- The AVERAGE function ignores empty cells
- The AVERAGE function ignores a cell reference argument that contains text, logical values. Cells with the value of zero are however counted
- The cell reference arguments must contain numbers
- To count logical values and text representation of numbers as part of the calculation, use the **AVERAGE** function
- To calculate the average of any value that meet certain condition or criteria, use the AVERAGE IF or AVERAGE IFS function

THE AVERAGEIF FUNCTION

The AVERAGEIF function is a function that is used to calculate the average of cells that meet a given criterion or condition. The AVERAGEIF function criteria include the use of logical operators (<,>, <>, =) and wildcards (*,?).

The AVERAGEIF function uses the following argument for its operations

=AVERAGEIF(range, criteria,[average_range])

- **Range (Required Argument):** This is the range of cell or cells to average and these cells may include numbers or names, arrays or references that contain numbers
- **Criteria (Required Argument):** The criteria are what determines how the cells will be average and it can come in form of a number, expression, cell reference, or texts. E.g., 13, <14 etc.
- **Average_range (Optional Range):** This is the actual or real range of cells to be averaged. When this is omitted, the function makes use of the given range

USING THE AVERAGEIF FUNCTION

Using the table given below, let's find out the average sales of cakes

	A	B	C	D
1	Goods	Sales		
2	Cakes	200		
3	Chocolate	300		
4	Vanilla	345		
5	Cakes	564		
6	Chocolate	232		
7				

To calculate the average sales of cakes using the AVERAGEIF function, follow the procedures given below

- Select an empty cell, type in the function name and its arguments;
  = AVERAGEIF(A2:A6, "chocolate", B2:B6)

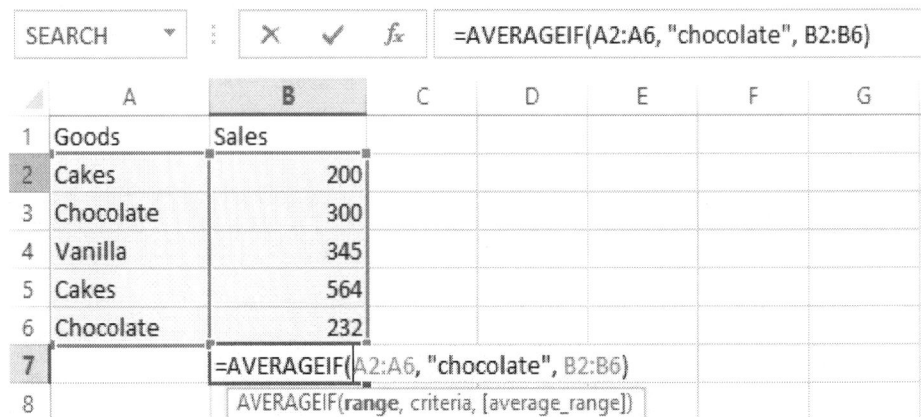

- Click on enter and the result will be **266** as shown in the table below

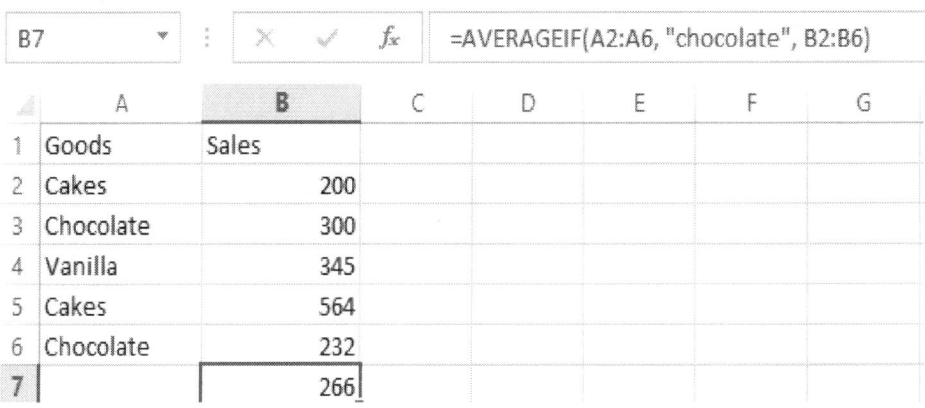

NOTE: Keep the following in mind when using the AVERAGEIF function

- #DVD! error takes place when
    - No cell in the range meets the criteria given
    - The range is blank or is a text value
- AVERAGEIF function treats a cell as zero when the criteria are given is empty
- The AVERAGEIF function ignores cells that contain TRUE or FALSE
- Wildcards such as asterisk and question mark can be used in criteria

THE AVERAGEIFS FUNCTION

The AVERAGEIFS function is a function that calculates the average (arithmetic mean) of the numbers in a given range of cells that meet more than one criterion. The AVERAGEIFS function also uses logical operators (<,>, <>) and wildcards (*?) as its criteria. This function was first introduced in Excel 2007.

The AVERAGEIFS uses the following argument for its operation
=AVERAGEIFS(average_range, criteria_range1 criteria1,,[criteria_range2, criteria2), ...)

- **Average_range (Required Argument):** This is the range of one or more cells to be average and the argument include names or numbers, arrays or references that contain numbers
- **Criteria_range1: (Required Argument):** This is the first range to be evaluated
- **Criteria_range2 (Optional Argument:** This is the second range to be evaluated it can be up to 127 ranges and related criteria
- **Criteria2 (Optional Argument):** This also determines how the cells will be averages and be up to 127 criteria in form of a number, cell reference, expression, or a text indicating which cells are to be averaged. This is used against critera_range2.

USING THE AVERGAEIFS FUNCTION

Using the table, let's find out the average salary of males that work full time using the AVERAGEIFS function

	A	B	C	D	E
1					
2		Name	Gender	Position	Salary
3		Jenny Davies	Female	Full Time	£17,883.00
4		Kevin Matthews	Male	Part Time	£15,966.00
5		Chris Sandford	Female	Part Time	£17,930.00
6		Peter Charkiw	Male	Full Time	£23,614.00
7		Paul Jones	Male	Full Time	£24,579.00

To find the average salary of males that work full time using the AVERAGEIFS functions, follow the steps below

- Select an empty cell and type in the function name and its arguments; = **AVERAGEIFS(E3:E7, C3:C7, "Male", D3:D7, "Full Time")**

	A	B	C	D	E	F	G	H	I
1									
2		Name	Gender	Position	Salary				
3		Jenny Davies	Female	Full Time	£17,883.00				
4		Kevin Matthews	Male	Part Time	£15,966.00				
5		Chris Sandford	Female	Part Time	£17,930.00				
6		Peter Charkiw	Male	Full Time	£23,614.00				
7		Paul Jones	Male	Full Time	£24,579.00				
8					=averageifs(E3:E7,C3:C7,"Male",D3:D7,"Full Time")				

- Click on enter and the result will be **£24,096.50** as shown in the table below

	A	B	C	D	E	F	G
1							
2		Name	Gender	Position	Salary		
3		Jenny Davies	Female	Full Time	£17,883.00		
4		Kevin Matthews	Male	Part Time	£15,966.00		
5		Chris Sandford	Female	Part Time	£17,930.00		
6		Peter Charkiw	Male	Full Time	£23,614.00		
7		Paul Jones	Male	Full Time	£24,579.00		
8					£24,096.50		

NOTE: Keep this in mind when using the AVERAGEIFS function
- The AVERAGEIFS function treats any cell as zero value when the criteria range is empty
- In the AVERAGEIFS function, all the criteria_range must be the same size and shape as the sum_range
- When a number or date is used together with a logical operator in the AVERAGEIFS' criteria, they must be enclosed in a double quote e.g., ">4/23/2018"
- In the AVERAGEIFS function, cells in a range that contains TRUE are evaluated as a 1 and the ones that contain FALSE are evaluated as zero

- #DIV0! Error occurs
    - When the argument average_range is blank or is a text value
    - When the average_range cannot be interpreted into numerical values
    - When all the criteria or conditions are not met
- The use of wildcards such as asterisks and question mark are allowed as criteria in the function

THE MIN FUNCTION

The MIN function returns the minimum or smallest number in a given set of values or arguments. The MIN function ignores numbers, texts, and logical values as well as text values

The MIN function uses the following argument

=MIN (number1, [number2],…)

- **Number1 (Required Argument):** This is the range of a cell or cells where the lowest number will be returned from
- **Number2 (Optional Argument):** Here, up to 255 numbers can be accepted

USING THE MIN FUNCTION

With the table given below, find the minimum number using the MIN function

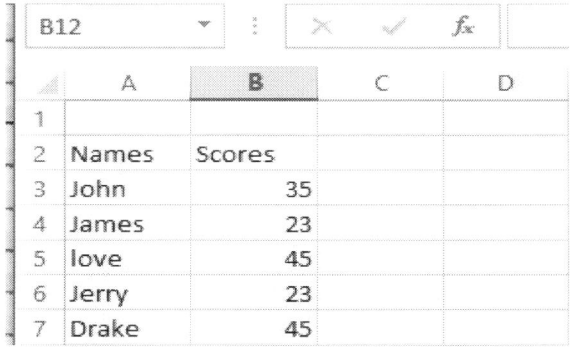

To find the minimum number using the MIN function, follow the steps below:

- Select an empty cell, type in the function name and its arguments; **=MIN(B3:B7)**

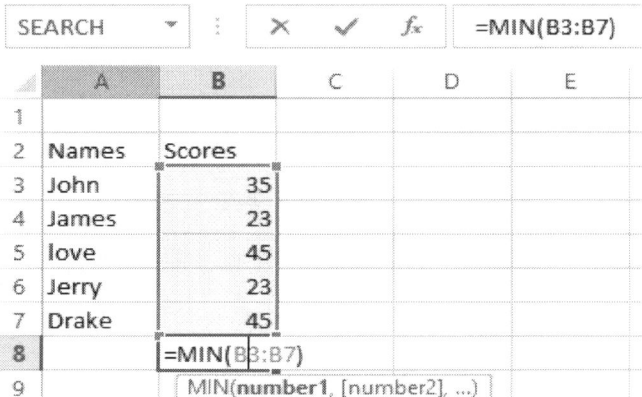

- Click on enter and the result will be **23** as shown in the table below

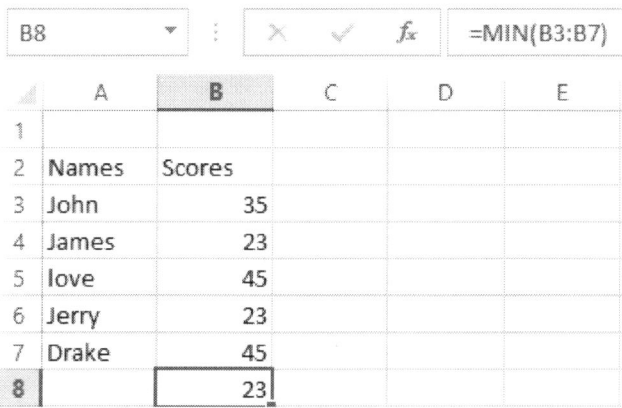

NOTE: Keep the following when using the MIN function

- When values provided into the MIN function are not numbers, VALUE! error occurs
- To use the logical values and text representation of numbers in a calculation, use the MINA function
- The arguments in the MIN function can be number or names, array or reference that contain numbers

- Empty cells, logical values, or text are ignored in the MIN function
- When an argument contains error values and text that cannot be interpreted, they cause errors to occur
- The MIN function returns any argument without numbers as 0

THE MAX FUNCTION

The MIN function returns the maximum or largest number in a given set of values or arguments. The MAX function ignores numbers, texts, and logical values as well as text values

The MAX function uses the following argument

=MAX(number1, [number2],…)

- **Number1 (Required Argument):** This is the range of a cell or cells where the highest number will be returned from
- **Number2(Optional Argument):** Here, up to 255 numbers can be accepted

USING THE MIN FUNCTION

With the table given below, find the minimum number using the MAX function

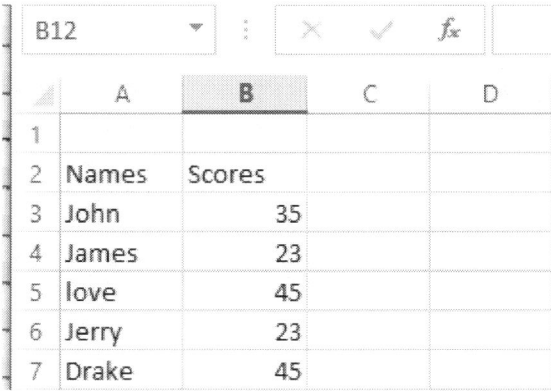

To find the minimum number using the MAX function, follow the steps below

- Select an empty cell and type in the function name and its arguments; **=MAX(B3:B7)**

	A	B	C	D	E
1					
2	Names	Scores			
3	John	35			
4	James	23			
5	love	45			
6	Jerry	23			
7	Drake	45			
8		=MAX(B3:B7)			

- Click on enter and the result will be **45** as shown in the table below

	A	B	C	D	E
1					
2	Names	Scores			
3	John	35			
4	James	23			
5	love	45			
6	Jerry	23			
7	Drake	45			
8		45			

NOTE: Keep these in mind when using the MAX function

- When values provided into the MAX function are not numbers, VALUE! error occurs
- The MAX function returns any argument without numbers as 0
- To use the logical values and text representation of numbers in a calculation, use the MAXA function
- The arguments in the MAX function can be number or names, array or reference that contain numbers
- Empty cells, logical values, or text are ignored in the MAX function
- When an argument contains error values and text that cannot be interpreted, they cause errors to occur

THE MEDIAN FUNCTION

The MEDIAN function calculates the middle value of a given set of numbers. For instance, the MEDIAN function returns 3 in the =MEDIAN (1, 2,3,4,5

The MEDIAN function contains the following arguments

=MEDIUM (number1, [number2],...)

- **Number1 (Required Argument):** This is the argument that contains the range of one or more cells that we wish to calculate or find the median.
- **Numnber2 (Optional Argument)** This can contain up to 255 numbers that we may wish to find the median

USING THE MEDIAN FUNCTION

With the table given below, let's calculate the median of the numeric data using the MEDIAN function

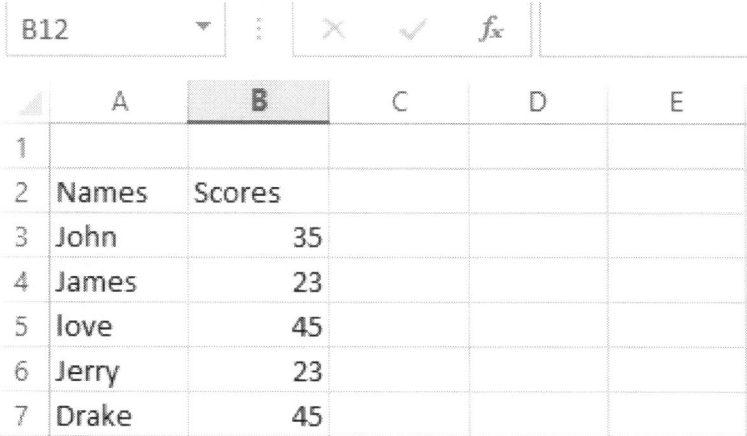

To calculate the median of the numeric values in the table, follow the steps given below

- Select an empty cell, type in the function name and its arguments; =MAX(B3:B7)

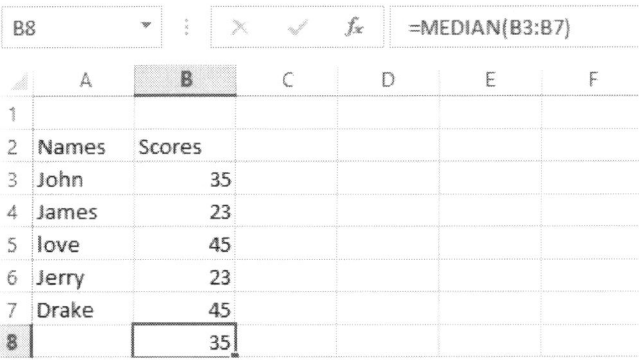

- Click on enter and the result will be **35** as shown in the table below

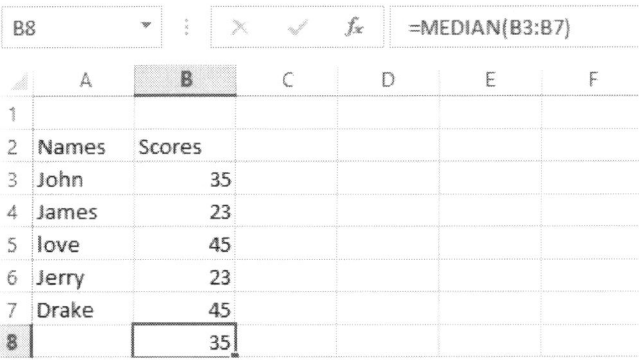

NOTE: Keep these in mind when using the MEDIAN function

- When an argument contains error values and text that cannot be interpreted, they cause errors to occur
- The arguments in the MEDIAN function can be number or names, array or reference that contain numbers
- Empty cells, logical values, or text are ignored in the MEDIAN function
- When there is an even number of values in the table, the average of the two middle number is returned.

CHAPTER EIGHT

THE FINANCIAL FUNCTION

Excel financial functions are designed to carry out varieties of financial operations such as calculation of yield, interest rates, internal rate of return, investment valuations, asset depreciation, etc. The functions are not available in earlier versions of Excel but from Excel 2013 and all later versions. The most commonly used financial functions in Excel are as follows:

THE PV FUNCTION

The PV function which stands for **Present Value** is a function designed to calculate the present value of an investment or loan which is based on a constant interest rate. The PV function can be used with periodic, constant payments e.g mortgage and other loans or a future value (investment goal)

The PV function uses the following arguments for its operations

=PV(rate, nper,pmt, [fv], [type])

- **Rate (Required Argument):** This is the interest rate per the compounding period. For instance, a loan with a 14% annual interest rate and monthly required payment will have monthly interest of 1.2% rate i.e 14/12= 1.2%
- **Nper(Required Argument)**: This is the number of the total payments made to clear the loans. For instance, If the loan year is 4 years, then the monthly payment period will be 48 months
- **Pmt (Required Argument)**: This is the payment that is done per period and it remains constant until the end of the investment or loan
- **Fv (Optional Argument):** This is the investment's future value when the payment period is over. In case there is input for this, Excel returns the value by default to 0

- **Type (Optional Argument):** This is used to indicate when the payment periods are issued and due. When 0 is inputted, the payment period is at the end of the period and when 1 is inputted, the payment period is at the beginning of the month.

USING THE PV FUNCTION

From the table below, we have an annuity that makes periodic payments of $500.00 with a 3.5 annual interest rate. The annuity will make payments for 6 years every month. Using the PV function, find the present value

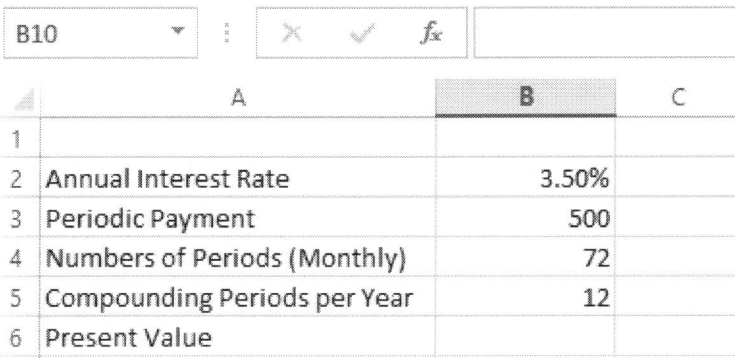

To find the present value of the table above using the PV function

- Select an empty cell, type in the function and its argument =PV(B2/B5,B4,B3,0,0)

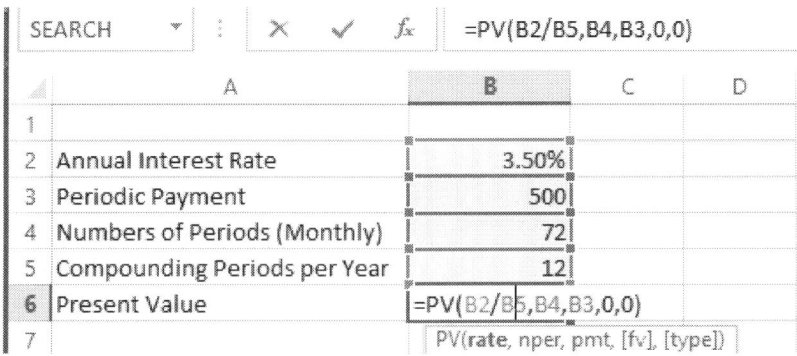

- Click on enter and the present value will be -£32,428.79 as shown in the table below

	A	B	C	D
1				
2	Annual Interest Rate	3.50%		
3	Periodic Payment	500		
4	Numbers of Periods (Monthly)	72		
5	Compounding Periods per Year	12		
6	Present Value	-£32,428.79		

NOTE: Keep these in mind while using the PV function

- When the arguments given are non-numeric, the PV function returns a #VALUE! error
- In the PV function, the annual interest rate cannot be converted to a periodic interest rate.

THE FV FUNCTION

The FV function is a function that is designed to help calculate the **future value** of an investment or loan with a periodic constant payment and a constant interest rate.

The FV function uses the following arguments to execute its operation

=FV(rate, nper, pmt, [pv], [type])

- **Rate (Required Argument):** This is the interest rate per the compounding period.
- **Nper (Required Argument):** This is the total period of payment made for a lifetime
- **Pmt (Optional Argument):** This indicates the payment per period. In case this argument is omitted, the PV argument must be provided
- **PV (Optional Argument):** This indicates the present value of the investment or loan. In case the PV argument is omitted, the Pmt argument must be provided

- **Type (Optional Argument):** This is used to indicate when the payment periods are made whether at the start or end of the year. When 0 is inputted, the payment period is at the end of the period and when 1 is inputted, the payment period is at the beginning of the month.

USING THE FV FUNCTION

Using the information in the table below, let's calculate the future value using the FV function

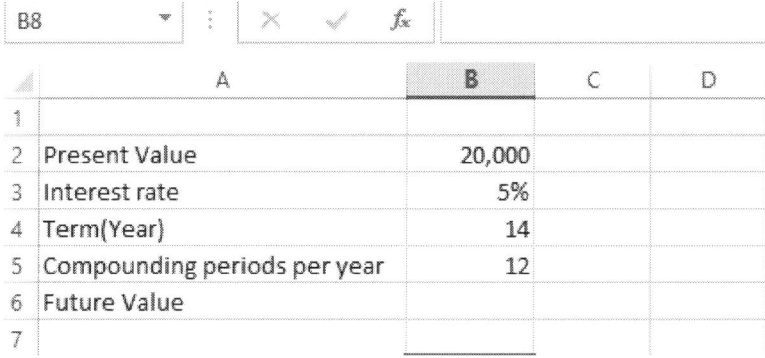

To find the future value of the table above using the FV function

- Select an empty cell and type in the function and its argument =FV(B3/B5,B4*B5,0,-B2)

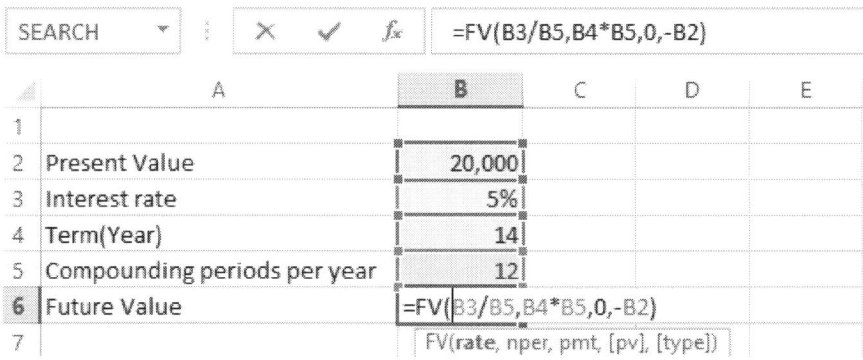

- Click on enter and the future value will be £40,216.52 as shown in the table below

	A	B	C	D
1				
2	Present Value	20,000		
3	Interest rate	5%		
4	Term(Year)	14		
5	Compounding periods per year	12		
6	Future Value	£40,216.52		
7				

NOTE: keep the following in mind when using the FV function

- When the argument is given is non-numeric #VALUE! error
- The payment value will be negative when the pmt argument is for the cash going out of a business

THE NPV FUNCTION

The NPV function is a function that is used to calculate the **net present value** of an investment by making use of discount rate and a series of future cash flows

The NPV function uses the following arguments for its operations

=NPV(rate,value1,[value2],...)

- **Rate (Required Argument):** This is the discount rate over the length of a period
- **Value1(Required Argument):** This is the first value that represents a series of payments and income. The negative payments connote outgoing payments while the positive payments connote incoming payments
- **Value2 (Optional Argument):** This is the second value that represents a series of payments and income

USING THE NPV FUNCTION

Given the table below, let's calculate the net present value using the NPV function

	A	B	C	D	E
4	1	200			
5	2	300			
6	3	400			
7	4	500			
8	5	600			
9	Required return	15%			
10					

To calculate the net present value;

- Select an empty cell, type in the function and its argument =NPV(B9,B3:B8)

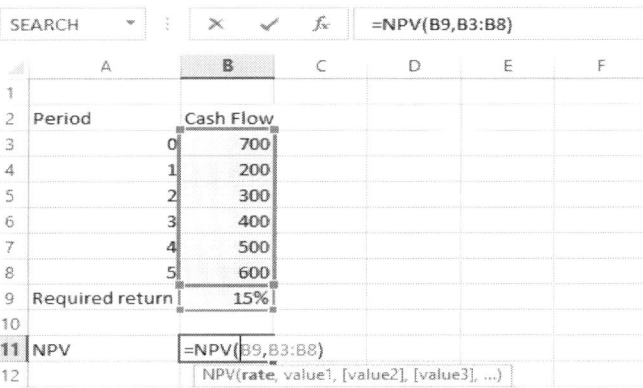

- Click on enter and the net present value will be £1,693.87 as shown in the table below

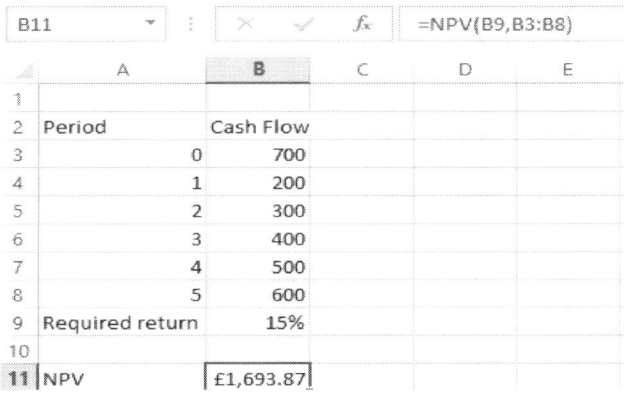

NOTE: Keep these in mind when using the NPV function

- Arguments must be numerical or a function with a numerical output. Other forms of input will be returned as an error
- In the NPV function, arrays with numerical values are evaluated and all other values are ignored.
- For the series of cash flow, the input order is important
- With the NPV function, there is an assumption that payments are spaced on equal periodic payments
- The NPV function and the IRR(Internal Rate of Return) are related to each other

THE PMT FUNCTION

The PMT function is a function that helps to calculate the **total payment** that is needed to pay up a loan or an investment with a fixed interest rate over a given period

The PMT function uses the following arguments for its operations

PMT(rate, nper, pv, [fv], [type])

- **Rate (Required Argument):** This is the interest rate for the loan
- **Nper (Required Argument):** This is the total number of payments to be made for the loan taken
- **PV (Required Argument):** This is the present value or the total amount that a series of future payment is worth now and this is also known as the principal
- **FV (Optional Argument):** This is the future value or the cash balance you wish to attain or get to after the last payment has been made. If the FV is omitted, it is assumed to be zero
- **Type (Optional Argument):** This indicates when payments are due. If it is omitted, it defaults to 0 and payments are due at the end of the month. When 1 is used in the argument, payments are due at the beginning of the period

USING THE PMT FUNCTION

Using the table below, let assume we need to invest for three years and we will receive £85,000 with an interest rate of 3.5% per year in which the payment will be made at the start of each month and with a future value of 0

	A	B
1		
2	Rate of Interest	3.50%
3	Nper	36
4	PV	85,000
5	FV	0
6		
7	PMT	

To calculate the PMT;

- Select an empty cell, type in the function and its argument
  =PMT(B2/12,B3,B4,B5)

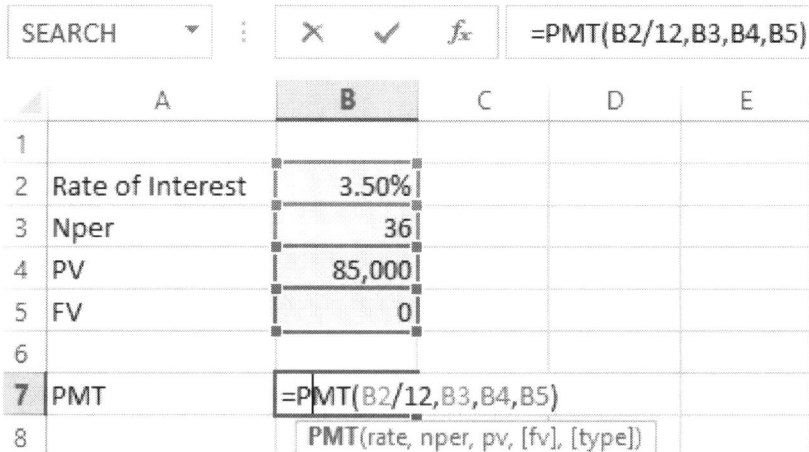

- Click on enter and the net present value will be -£2,490.87 as shown in the table below

	A	B	C	D	E
1					
2	Rate of Interest	3.50%			
3	Nper	36			
4	PV	85,000			
5	FV	0			
6					
7	PMT	-£2,490.68			

B7 =PMT(B2/12,B3,B4,B5)

NOTE: Keep these in mind when using the PMT function

- #VALUE! occurs when the arguments provided is non-numeric
- #NUM! error occurs when the given rate is less than or equal to -1
- #NUM! error also occurs when given nper is equal to 0
- When calculating monthly or quarterly payment using the PMT function, convert the annual interest rates to months or quarters
- To find the total amount that was paid for the duration of the loan, multiply the PMT as calculated by nper

THE SLN FUNCTION

The SLN function helps to calculate the depreciation of an asset using a straight-line depreciation method for one period of time

The SLN function uses the following arguments to perform its operations

=SLN(cost, salvage, life)

- **Cost (Required Argument):** This is the initial cost of an asset
- **Salvage (Required Argument):** This is the value at the end of the depreciation which is also known as the salvage value of the asset
- **Life(Required Argument):** This is the number of periods at which the asset depreciates and this can also be called useful life of the asset.

USING THE SLN FUNCTION

From the table below, let calculate the depreciation of an asset given the cost of the asset to be £55,000, the salvage value to be £8,500, and the useful life to be 10 years

	A	B	C	D	E
1					
2					
3	Cost of the asset	55,000			
4	Salvage value	8,500			
5	Useful life	10			
6					

To find the depreciation of the asset in the table below

- Select an empty cell, type in the function and its argument =SLN(B3,B4,B5)

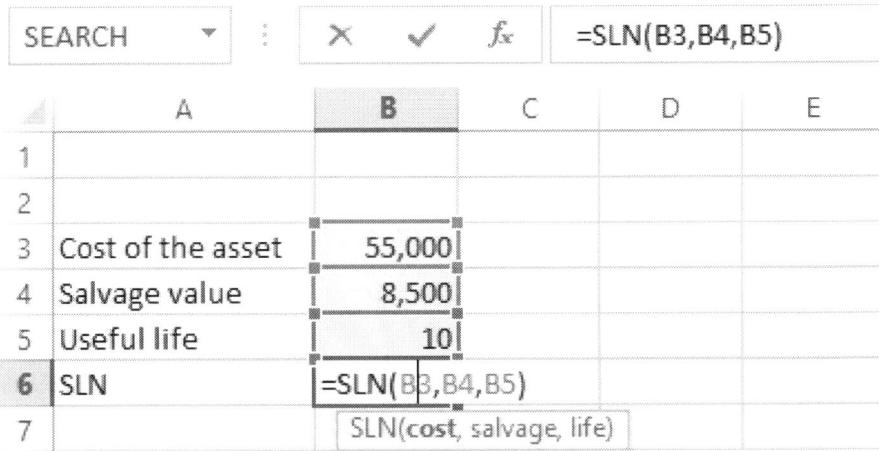

- Click on enter and the depreciation value of the asset will be £4,650.00 as shown in the table below

	A	B	C	D	E
1					
2					
3	Cost of the asset	55,000			
4	Salvage value	8,500			
5	Useful life	10			
6	SLN	£4,650.00			
7					

NOTE: Observe the following when using the SLN function

- #DIV/0! error occurs when the arguments that are given is equal to zero
- #VALUE! error occurs when the arguments that are given are non-numeric

The SYD Function

The SYD function is a function that helps to calculate the sum of years depreciation of an asset over a specific period in the lifetime of the asset. This function is centered on the cost of the asset, the salvage value, and the number of periods the asset depreciated

The SYD function uses the following arguments to carry out its operation

=SYD(cost, salvage, life, per)

- **Cost (Required Argument):** This is the initial cost of an asset
- **Salvage (Required Argument):** This is the value at the end of the depreciation which is also known as the salvage value of the asset
- **Life (Required Argument):** This is the number of periods at which the asset depreciates and this can also be called useful life of the asset.
- **Per (Required Argument):** This is the period in which the depreciation will be calculated for

USING THE SYD FUNCTION

Assuming we want to calculate the depreciation of an asset with an initial cost of £400,000 with a salvage cost of £6,000 after 8 years with a period of 3 years to calculate the depreciation

	A	B	C	D	E
1					
2	Initial cost	400,000			
3	Salvage value	6,000			
4	Life	8			
5	Period	3			
6					

To calculate the sum of years depreciation of the asset given in the table above

- Select an empty cell, type in the function and its argument **=SYD(B2,B3,B4,B5)**

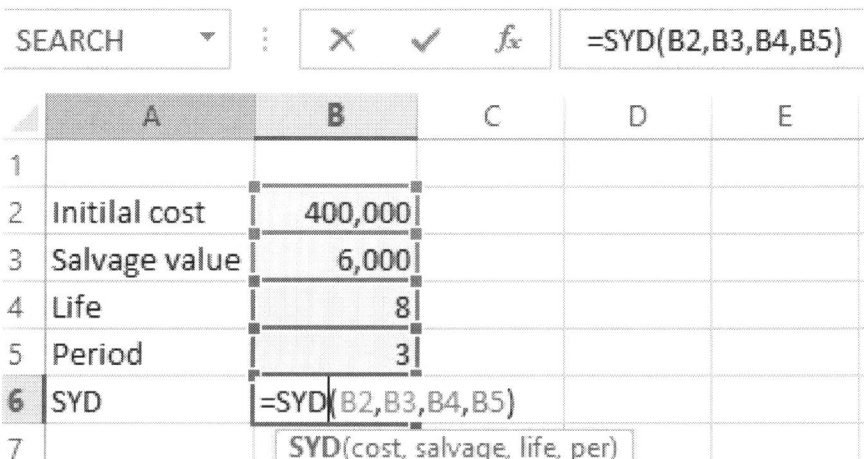

- Click on enter and the sum years of the depreciation value of the asset will be £65,666.67 as shown in the table below

	A	B	C	D	E
1					
2	Initilal cost	400,000			
3	Salvage value	6,000			
4	Life	8			
5	Period	3			
6	SYD	£65,666.67			

B6 =SYD(B2,B3,B4,B5)

NOTE: Observe the following when using the SYD function

- When inputting *life* and *per* arguments, they must be in the same units of time e.g., days, months, and years
- When the arguments given are non-numeric, it returns a #VALUE! error
- #NUM! error occurs due to the following reasons
    - When the salvage argument supplied is less than zero
    - When the life or per argument provided is less than or equal to zero
    - When the per argument provided or supplied is greater than the life argument supplied in the formula

THE DB FUNCTION

The DB function is a function that calculates the depreciation of an asset using the fixed declining balance method for a specified period.

The DB function uses the following arguments to execute its operations

=DB(cost, salvage, life, period,[month)

- **Cost (Required Argument):** This is the initial cost of an asset
- **Salvage (Required Argument):** This is the value at the end of the depreciation which is also known as the salvage value of the asset
- **Life (Required Argument):** This is the number of periods at which the asset depreciates and this can also be called useful life of the asset.

- **Period (Required Argument):** This is the period in which the depreciation will be calculated for
- **Month (Optional Argument):** This indicates how many months of the year are used in the calculation of the first period of depreciation. If this is omitted, the function defaults the value to 12.

USING THE DB FUNCTION

Let's calculate the depreciation of an asset with an initial cost of £200,000 with the salvage value of £8,000 after 5 years with a period of 2 years and 4 months in the first year

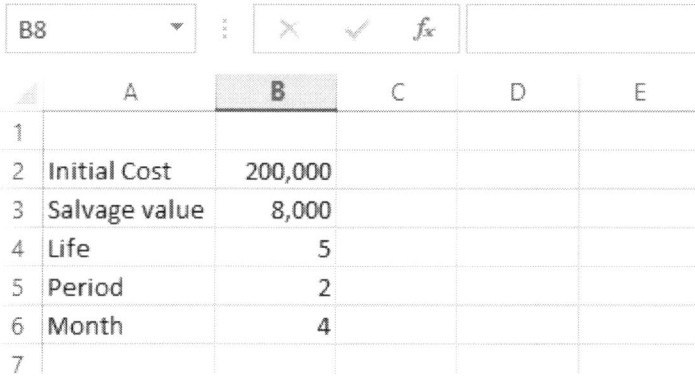

To find the depreciation value using the DB function

- Select an empty cell, type in the function and its argument **=DB(B2,B3,B4,B5,B6)**

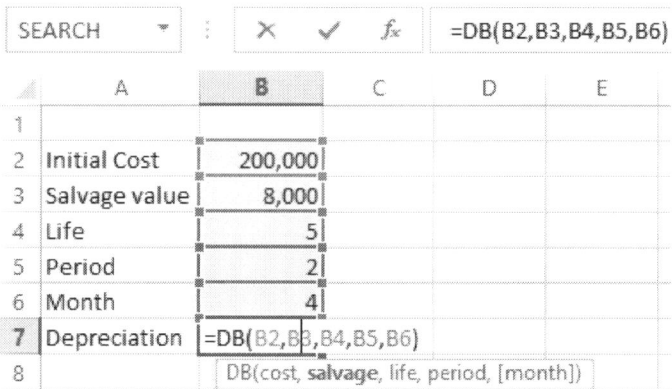

- Click on enter and the depreciation value of the asset will be £79,958.33 as shown in the table below

	A	B	C	D	E
1					
2	Initial Cost	200,000			
3	Salvage value	8,000			
4	Life	5			
5	Period	2			
6	Month	4			
7	Depreciation	£79,958.33			

B7 fx =DB(B2,B3,B4,B5,B6)

NOTE: Keep these in mind when using the DB function

- #VALUE error occurs when the argument supplied is non-numeric
- #NUM! error occurs due to the following reasons
- When the given cost or salvage is less than zero
- When the life or period argument provided is less than or equal to zero
- When the month argument provided is less than or equal to zero is greater than 12
- When the period argument provided is greater than the life argument and when the month argument is omitted
- When the period provided is greater than life +1

THE DDB FUNCTION

The DDB function is a function that calculates the depreciation of an asset for a specific period using the double-declining balance method or any other method that is specified by changing the factor argument

The DDB function uses the following arguments

=DDB (cost, salvage, life, period, [factor})

- **Cost (Required Argument):** This is the initial cost of an asset

- **Salvage (Required Argument):** This is the value at the end of the depreciation which is also known as the salvage value of the asset
- **Life (Required Argument):** This is the number of periods at which the asset depreciates and this can also be called useful life of the asset.
- **Period (Required Argument):** This is the period where the depreciation of the asset will be calculated.
- **Factor (Optional Argument):** This is the rate at which the balance declines. If the factor is omitted, it defaults to 2.

USING THE DDB FUNCTION

Let's calculate the depreciation of an asset with an initial cost of £300,000 with the salvage value of £5,000 after 5 years with a period of 2 years. Use the DBB function to calculate the depreciation by a factor of 1.

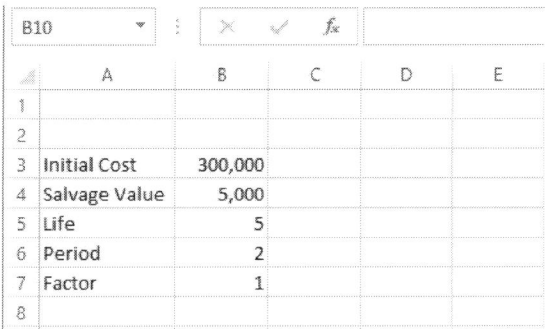

To calculate depreciation using the DDB

- Select an empty cell, type in the function and its argument =DDB(B3,B4,B5,B6,B7)

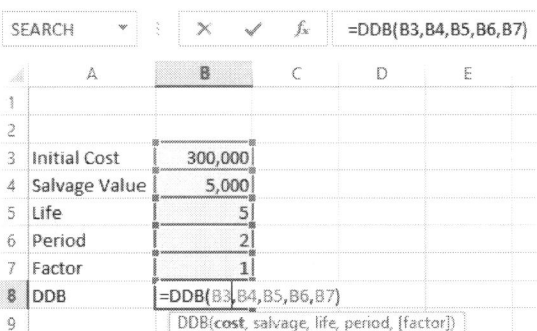

- Click on enter and the depreciation value of the asset will be £48,000.00 as shown in the table below

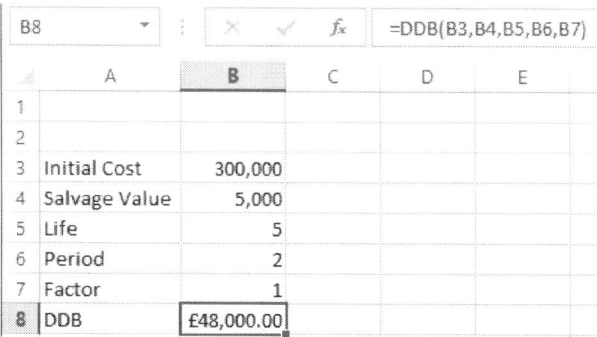

NOTE: Keep the following in mind when using the DDB function

- #VALUE! error occurs when the argument provided in the function is non-numeric
- #NUM! error occurs due to the following reasons
    - When the value of the coat and that of salvage is less than 0
    - When the value of the life of the asset is less than or equal to zero
    - When the period argument is less than or equal to 0 or greater than the life value
    - When the factor argument is less than 1

THE SEARCH FUNCTION

The SEARCH Function locates or finds the position of a substring within a string. This is just like locating the position of **S** in the word **JOURNALISM**. The SEARCH function in this case is insensitive, that is, it doesn't mind whether the text to find is in capital letter or small letter

The syntax for SEARCH function is =SEARCH (find text, within text, [start_num]

- find text= The text to find
- within text= The text to search from

- start_num = Where to start the search for the text within the text.

Let's get practical with the SEARCH function

Example 1

Search for the position T in cell A1 in the table below

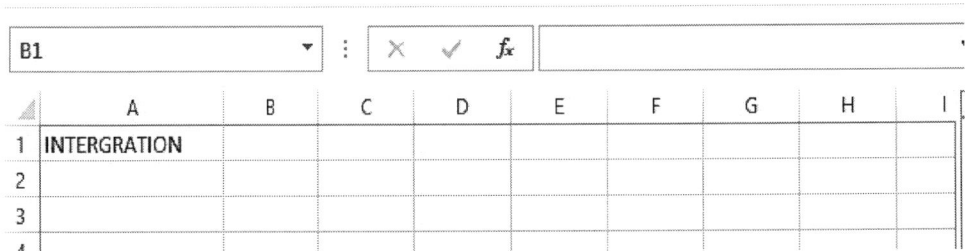

To search for the position of T in cell A1

- Go to cell B2 to type **=SEARCH ("T", A1,1)** and press **Enter**

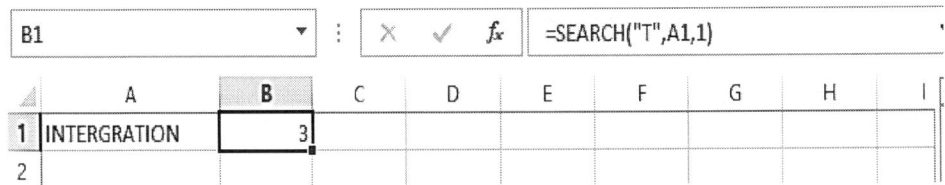

The position of T in cell A1 is 3

Example 2

Search for the position MAN in cell C1 in the table below

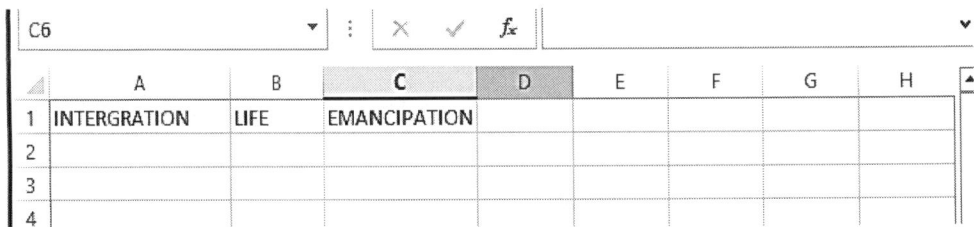

To search for the position of MAN in cell D2

- Go to cell D2 to type **=SEARCH("MAN",C1,1)** and press **Enter**

	A	B	C	D	E	F	G	H
1	INTERGRATION	LIFE	EMANCIPATION	2				
2								
3								
4								

The position of MAN in cell C1 is 3

THE FIND FUNCTION

Just like the SEARCH Function, the FIND Function also locates or finds the position of a substring within a string. The SEARCH function in this case is sensitive i.e., it observes the capital and small letter before searching for a text therefore, searching for the exact text.

The syntax for FIND function is =FIND (find text, within text, [start_num]

- find text= The text to find
- within text= The text to search from
- start_num = Where to start the search for the text within the text.

Example 1

Find the position of GROWTH In cell B2 in the table below

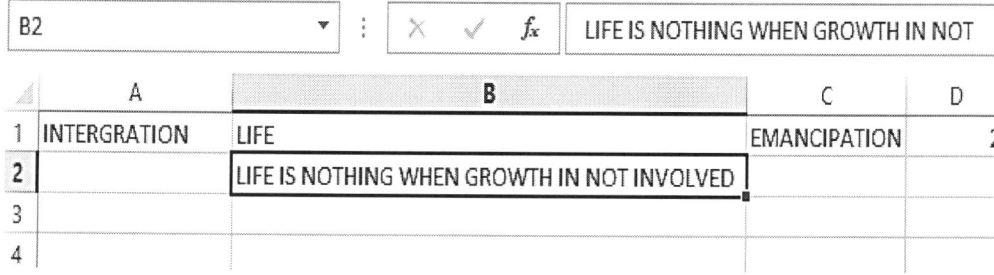

To find the position of GROWTH in cell B2

- Go to cell C2 to type **=FIND ("GROWTH", B2,1)** and press **Enter**

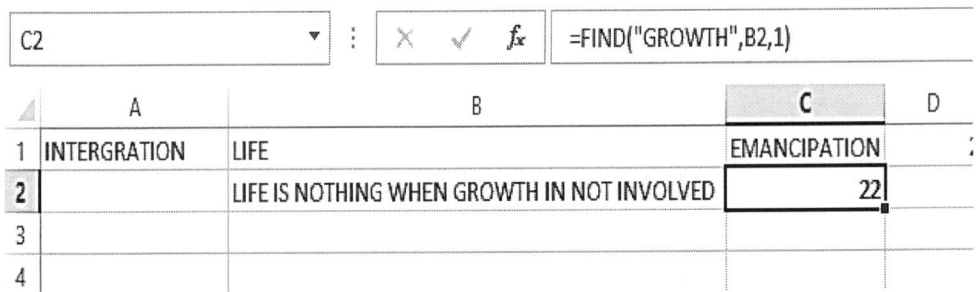

The position of GROWTH in cell B2 is 22.

CHAPTER NINE

LOGICAL FUNCTIONS

Logical functions are the functions that provide decision-making tools that allow you to look at the content of a cell, execute a calculation, and then test the result against a required value. The logical function is also used to test if a situation is true or false and these results can be used to display information and execute all kinds of calculations. Examples of the logical functions are IF, NOT, OR, IFS, etc.

THE IF FUNCTION

The IF function is a function that tests a given condition and returns one value for a TRUE result and another value for a FALSE result. This function allows you to make a logical comparison between a value and what you expect.

The IF function uses the following arguments

=IF (Logical_text,[Value_if_true],[Value_if_false])

- **Logical_text (Required Argument):** This is the value or logical expression that are to be tested and evaluated as either TRUE or FALSE
- **Value_if_true (Optional Argument):** This is the value that will be returned if the logical test evaluates to TRUE
- **Value_if_false (Optional Argument):** This is the value that will be returned if the logical test evaluates to FALSE

While using this function, the following logical operators can be used

- Equal to (=)
- Greater than (>)
- Greater than or equal to (≥)
- Less than (<)
- Less than or equal to (≤)

- Not equal (≠)

USING THE IF FUNCTION

In the table below, we want to test if the values in the cells are greater than 500 or not, if it is true, the value will be returned stating **Yes** and if it is false, the value will be returned stating **No**

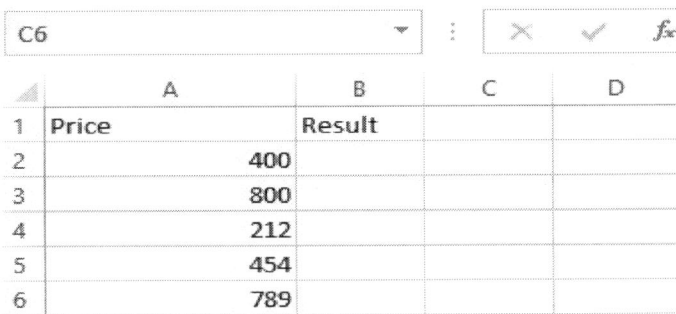

- To check if cell A2 is greater than 500, type in =IF(A2>500," Yes", "No")

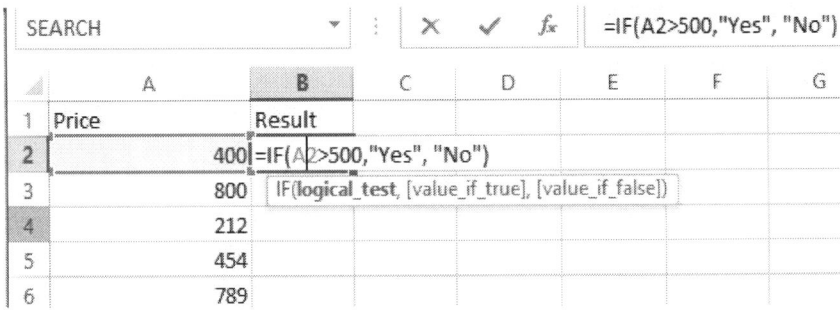

- Click on enter and the return value will be **No**

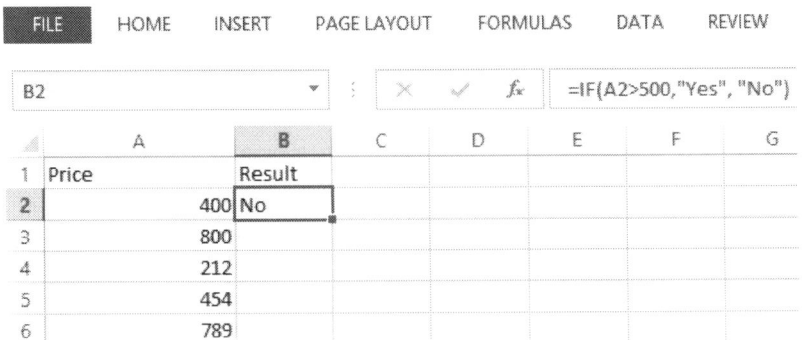

- Use the steps above to get the value of A3 to B6; **=IF(A3>500," Yes", "No"), =IF(A4>500," Yes", "No"), =IF(A5>500," Yes", "No"), =IF(A6>500," Yes", "No")** respectively

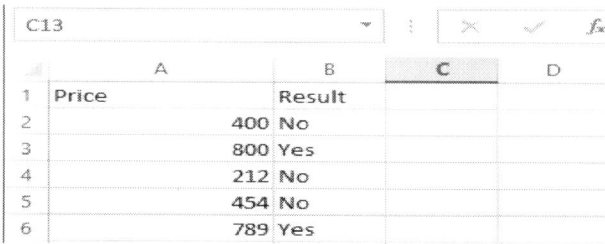

NOTE: Keep these in mind when using the IF functions:

- The IF function works if the logical_test returns a numeric value.
- The IF function treats any non-zero values as TRUE and zero value as FALSE
- #VALUE! occurs when the logical_test argument cannot be evaluated to be TRUE or FALSE
- The IF function evaluates every element of the array when any of the arguments is supplied to the function as an array
- To count condition, use the COUNTIF and COUNTIFS functions
- To add up conditions, use the SUMIF and SUMIFS functions

THE NESTED IF FUNCTION

The Nested IF function means one IF function located inside another nest IF function thereby allowing you to test multiple criteria and increasing the number of possible outcomes. You can get the same result with the nested IF function when used individually with just the IF function. Now let's use the Nested IF function in the table below to check the prices that are greater or lesser than 500

161

- To use the Nested IF to get the value that is greater 500, type in the function in an empty cell; =IF(A2>500, "Yes", "No" =IF(A3>500, "Yes", "No "=IF(A4>500, "Yes", "No" =IF(A5>500, "Yes", "No") =IF(A6>500, "Yes", "No")))) and then click enter

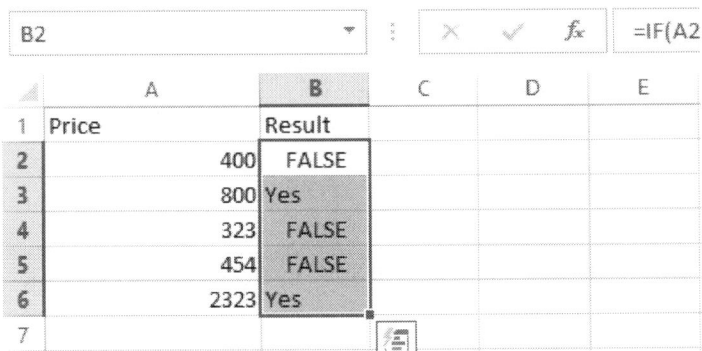

- You will get the value of the first cell referenced

- To get the values of the remaining cells, use the fill handle to drag the function to reflect on the other cells.

NOTE: When using the Nested IF functions, take note of the following:

- The Nested IF function involves a lot of thinking and accuracy when building so that the logic can calculate correctly with the condition given to the very end.
- The Nested IF functions can be confusing at times, especially when there are a lot of IF functions to be nested

THE IFS FUNCTION

The IFS function is a function that is used as a substitute to the nested IF function. This function checks whether one or more conditions or criteria are met and returns the values that correspond to or meet the first TRUE condition

The IFS function uses the following for its operations

=IFS (Logical_test1, value1[logical_test2, value2] ..., [logical_test127, value127])

- **Logical_test1 (Required Argument):** This is a condition that Excel uses to evaluate whether a value is TRUE or FALSE
- **Value1 (Required Argument):** This is when the logical_test 1 is true. Other logical values are optional.

USING THE IFS FUNCTION

Let's use the IFS function to assign grades to the marks of students given in the table below

	A	B	C	D	E
1					
2	Marks	Grade			
3	80				
4	75				
5	70				
6	65				
7	60				
8	55				

To assign grades to the marks above;

- Select an empty cell and type in the function name and its arguments; **=IFS(A3>75,"A", A3>70, "B", A3>65, "C", A3>60, "D", A3>55, "E", A3>50, "F")**

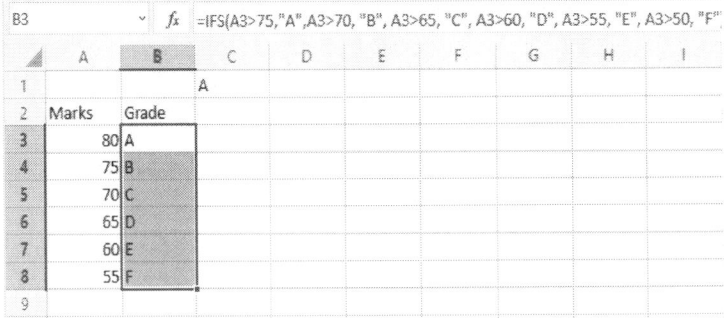

- To get the values of the remaining cells, use the fill handle to drag the function to reflect on the other cells.

NOTE: Keep these in mind when using the IFS function

- #N/A error occurs when there are no TRUE conditions found by the IFS function
- When the logical_test argument resolves to a value other than TRUE or FALSE, #VALUE! error occurs

The IFFEROR Function

The IFFEROR function is a function that is used to custom result when a formula generates an error. The IFERROR is to trap and manage errors without using more complicating nested IF statements.

The IFERROR uses the following arguments

=IFFERROR (value, value_if_error)

- **Value (Required Argument):** This is a value or expression that is checked or tested for error
- **Value_if_error (Required Argument):** This is the value that will be returned when an error is found in the formula

USING THE IFERROR FORMULAS

With the table given below, let's use the IFFEROR function to remove the errors and put in a customized message "invalid data"

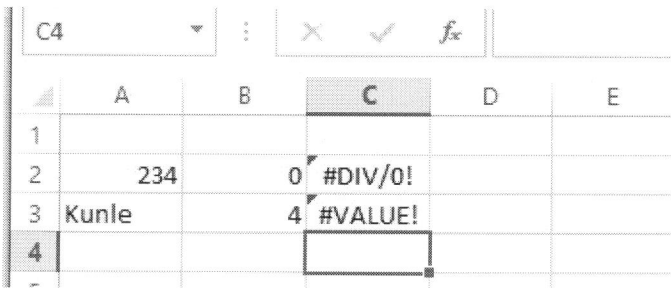

To change the error in cell C2

- Select an empty cell and type in the function name and its arguments; =IFERROR (A2/B2, "invalid data")

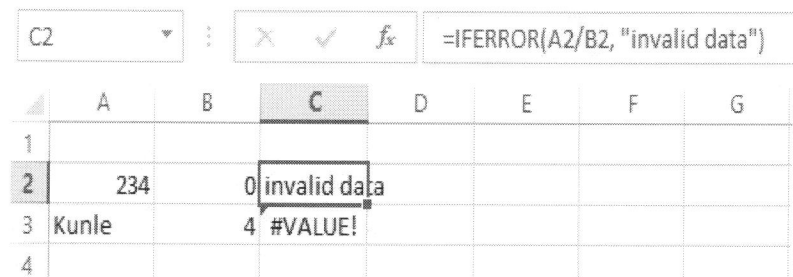

To change the error in cell C3

- Select an empty cell and type in the function name and its arguments; =IFERROR (A3/B3, "invalid data")

	A	B	C	D	E	F	G
1							
2		234	0	invalid data			
3	Kunle		4	invalid data			

C3 =IFERROR(A3/B3, "invalid data")

NOTE: Keep these in mind when using the IFERROR FUNCTION

- When the value or value_if_error is an empty cell, the IFERROR function treats it as an empty string value
- The IFFEROR returns an array of results for each cell in the range specified in the value if the value is an array formula

THE AND FUNCTION

The AND function is a function that is used to determine if the conditions given in a data set are TRUE and when any of the conditions is not met, it returns a FALSE value e.g., B1 is greater than 50 and less than 100

The AND function uses the following arguments to execute

=AND (logical1, [logical2},)

- **Logical1 (Required Argument):** This is the first condition or logical value to be evaluated
- **Logical2 (Optional Argument):** This is the second condition or logical value to be evaluated

USING THE AND FUNCTION

Using the table given below, let's examine if cell A2 is greater than 67 and less than cell A3 using the AND function to return TRUE or FALSE value depending on the result.

	A	B	C	D
1				
2		23		
3		56		

To get the result of the table above;

- Select an empty cell and type in the function name and its arguments; =**AND(A2>67, A2<A3)**

	A	B	C	D
1				
2	23	FALSE		
3	56			
4				

Formula bar: =AND(A2>67,A2<A3)

- The AND function returns FALSE in the table above because one of the conditions given in the data set was not met i.e. A2 is not greater than 67
- When the conditions given in a dataset are met, the AND function will return TRUE as shown in the table below

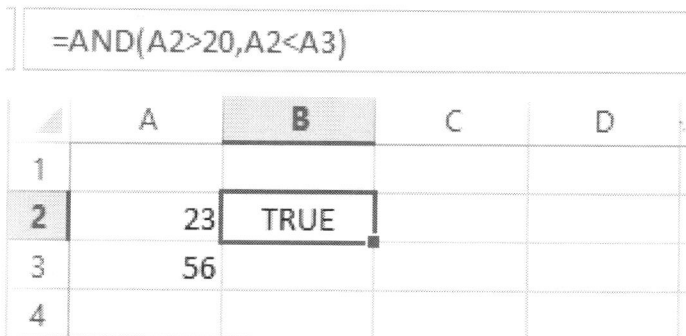

NOTE: Keep the following in mind when using the AND function

- When there is no logical value found or created during the evaluation, the AND function returns a VALUE! error
- The AND function ignores test values and empty cell provided as arguments
- The AND function can contain 255 conditions
- The AND function returns TRUE when all the conditions are met

THE OR FUNCTION

The OR function is a function that returns TRUE if any of the conditions are TRUE and returns FALSE if all conditions are false. Unlike the AND function, when one of all the conditions is false, it will be returned as FALSE.

The OR function uses the following arguments

=OR (logical1, [logical2},...)

- **Logical1 (Required Argument):** This is the first condition or logical value to evaluate.
- **Logical (Required Argument):** The second condition or logical value to evaluate

USING THE OR FUNCTION

let's examine if cell A2 is greater than 30, B2 is less than 50 and B3 is equal to 45 using the OR function to return TRUE or FALSE value depending on the result.

To get the result of the table above;

- Select an empty cell and type in the function name and its arguments; **=OR(A2>30,B2<50, B3=45)**

- Click on enter and the result will be returned as FALSE as shown in the table below

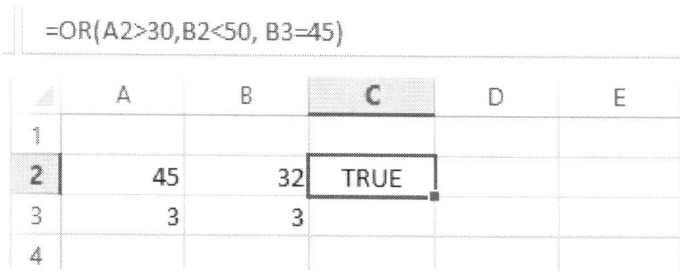

NOTE: Keep the following in mind when using the OR function

- When any of the logical_test cannot be interpreted as numeric or logical values, the function returns a #VALUE! error
- This function ignores text values or empty cells supplied in the arguments
- The function can contain 255 conditions in total
- This function can also be used together with the AND function depending on the arguments

CHAPTER TEN

LOOKUP AND REFERENCE FUNCTIONS

The Lookup functions are used for retrieving information from a list of data or tables and used on the worksheet or workbook. Examples of the lookup functions are HLOOK UP, VLOOK UP, etc.

The Reference functions return information about cell references as text values such as the entire address, row, and column. Examples of these functions are ADDRESS function, ROW function, etc. Now let's talk about the lookup and reference functions and how they can be applied to the worksheet.

THE VLOOKUP FUNCTION

The VLOOKUP function in which the V means **Vertical** is a quick way to lookup up a piece of information in the first column of a table or dataset and extracting or returning some corresponding data or information in the same row from another column of the data set or table.
The VLOOKUP function uses the following arguments to execute its operation:

=VLOOKUP (lookup_value, table_array, col_index_num, [range_lookup])

- **Lookup_value (required argument):** This is the value to look up for in the first column of the table or dataset
- **Table_array (required argument):** This is the data array that is to be searched by the lookup value in the left part of the column
- **Col_index_num (required argument):** This is the column number or integer in the table array where the matching value must be returned.
- **Range_lookup (optional argument):** This part of the function specifies if you want the VLOOK to find an exact match or the appropriate match. The argument is set to either TRUE or FALSE. TRUE stands for appropriate match and if not found, the next

largest value is returned. FALSE on its stands for exact match and if not found, it returns as error #N/A

USING THE VLOOKUP FUNCTION

Let's look at the example below; this is a table containing 4 fruits and their prices. With the VLOOKUP function, let's find out the price of yam in the table

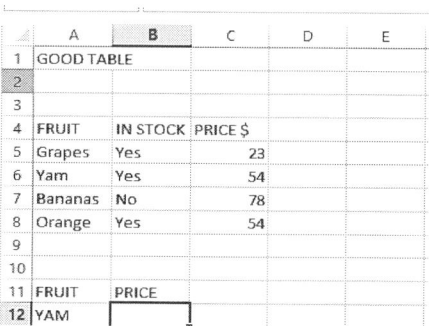

To find the price of yam in the table above using the VLOOKUP function, follow the steps below:

- Select an empty cell and type in the function to be used with the **lookup_value** i.e., the cell that contains the information to lookup for. The lookup cell here is A12 which contains **Yam =VLOOKUP (A12**

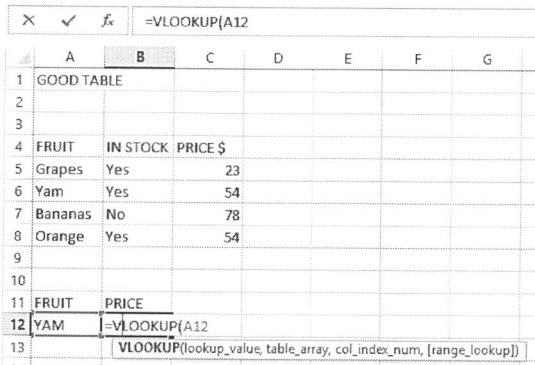

- Select the table where the data is to be searched from by inputting the **table_array: =VLOOKUP (A12, A4:C8**

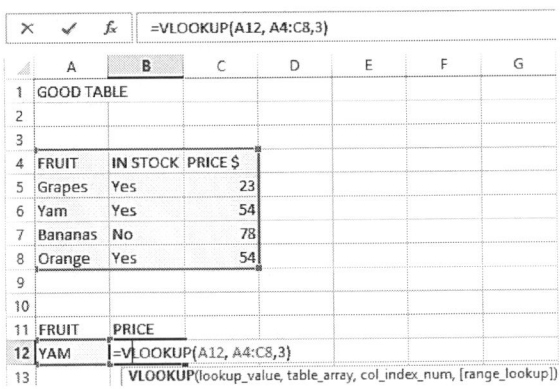

- Tell Excel the column that contains the data you want the VLOOKUP to use as output by inputting the **col_index_num** which is **3: =VLOOKUP (A12, A4:C8,3**

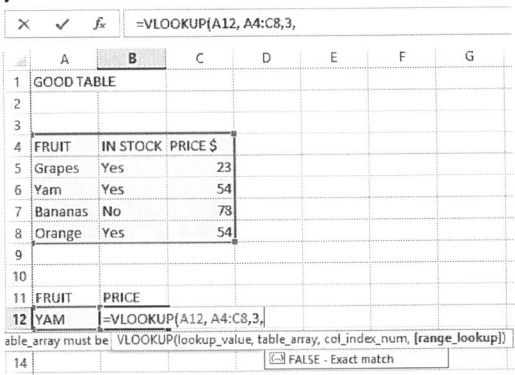

- The final step which is optional is to tell Excel if you are looking for an appropriate match or exact match by inputting either TRUE or FALSE; **=VLOOKUP (A12, A4:C8,3, FALSE)** or **=VLOOKUP (A12, A4:C8,3, TRUE)**

- If you have followed the steps above, the result of your operation using the VLOOKUP function with the table must be **54**

	A	B	C	D	E
		=VLOOKUP(A12, A4:C8,3,FALSE)			
1	GOOD TABLE				
2					
3					
4	FRUIT	IN STOCK	PRICE $		
5	Grapes	Yes	23		
6	Yam	Yes	54		
7	Bananas	No	78		
8	Orange	Yes	54		
9					
10					
11	FRUIT	PRICE			
12	YAM	54			

NOTE: When using the VLOOKUP function, keep the following in mind:

- When the range lookup is not used, the VLOOKUP function will not permit a non-exact match, rather it will use an exact match if it does exist.
- If the dataset contains duplicate values, the VLOOKUP function will only pick the first one
- The VLOOKUP function is not case-sensitive i.e., it works with both upper case and higher case characters
- This function permits the use of wildcards such as asterisks, question marks, and tilde
- #N/A! error occurs when the VLOOKUP function cannot find a match to the given lookup value
- #VALUE! error can occur due to two reasons
    - When the col_index_num argument is less than one or not even seen as a numeric value
    - If the range_lookup value argument is not seen or recognized as one of the logical values TRUE or FALSE
- #REF! error can occur when the col_index_num argument is bigger than the number of columns in the given table_array or when the formula used in the table to reference a cell does not exist.

THE HLOOKUP FUNCTION

The HLOOKUP function in which the H means Horizontal is a tool that is used to lookup for a value or a piece of information in the top row of a table array or dataset and then return the value or information in the same column from another row specified in the table array or dataset.

The HLOOKUP function uses the following arguments to execute its operation

=HLOOKUP (lookup_value, table_array, col_index_num, [range_lookup])

- **Lookup_value (required argument):** This is the value to look up for in the first row of the table or dataset
- **Table_array (required argument):** This is the data array that is to be searched by the lookup value in the left part of the column
- **Row_index_num (required argument):** This is the row number or integer in the table array where the matching value must be returned.
- **Range_lookup (optional argument):** This part of the function specifies if you want the VLOOK to find an exact match or the appropriate match. The argument is set to either TRUE or FALSE. TRUE stands for appropriate match and if not found, the next largest value is returned. FALSE on its own stands for exact match and if not found, it returns back as error #N/A

USING THE HLOOKUP FUNCTION

With the table below, let's find out the score of Joy in Mathematics using the HLOOKUP function

A	B	C	D	E
STUDENT SCORES	JOY	LOVETH	JOHN	ADEX
MATHEMATICS	59	45	68	98
ENGLISH	69	78	43	76
ECONOMICS	34	56	65	89
PHE	23	89	24	97
THE TOTAL SCORE OF JOY IN MATHEMATICS				

To find the total score of Joy in Mathematics, follow the steps below

- Select an empty cell and type in the function to be used with the **lookup_value** i.e., the cell that contains the information to lookup for. The lookup cell here is B1 which carries the name **Joy;** =HLOOKUP (B1

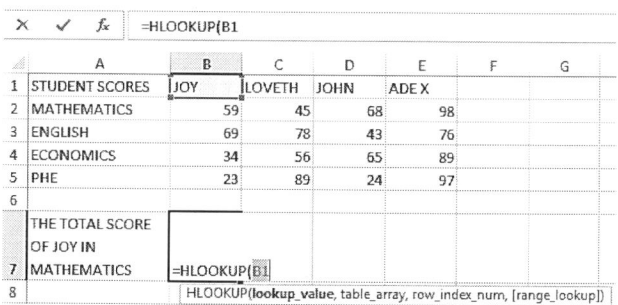

- Select the table where the data is to be searched from by inputting the **table_array**: =HLOOKUP (B1, A1:E5

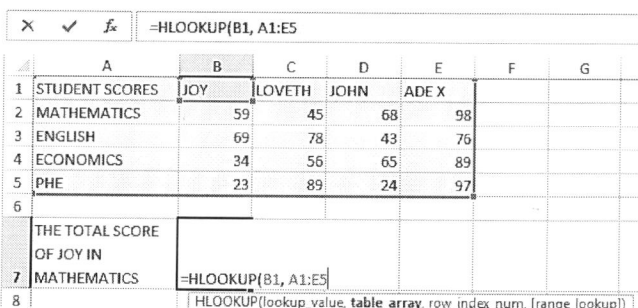

- Tell Excel the row that contains the data you want the HLOOKUP to use as output by inputting the **row_index_num** which is 2: =HLOOKUP (B1, A1:E5, 3

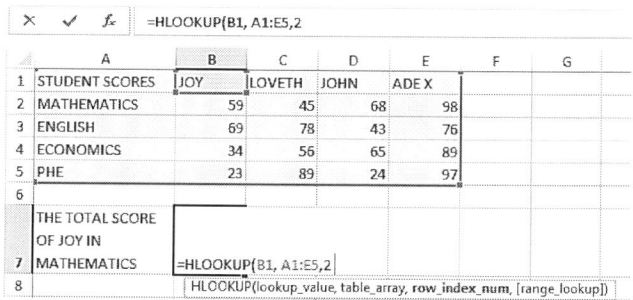

- The final step which is optional is to tell Excel if you are looking for an appropriate match or exact match by inputting either TRUE or FALSE; = **HLOOKUP (B1, A1:E5,3, FALSE)** or **=HLOOKUP (B1, A1:E5,3, TRUE)**

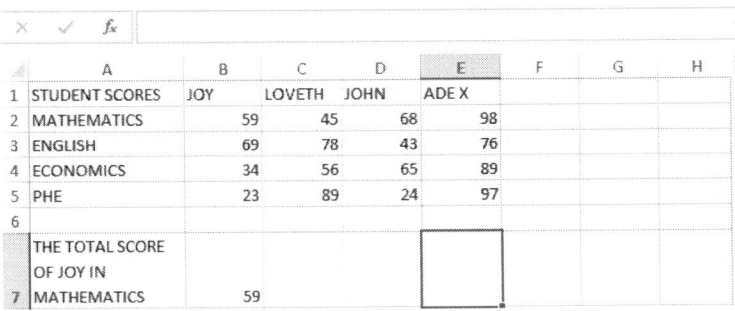

- If you have followed the steps above, the result of your operation using the VLOOKUP function with the table must be **59**

NOTE: When using the HLOOKUP functions, ensure to keep these in mind

- Just like the VLOOKUP, the HLOOKUP function is also case insensitive
- It also supports wildcard characters such as asterisks and question mark
- #N/A! error occurs when the range_lookup is FALSE and the HLOOKUP function is not able to find the lookup_value in the range
- #REF! error occurs when the row_index_num is greater than the number of columns in table_array

- #VALUE! error surfaces when the row_index_num is lesser than 1
- HLOOKUP function will only return one value and this is always the first value that matches the lookup value

THE CHOOSE FUNCTION

The CHOOSE function is a tool that uses an index number provided to return a value from the list of value arguments.

The CHOOSE function uses the following arguments to execute its operation

=CHOOSE (index_num, value1, [value2] ...)

- **Index_num (required argument):** This is an integer that specifies the position of the value to return. This must contain any number between 1 and 254, formula, or a reference to a cell ranging between 1 and 254
- **Value1, Value2...** This is a list that ranges from 1 and 254 values from which the CHOOSE function is to look from. The value 1 is required while others are optional. These values can come in form of numbers, text values, formulas, cell references, or defined names.

USING THE CHOOSE FUNCTION

With the table below, let's return the second value from a list using the CHOOSE function

	A	B	C	D	E
1	Names of students				
2	Joy				
3	Loveth				
4	Jasmine				
5	Anita				

To return the second value in the list

- Select an empty cell and type in the function name and its arguments; **=CHOOSE (3, A2, A3, A4, A5)**

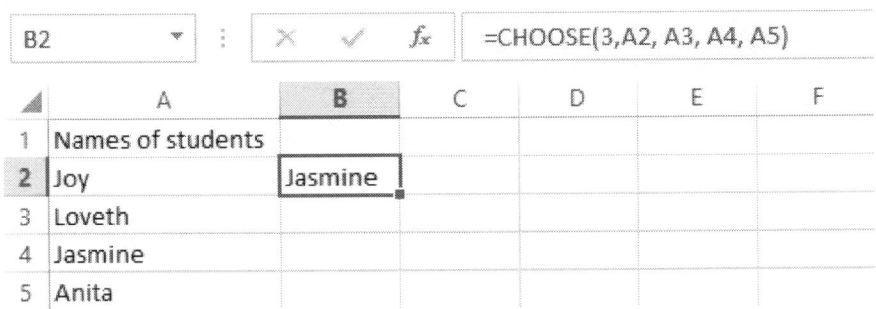

- Click on Enter and the function will return the third value as **Jasmine** as shown in the table below

NOTE: Keep these in mind when using the CHOOSE function:

- When the text values in an argument are not enclosed in quotes and are not invalid cell reference, it returns #NAME? error
- #VALUE! error occurs when the index_num provided is less than 1 or greater than the given number of values or when the index_num argument is non-numeric

THE MATCH FUNCTION

The MATCH function is a tool that is used to look up a value within a range and then returns the relative position of that value within that range.

The MATCH function uses the following arguments for its operations

=MATCH (lookup_value, lookup_array, [match_type])

- **Lookup_value (Required Argument):** This is the value to be looked up
- **Lookup_array (Required Argument):** This is the data array where the value will be looked up from
- **Match_type (Optional Argument):** This argument indicates how the Lookup_value with values in lookup_array are matched together.

Match_type	Behaviour
1 or omitted	This match_type finds the largest value that is less or equal to the lookup_value. When this argument is used, the lookup_array must be in ascending order.
0	This match_type finds the first value that is equal to the lookup_value. when this argument is used, the lookup_array can be ordered anyhow
-1	This match_type finds the smallest value that is greater than or equal to the lookup_value. When this argument is used, the lookup_array must be in descending

USING THE MATCH FUNCTION

With the table below, let's find the value of Apple

	A	B	C	D	E
1					
2	Items	Value			
3	Spinach	Apple			
4	Pineaple				
5	Cucumber				
6	Apple				

To find the value of Apple;

- Select an empty cell and type in the function name and its arguments; =MATCH (B3, A3:A6,0)

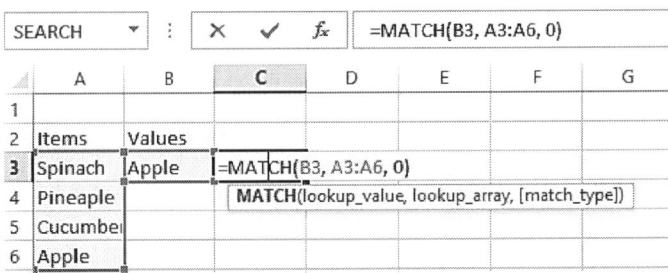

- Click on Enter and the function will return the value of Apple to be 4 as shown in the table below

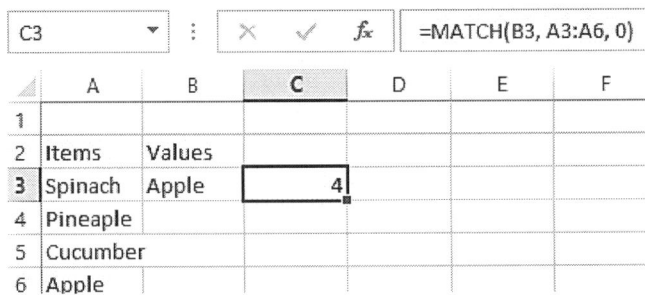

NOTE: keep the following in mind when using the MATCH function

- The MATCH function is case insensitive i.e., it does not distinguish between lowercase and uppercase letters when looking up the values in the dataset
- When the MATCH function cannot find a match for the lookup_value, #N/A! error is returned
- The Function allows for appropriate and exact matching and also the use of wildcards for partial matches

THE TRANSPOSE FUNCTION

The TRANSPOSE function is a tool that is used to change the orientation of a given range or array; TRANSPOSE changes a vertical range to horizontal range and vice versa.

The TRANSPOSE function uses just an argument

=TRANSPOSE (array)

The array argument contains the range of cells to be transposed. When an array is transposed, the first row becomes the first column of the new array and the second row also becomes the second column of the new array and it continues like that.

USING THE TRANSPOSE FUNCTION

With the example below, let's change the orientation display of the array from vertical portrait to horizontal portrait using the TRANSPOSE function

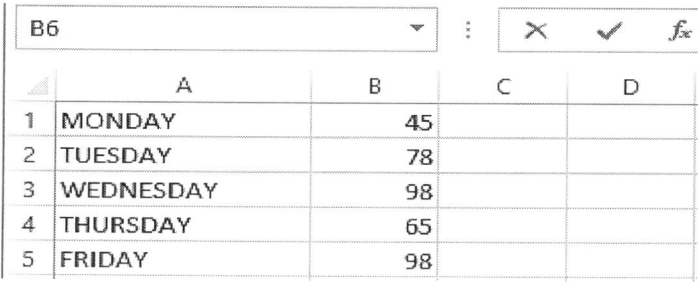

To do this, follow the procedures below:

- The first thing to do is to select some blank cells. Ensure that the cells selected are the same as the numbers of the original set of the cell but in the other direction

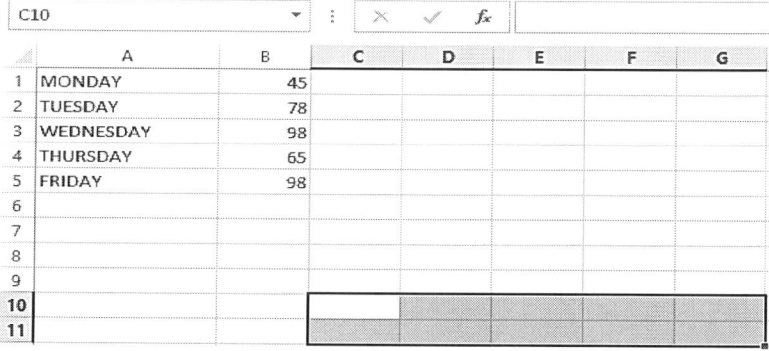

- In the selected blanks cells, type **=TRANSPOSE**

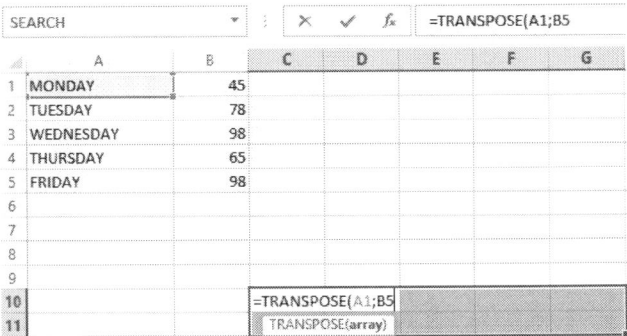

- Type in the range of the original set of cells in the TRANSPOSE function; **=TRANSPOSE (A1:B5)**

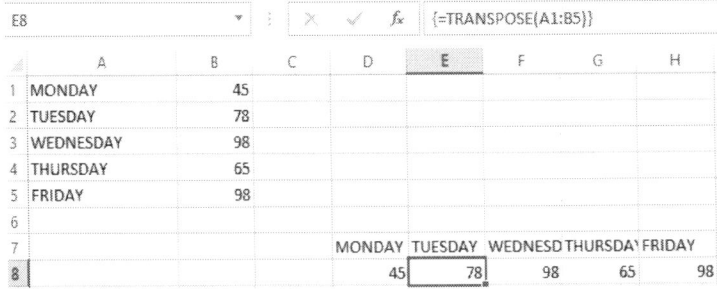

- Finally, press **CTRL+SHIF+ENTER,** then the cell range will be transposed

NOTE: Observe the following points in mind when using the TRANSPOSE function**:**

- The TRANSPOSE function being an array function does not permit changing any part of the array it returns. However, you can still

edit the TRANSPOSE function by selecting the entire range used with the function and then make any corrections. When this is done, press **Ctrl +Shift +Enter** to save the changes made.
- The TRANSPOSE location range must have the same numbers of rows and columns as the original set of cells
- The TRANSPOSE formula must be inputted as an array formula by pressing **Ctrl +Shift +Enter.**

THE FORMULATEXTS FUNCTION

The FORMULATEXT function is used to get a formula in a text form from a given reference or referred cell. With the FORMULATEXT function, you can extract a formula as a text from a cell. This function was first introduced in MS Excel 2013.

The FORMULATEXT function uses just one argument

= FORMULATEXT (reference)

- **Reference (Required argument):** This is the reference to the cell or range of cells you want the formula as texts.

USING THE FORMULATEXT FUNCTION

With the table below, let's use the FORMULATEXT function to check the formula used to find the total score of Joy in mathematics

	A	B	C	D	E
1	STUDENT SCORES	JOY	LOVETH	JOHN	ADE X
2	MATHEMATICS	59	45	68	98
3	ENGLISH	69	78	43	76
4	ECONOMICS	34	56	65	89
5	PHE	23	89	24	97
6					
7	THE TOTAL SCORE OF JOY IN MATHEMATICS	59			

To check the formula used, using the FORMULATEXT, follow the steps below:

- Select an empty cell and type in the function **=FORMULATEXT**

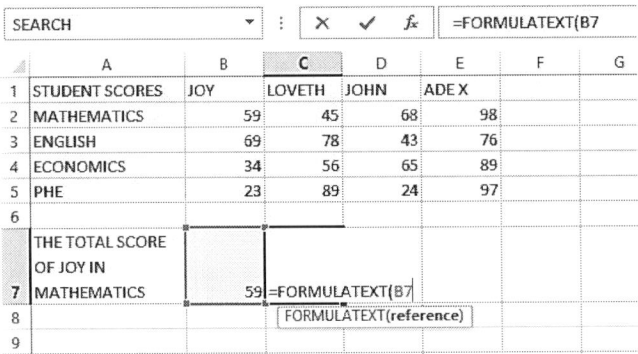

- Type the reference which is **B7** to the function; **=FORMULATEXT(B7)**

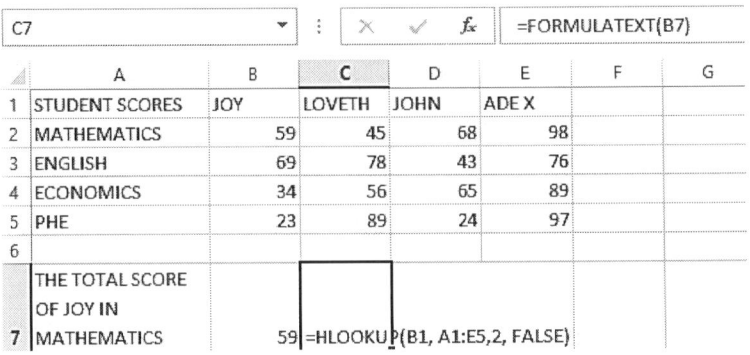

- Finally, click on enter and the formula used in the table will be displayed for you to see

NOTE: Keep the following points in mind when using the FORMULATEXT function:

- #VALUE error occurs when invalid data types are used as inputs
- The N/A error can occur due to the following reasons:
    - When you use the FORMULATEXT on a cell that does not contain a formula
    - When a reference argument is to another workbook that is not open.
    - When the formula input in the cell is longer than 8192 characters
    - When the worksheet cannot be opened because it is protected
- VBA is needed in an older version of Excel to use the formula in the cell
- The Reference argument can be used in another worksheet or workbook

THE COLUMN FUNCTION

The column function returns the column number of a given cell reference in a worksheet. It helps to give or provide the column number of a given cell reference

The COLUMN function uses one argument

= COLUMN (reference)

- **Reference (Optional Argument):** This is the cell or range for which to find the column number

USING THE COLUMN FUNCTION

In the table below, we will be using the COLUMN function to find out the column numbers of the targeted cells A4, B3, and C4

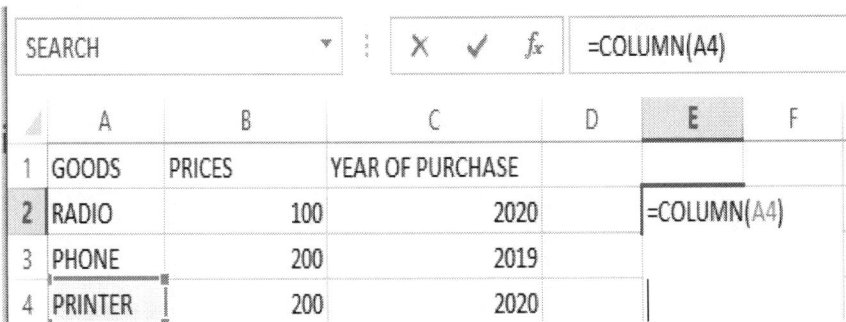

To find the column number of cell A4

- Click on a blank cell and then type the function and the cell reference you wish to know its column number =COLUMN(A4)

Click on Enter and the column number will be displayed

To find the column number of cell B3

- Click on a blank cell and then type the function and the cell reference you wish to know its column number =COLUMN(B4)

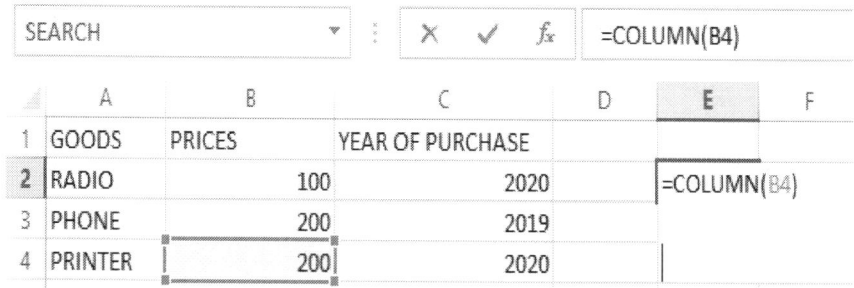

- Click on Enter and the column number will be displayed

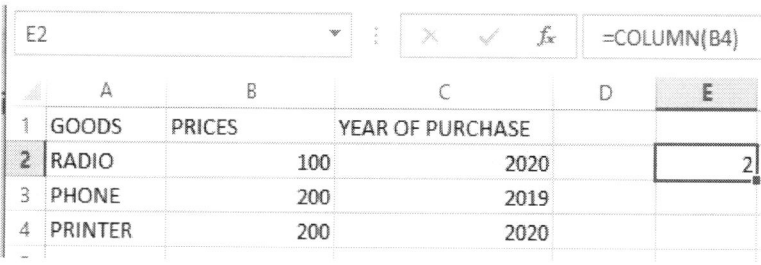

To find the column number of cell C1;

- Click on a blank cell and then type the function and the cell reference you wish to know its column number **=COLUMN(C4)**

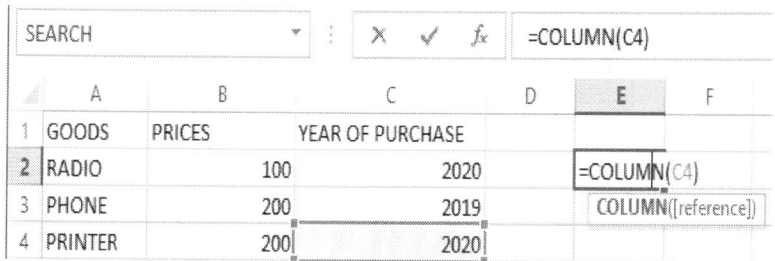

- Click on Enter and the column number will be displayed

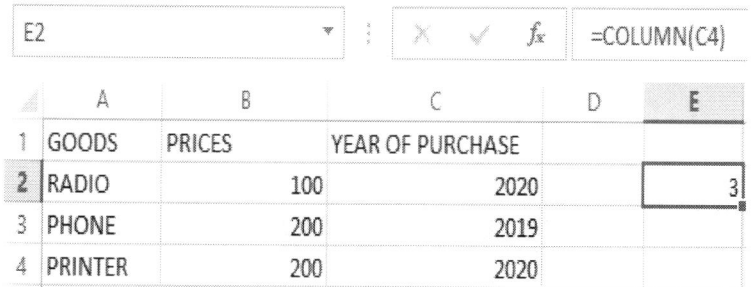

When you use the COLUMN function without specifying the reference, the function will automatically pick the column number of the cell it is inserted into =COLUMN ()

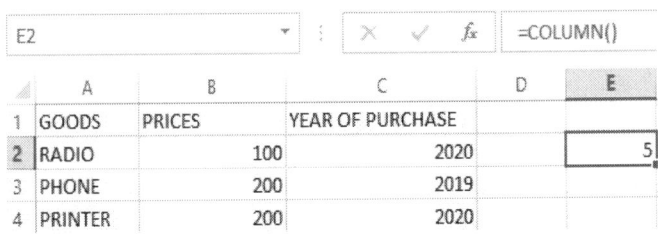

NOTE: Keep the following points in mind while using the COLUMN function

- The COLUMN function cannot include more than one cell reference or address
- The cell reference in a COLUMN function can be a single cell or a range of cells
- The reference argument in the COLUMN function is optional

THE ROW FUNCTION

The ROWS function returns the row number of a given cell reference in a worksheet. This function helps to look up and give the number of rows in a dataset or table. For instance, the formula =ROW(C6) returns 6 since C5 is the fifth row in the worksheet. To use the ROW function, all you need is to select the cell reference of the row number you wish to know.

The ROWS function uses an argument

=ROWS (reference)

- **Reference (Optional Argument):** This is the cell or range of cells to find the row numbers

USING THE ROW FUNCTION

In the table below, we will be using the ROWS function to find out the row numbers of the targeted cells A3, B4 and C3

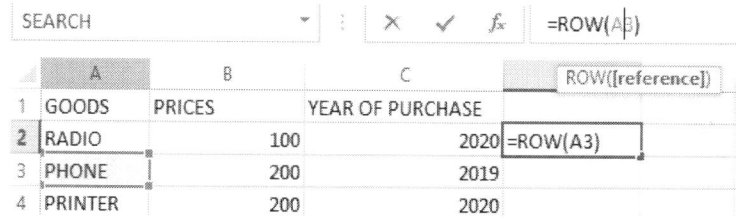

To find the row number of cell A3;

- Click on a blank cell, type the function and the cell reference you wish to know its row number **=ROW(A3)**

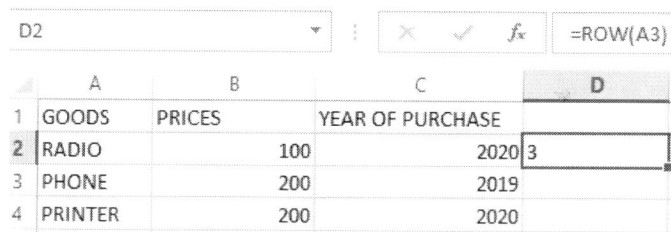

- Click on Enter and the column number will be displayed

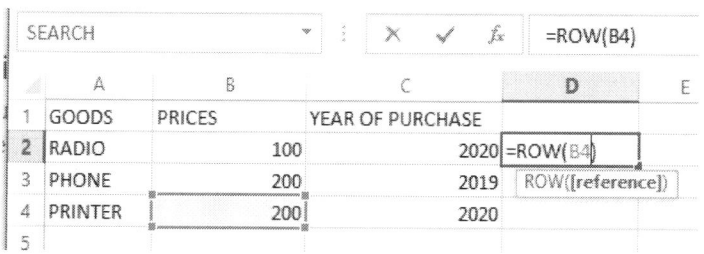

To find the row number of cell B4;

- Click on a blank cell and then type the function and the cell reference you wish to know its column number **=ROW(B4)**

- Click on Enter and the column number will be displayed

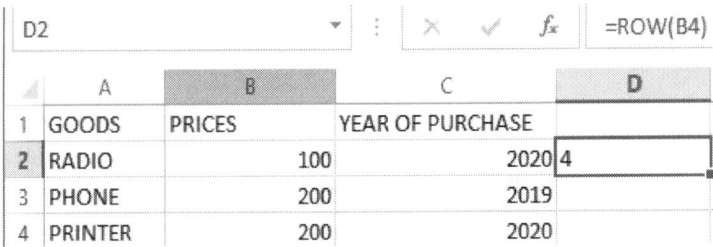

To find the row number of cell **C3**;

- Click on a blank cell and then type the function and the cell reference you wish to know its column number **=ROW(C3)**

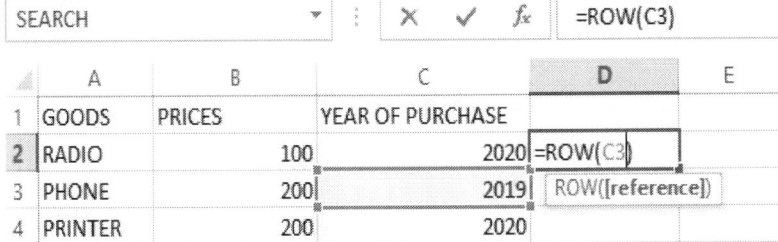

- Click on Enter and the column number will be displayed

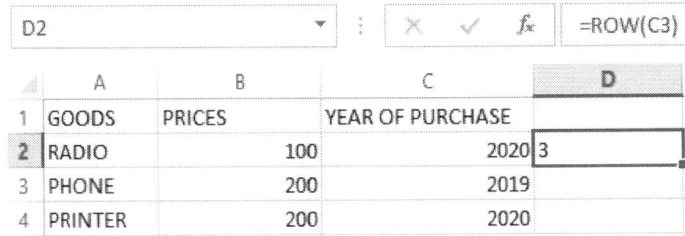

Just like the COLUMN function, you can also use the ROW function without specifying the reference. The function automatically picks the row number of the cell it is inserted into **=ROW ()**

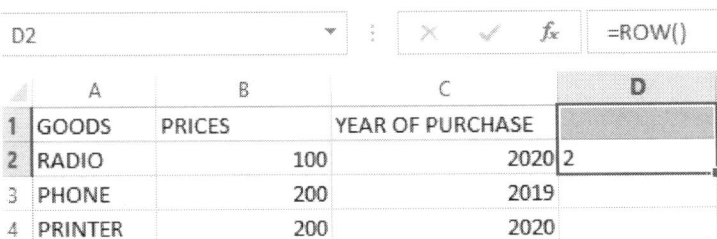

NOTE: Keep the following points in mind while using the COLUMN function

- The ROW function cannot include more than one cell reference or address
- The cell reference in a ROW function can be a single cell or a range of cells
- The reference argument in the COLUMN function is optional
- If the reference in the ROW function is entered as an array, the ROW function returns the row of numbers of all the rows in that array

THE INDEX FUNCTION

The INDEX function returns a value or a reference to a value within a table based on the intersection of rows and columns within the dataset or table. The INDEX function is mostly used with the MATCH function and can also be used in the replacement of VLOOKUP. There are two formats for the INDEX function

- Array Format
- Reference Format

THE ARRAY FORMAT OF THE INDEX FUNCTION

The array format of the INDEX function is used to return the value of a specific cell or an array of cells.

The array format of the INDEX functions takes the following arguments:

=INDEX (array, row_num, [col_num]

- **Array (Required Argument):** This is the specific array or range of cells to look up From.
- **Row_num (Required Argument):** This indicates the row number of the specified array from which to return a value from. When this argument is set to zero or blank, all rows in the array will default to zero or blank.

- **Column_num (Optional Argument):** This indicates the row number of the specified array from which to return a value from. When this argument is set to zero or blank, all columns in the array will default to zero or blank.

USING THE ARRAY FORMAT OF THE INDEX FUNCTION

From the table below, we will use the array format of the INDEX function to find out the numbers of goals scored by LOVETH

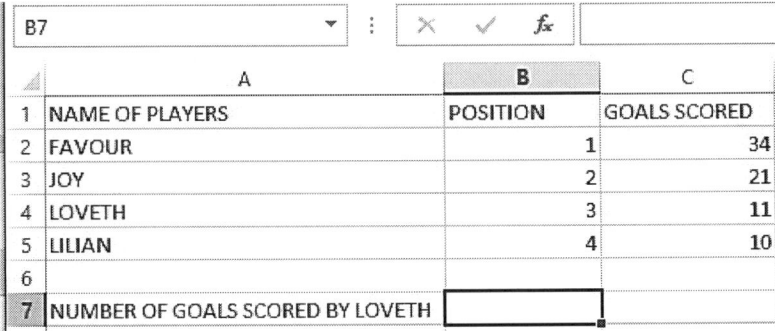

To find out the total number of scores by LOVETH, follow the steps below:

- Select an empty cell and type in the function to be used with the **array** i.e., the specified range of cells which are A2:C5=**INDEX (A2:C5**

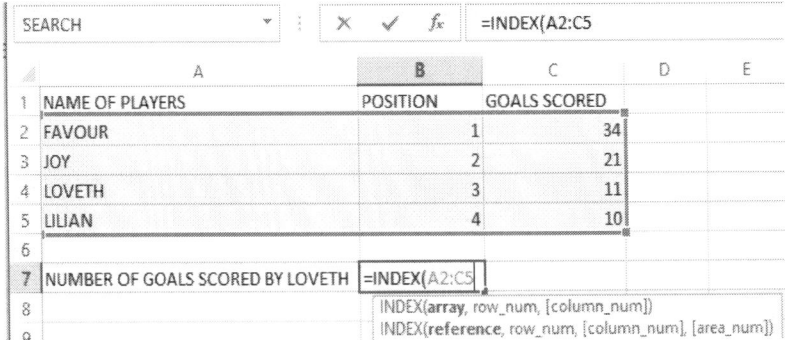

- Put in the row and column number alongside the array; **INDEX (A2:C5,3,3)**

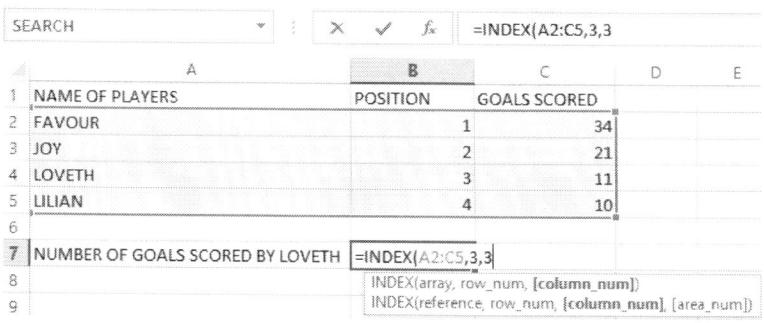

- If you have followed the steps above, the result of your operation using the array format of the INDEX function with the table will be **11**

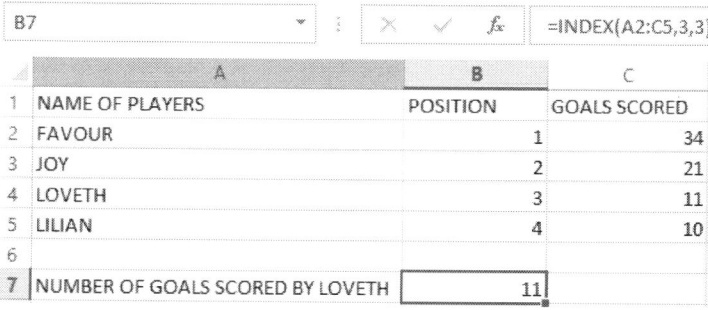

THE REFERENCE FORMAT OF THE INDEX FUNCTION

The reference format of the INDEX function returns the reference of the cell when the row_num and col_num are intersected.

The reference format of the INDEX functions takes the following arguments:

=INDEX((reference,row_num,[column_num],[area_num])

- **Reference (Required Argument):** This is a reference to one or more cells. When multiple areas are inputted into the function, each is separated by commas e.g. (A1:B2, D5:E6)
- **Row_num (Required Argument):** This indicates the row number of the specified reference from which to return a value from. When this argument is set to zero or blank, all rows in the array will default to zero or blank.

- **Col_num (Optional Argument):** This indicates the col number of the specified reference from which to return a value from. When this argument is set to zero or blank, all columns in the array will default to zero or blank.
- **Area_num (Optional Argument):** When the reference supplied is a multiple range, the area_num specifies the range in reference from which to return the intersection of row_num and column_num

USING THE REFERENCE FORMAT OF THE INDEX FUNCTION

From the table below, we will be using the reference format of the INDEX function to find out the price of mango

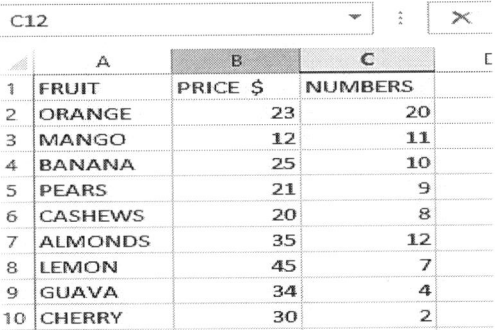

To find out the price of mango in the table, follow the steps below:

- Select an empty cell and type in the function to be used with the reference i.e., the specified range of cells which is A2:C10=**INDEX (A2:C10**

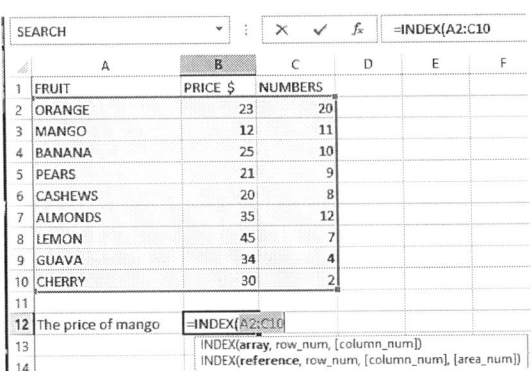

- Put in the row and column number alongside the reference; **INDEX (A2:C10,2,2,1)**

- If you have followed the steps above, the result of your operation using the reference format of the INDEX function with the table will be **12**

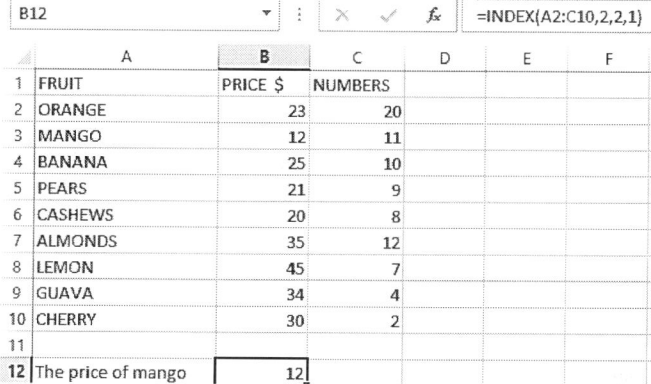

NOTE: Keep these in mind when using the array and reference format of the INDEX function:

- The INDEX function returns the value in the cell at the intersection of row_num and column_num when both the rows_num and column_num arguments are used.
- When the row_num or column_num is set to 0, the INDEX function automatically returns the array of values for the entire column or row.
- #VALUE! error occurs when the given row_num, col_num or area_num arguments are non-numeric
- #REF! error occurs:

- When the row_num argument given is greater than the number of rows in the given range
- When the col_num argument given is greater than the number of columns provided in the range
- When the area_num argument is more than the number of areas provided in the range given.

CHAPTER ELEVEN

LOGICAL FUNCTIONS

Logical functions are the functions that provide decision-making tools that allow you to look at the content of a cell, execute a calculation, and then test the result against a required value. The logical function is also used to test if a situation is true or false and these results can be used to display information and execute all kinds of calculations. Examples of the logical functions are IF, NOT, OR, IFS, etc.

THE IF FUNCTION

The IF function is a function that tests a given condition and returns one value for a TRUE result and another value for a FALSE result. This function allows you to make a logical comparison between a value and what you expect.

The IF function uses the following arguments

=IF (Logical_text,[Value_if_true],[Value_if_false])

- **Logical_text (Required Argument):** This is the value or logical expression that are to be tested and evaluated as either TRUE or FALSE
- **Value_if_true (Optional Argument):** This is the value that will be returned if the logical test evaluates to TRUE
- **Value_if_false (Optional Argument):** This is the value that will be returned if the logical test evaluates to FALSE

While using this function, the following logical operators can be used

- Equal to (=)
- Greater than (>)
- Greater than or equal to (≥)
- Less than (<)
- Less than or equal to (≤)

- Not equal (≠)

USING THE IF FUNCTION

In the table below, we want to test if the values in the cells are greater than 500 or not, if it is true, the value will be returned stating **Yes** and if it is false, the value will be returned stating **No**

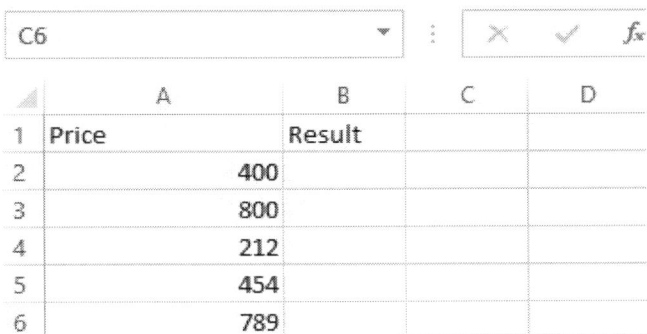

- To check if cell A2 is greater than 500, type in =IF(A2>500," Yes", "No")

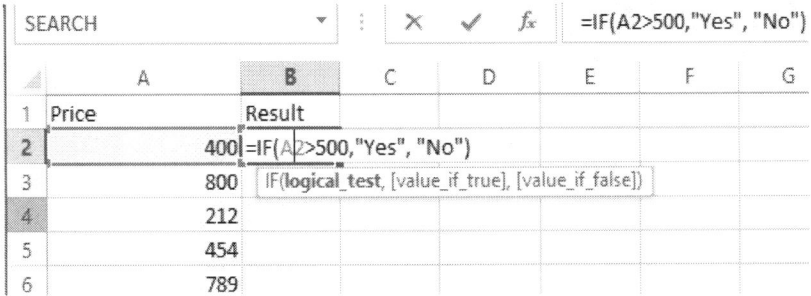

- Click on enter and the return value will be **No**

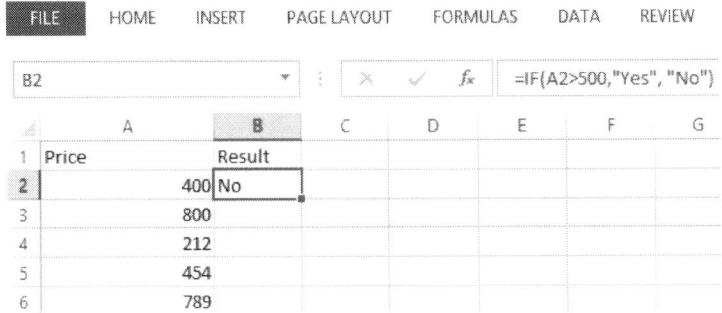

- Use the steps above to get the value of A3 to B6; **=IF(A3>500," Yes", "No"), =IF(A4>500," Yes", "No"), =IF(A5>500," Yes", "No"), =IF(A6>500," Yes", "No")** respectively

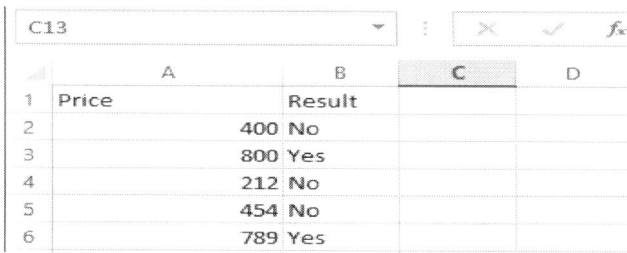

NOTE: Keep these in mind when using the IF functions:

- The IF function works if the logical_test returns a numeric value.
- The IF function treats any non-zero values as TRUE and zero value as FALSE
- #VALUE! occurs when the logical_test argument cannot be evaluated to be TRUE or FALSE
- The IF function evaluates every element of the array when any of the arguments is supplied to the function as an array
- To count condition, use the COUNTIF and COUNTIFS functions
- To add up conditions, use the SUMIF and SUMIFS functions

THE NESTED IF FUNCTION

The Nested IF function means one IF function located inside another nest IF function thereby allowing you to test multiple criteria and increasing the number of possible outcomes. You can get the same result with the nested IF function when used individually with just the IF function. Now let's use the Nested IF function in the table below to check the prices that are greater or lesser than 500

	A	B	C	D
1	Price	Result		
2		400		
3		800		
4		323		
5		454		
6		2323		

- To use the Nested IF to get the value that is greater 500, type in the function in an empty cell; **=IF(A2>500, "Yes", "No" =IF(A3>500, "Yes", "No "=IF(A4>500, "Yes", "No" =IF(A5>500, "Yes", "No") =IF(A6>500, "Yes", "No"))))** and then click enter

- You will get the value of the first cell referenced

- To get the values of the remaining cells, use the fill handle to drag the function to reflect on the other cells.

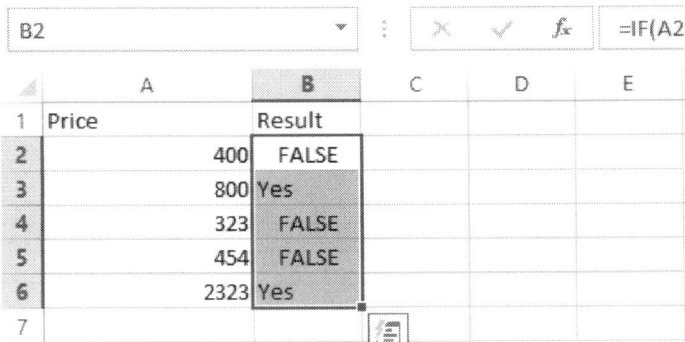

200

NOTE: When using the Nested IF functions, take note of the following:

- The Nested IF function involves a lot of thinking and accuracy when building so that the logic can calculate correctly with the condition given to the very end.
- The Nested IF functions can be confusing at times, especially when there are a lot of IF functions to be nested

THE IFS FUNCTION

The IFS function is a function that is used as a substitute to the nested IF function. This function checks whether one or more conditions or criteria are met and returns the values that correspond to or meet the first TRUE condition

The IFS function uses the following for its operations

=IFS (Logical_test1, value1[logical_test2, value2] ..., [logical_test127, value127])

- **Logical_test1 (Required Argument):** This is a condition that Excel uses to evaluate whether a value is TRUE or FALSE
- **Value1 (Required Argument):** This is when the logical_test 1 is true. Other logical values are optional.

USING THE IFS FUNCTION

Let's use the IFS function to assign grades to the marks of students given in the table below

	A	B	C	D	E
1					
2	Marks	Grade			
3		80			
4		75			
5		70			
6		65			
7		60			
8		55			

To assign grades to the marks below;

- Select an empty cell and type in the function name and its arguments; =IFS(A3>75,"A", A3>70, "B", A3>65, "C", A3>60, "D", A3>55, "E", A3>50, "F")

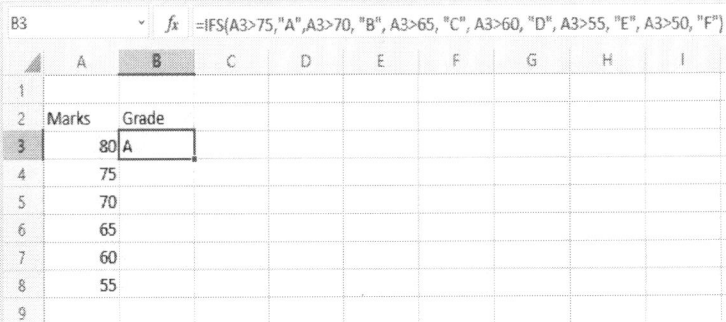

- To get the values of the remaining cells, use the fill handle to drag the function to reflect on the other cells.

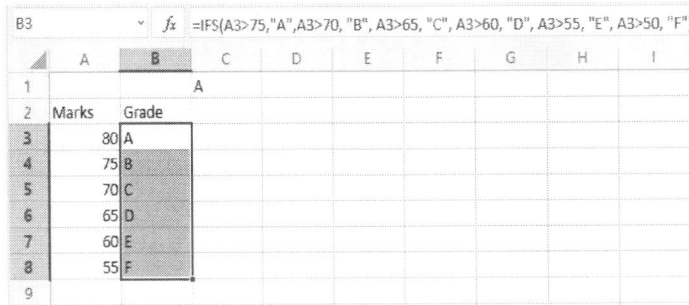

NOTE: Keep these in mind when using the IFS function

- #N/A error occurs when there are no TRUE conditions found by the IFS function
- When the logical_test argument resolves to a value other than TRUE or FALSE, #VALUE! error occurs

THE IFFEROR FUNCTION

The IFFEROR function is a function that is used to custom result when a formula generates an error. The IFERROR is to trap and manage errors without using more complicating nested IF statements.

The IFERROR uses the following arguments

=IFFERROR (value, value_if_error)

- **Value (Required Argument):** This is a value or expression that is checked or tested for error
- **Value_if_error (Required Argument):** This is the value that will be returned when an error is found in the formula

USING THE IFERROR FORMULAS

With the table given below, let's use the IFFEROR function to remove the errors and put in a customized message "invalid data"

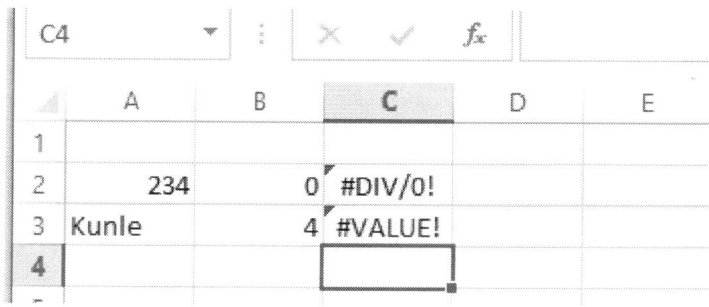

To change the error in cell C2

- Select an empty cell and type in the function name and its arguments; **=IFERROR (A2/B2, "invalid data")**

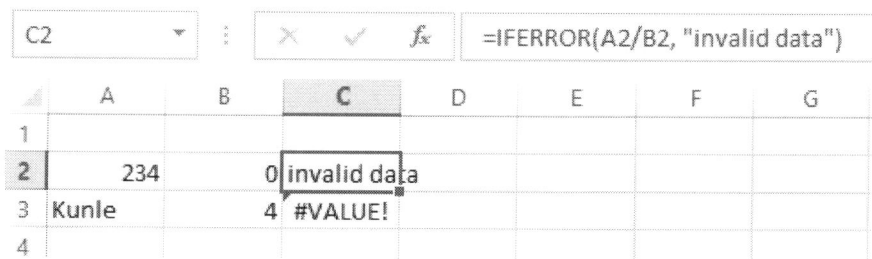

To change the error in cell C3

- Select an empty cell and type in the function name and its arguments; **=IFERROR (A3/B3, "invalid data")**

	A	B	C	D	E	F	G
1							
2	234		0	invalid data			
3	Kunle		4	invalid data			

C3 =IFERROR(A3/B3, "invalid data")

NOTE: Keep these in mind when using the IFERROR FUNCTION

- When the value or value_if_error is an empty cell, the IFERROR function treats it as an empty string value
- The IFFEROR returns an array of results for each cell in the range specified in the value if the value is an array formula

THE AND FUNCTION

The AND function is a function that is used to determine if the conditions given in a data set are TRUE and when any of the conditions is not met, it returns a FALSE value e.g., B1 is greater than 50 and less than 100

The AND function uses the following arguments to execute

=AND (logical1, [logical2},)

- **Logical1 (Required Argument):** This is the first condition or logical value to be evaluated
- **Logical2 (Optional Argument):** This is the second condition or logical value to be evaluated

USING THE AND FUNCTION

Using the table given below, let's examine if cell A2 is greater than 67 and less than cell A3 using the AND function to return TRUE or FALSE value depending on the result.

	A	B	C	D
1				
2		23		
3		56		
4				

To get the result of the table above:

- Select an empty cell and type in the function name and its arguments; =AND(A2>67, A2<A3)

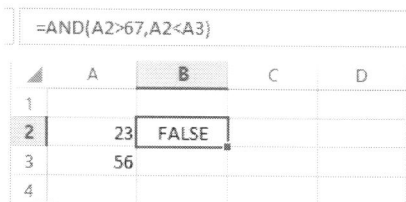

- The AND function returns FALSE in the table above because one of the conditions given in the data set was not met i.e. A2 is not greater than 67
- When the conditions given in a dataset are met, the AND function will return TRUE as shown in the table below

	A	B	C	D
1				
2		23	TRUE	
3		56		
4				

=AND(A2>20,A2<A3)

NOTE: Keep the following in mind when using the AND function

- When there is no logical value found or created during the evaluation, the AND function returns a VALUE! error
- The AND function ignores test values and empty cell provided as arguments
- The AND function can contain 255 conditions
- The AND function returns TRUE when all the conditions are met

THE OR FUNCTION

The OR function is a function that returns TRUE if any of the conditions are TRUE and returns FALSE if all conditions are false. Unlike the AND function, when one of all the conditions is false, it will be returned as FALSE

The OR function uses the following arguments

=OR (logical1, [logical2},...)

- **Logical1 (Required Argument):** This is the first condition or logical value to evaluate.
- **Logical (Required Argument):** The second condition or logical value to evaluate

USING THE OR FUNCTION

let's examine if cell A2 is greater than 30, B2 is less than 50 and B3 is equal to 45 using the OR function to return TRUE or FALSE value depending on the result.

	A	B	C	D	E
1					
2	45	32			
3	3	3			
4					
5					

To get the result of the table above

- Select an empty cell and type in the function name and its arguments; =OR**(A2>30,B2<50, B3=45)**

=OR(A2>30,B2<50, B3=45)

	A	B	C	D	E	F	G
1							
2	45	32	=OR(A2>30,B2<50, B3=45)				
3	3	3	OR(logical1, [logical2], [logical3], [logical4], ...)				
4							
5							

- Click on enter and the result will be returned as FALSE as shown in the table below

```
=OR(A2>30,B2<50, B3=45)
```

	A	B	C	D	E
1					
2	45	32	TRUE		
3	3	3			
4					

NOTE: Keep the following in mind when using the OR function

- When any of the logical_test cannot be interpreted as numeric or logical values, the function returns a #VALUE! error
- This function ignores text values or empty cells supplied in the arguments
- The function can contain 255 conditions in total
- This function can also be used together with the AND function depending on the arguments

CHAPTER TWELVE

LOOKUP AND REFERENCE FUNCTIONS

The Lookup functions are used for retrieving information from a list of data or tables and used on the worksheet or workbook. Examples of the lookup functions are HLOOK UP, VLOOK UP, etc.

The Reference functions return information about cell references as text values such as the entire address, row, and column. Examples of these functions are ADDRESS function, ROW function, etc. Now let's talk about the lookup and reference functions and how they can be applied to the worksheet.

THE VLOOKUP FUNCTION

The VLOOKUP function in which the V means **Vertical** is a quick way to lookup up a piece of information in the first column of a table or dataset and extracting or returning some corresponding data or information in the same row from another column of the data set or table.
The VLOOKUP function uses the following arguments to execute its operation:

=VLOOKUP (lookup_value, table_array, col_index_num, [range_lookup])

- **Lookup_value (required argument):** This is the value to look up for in the first column of the table or dataset
- **Table_array (required argument):** This is the data array that is to be searched by the lookup value in the left part of the column
- **Col_index_num (required argument):** This is the column number or integer in the table array where the matching value must be returned.
- **Range_lookup (optional argument):** This part of the function specifies if you want the VLOOK to find an exact match or the appropriate match. The argument is set to either TRUE or FALSE. TRUE stands for appropriate match and if not found, the next

largest value is returned. FALSE on its stands for exact match and if not found, it returns as error #N/A

USING THE VLOOKUP FUNCTION

Let's look at the example below; this is a table containing 4 fruits and their prices. With the VLOOKUP function, let's find out the price of yam in the table

	A	B	C	D	E
1	GOOD TABLE				
2					
3					
4	FRUIT	IN STOCK	PRICE $		
5	Grapes	Yes	23		
6	Yam	Yes	54		
7	Bananas	No	78		
8	Orange	Yes	54		
9					
10					
11	FRUIT		PRICE		
12	YAM				

To find the price of yam in the table above using the VLOOKUP function, follow the steps below:

- Select an empty cell and type in the function to be used with the **lookup_value** i.e., the cell that contains the information to lookup for. The lookup cell here is A12 which contains **Yam =VLOOKUP (A12**

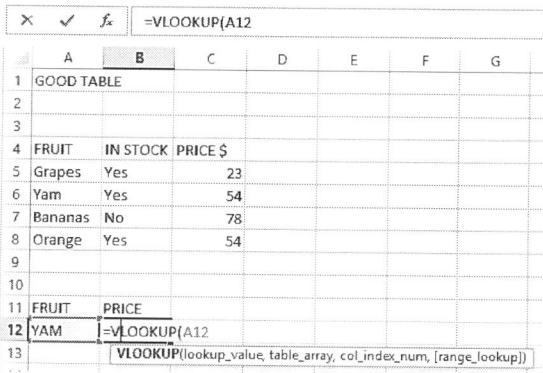

- Select the table where the data is to be searched from by inputting the **table_array: =VLOOKUP (A12, A4:C8**

209

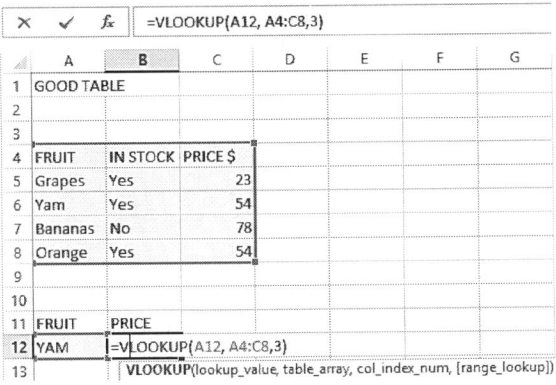

- Tell Excel the column that contains the data you want the VLOOKUP to use as output by inputting the **col_index_num** which is **3: =VLOOKUP (A12, A4:C8,3**

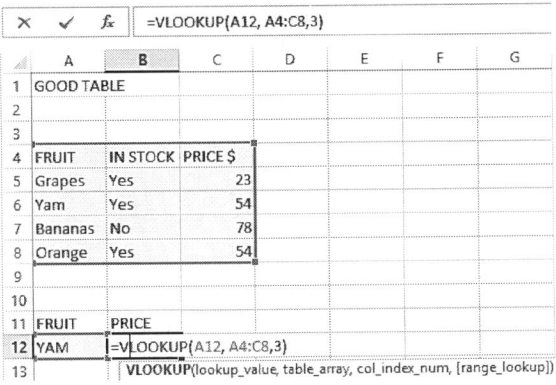

- The final step which is optional is to tell Excel if you are looking for an appropriate match or exact match by inputting either TRUE or FALSE; **=VLOOKUP (A12, A4:C8,3, FALSE) or =VLOOKUP (A12, A4:C8,3, TRUE)**

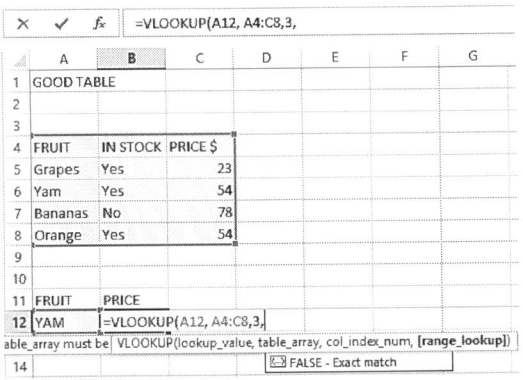

- If you have followed the steps above, the result of your operation using the VLOOKUP function with the table must be **54**

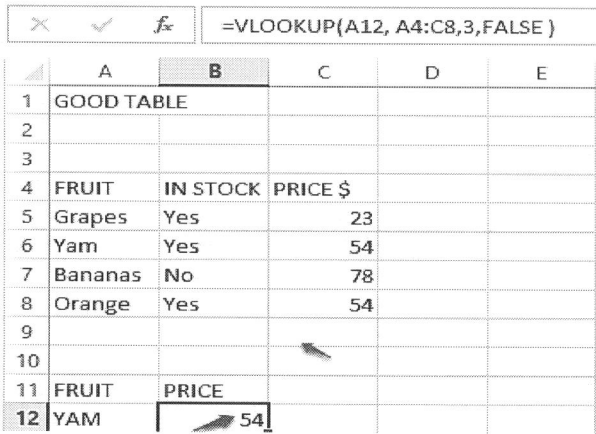

NOTE: When using the VLOOKUP function, keep the following in mind:

- When the range lookup is not used, the VLOOKUP function will not permit a non-exact match, rather it will use an exact match if it does exist.
- If the dataset contains duplicate values, the VLOOKUP function will only pick the first one
- The VLOOKUP function is not case-sensitive i.e., it works with both upper case and higher case characters
- This function permits the use of wildcards such as asterisks, question marks, and tilde
- #N/A! error occurs when the VLOOKUP function cannot find a match to the given lookup value
- #VALUE! error can occur due to two reasons
    - When the col_index_num argument is less than one or not even seen as a numeric value
    - If the range_lookup value argument is not seen or recognized as one of the logical values TRUE or FALSE
- #REF! error can occur when the col_index_num argument is bigger than the number of columns in the given table_array or when the formula used in the table to reference a cell does not exist.

THE HLOOKUP FUNCTION

The HLOOKUP function in which the H means Horizontal is a tool that is used to lookup for a value or a piece of information in the top row of a table array or dataset and then return the value or information in the same column from another row specified in the table array or dataset.

The HLOOKUP function uses the following arguments to execute its operation

=HLOOKUP (lookup_value, table_array, col_index_num, [range_lookup])

- **Lookup_value (required argument):** This is the value to look up for in the first row of the table or dataset
- **Table_array (required argument):** This is the data array that is to be searched by the lookup value in the left part of the column
- **Row_index_num (required argument):** This is the row number or integer in the table array where the matching value must be returned.
- **Range_lookup (optional argument):** This part of the function specifies if you want the VLOOK to find an exact match or the appropriate match. The argument is set to either TRUE or FALSE. TRUE stands for appropriate match and if not found, the next largest value is returned. FALSE on its own stands for exact match and if not found, it returns back as error #N/A

USING THE HLOOKUP FUNCTION

With the table below, let's find out the score of Joy in Mathematics using the HLOOKUP function

A	B	C	D	E
STUDENT SCORES	JOY	LOVETH	JOHN	ADE X
MATHEMATICS	59	45	68	98
ENGLISH	69	78	43	76
ECONOMICS	34	56	65	89
PHE	23	89	24	97
THE TOTAL SCORE OF JOY IN MATHEMATICS				

To find the total score of Joy in Mathematics, follow the steps below

- Select an empty cell and type in the function to be used with the **lookup_value** i.e., the cell that contains the information to lookup for. The lookup cell here is B1 which carries the name **Joy**; =HLOOKUP (B1

	A	B	C	D	E	F	G
1	STUDENT SCORES	JOY	LOVETH	JOHN	ADE X		
2	MATHEMATICS	59	45	68	98		
3	ENGLISH	69	78	43	76		
4	ECONOMICS	34	56	65	89		
5	PHE	23	89	24	97		
6							
7	THE TOTAL SCORE OF JOY IN MATHEMATICS	=HLOOKUP(B1					
8		HLOOKUP(lookup_value, table_array, row_index_num, [range_lookup])					

- Select the table where the data is to be searched from by inputting the **table_array**: =HLOOKUP (B1, A1:E5

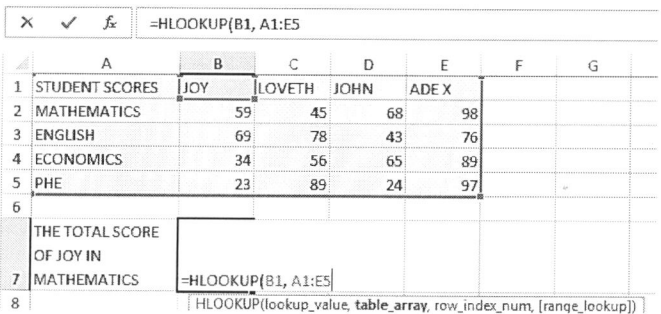

- Tell Excel the row that contains the data you want the HLOOKUP to use as output by inputting the **row_index_num** which is **2**: =HLOOKUP (B1, A1:E5, 3

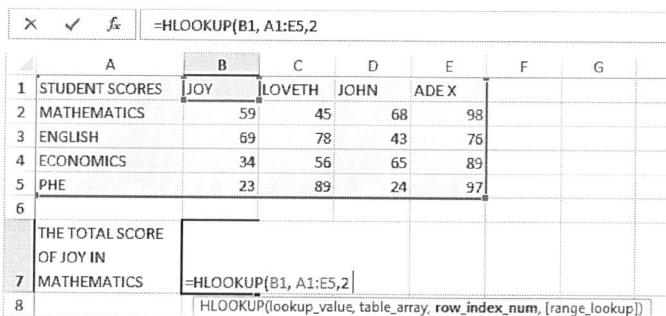

213

- The final step which is optional is to tell Excel if you are looking for an appropriate match or exact match by inputting either TRUE or FALSE; = **HLOOKUP (B1, A1:E5,3, FALSE)** or =**HLOOKUP (B1, A1:E5,3, TRUE)**

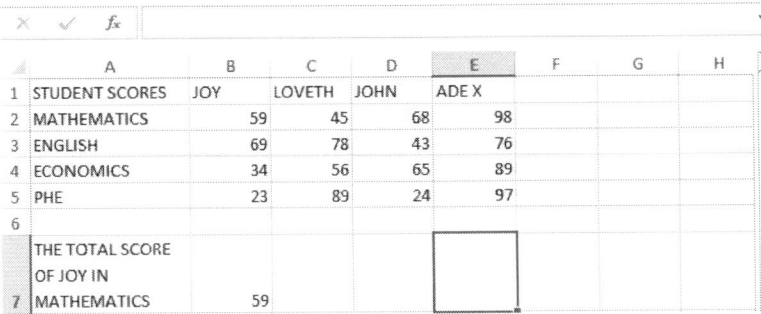

- If you have followed the steps above, the result of your operation using the VLOOKUP function with the table must be **59**

NOTE: When using the HLOOKUP functions, ensure to keep these in mind

- Just like the VLOOKUP, the HLOOKUP function is also case insensitive
- It also supports wildcard characters such as asterisks and question mark
- #N/A! error occurs when the range_lookup is FALSE and the HLOOKUP function is not able to find the lookup_value in the range
- #REF! error occurs when the row_index_num is greater than the number of columns in table_array
- #VALUE! error surfaces when the row_index_num is lesser than 1

- HLOOKUP function will only return one value and this is always the first value that matches the lookup value

THE CHOOSE FUNCTION

The CHOOSE function is a tool that uses an index number provided to return a value from the list of value arguments.

The CHOOSE function uses the following arguments to execute its operation

=CHOOSE (index_num, value1, [value2] ...)

- **Index_num (required argument):** This is an integer that specifies the position of the value to return. This must contain any number between 1 and 254, formula, or a reference to a cell ranging between 1 and 254
- **Value1, Value2...** This is a list that ranges from 1 and 254 values from which the CHOOSE function is to look from. The value 1 is required while others are optional. These values can come in form of numbers, text values, formulas, cell references, or defined names.

USING THE CHOOSE FUNCTION

With the table below, let's return the second value from a list using the CHOOSE function

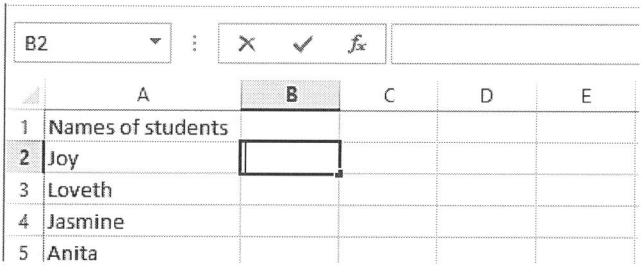

To return the second value in the list

Select an empty cell and type in the function name and its arguments;
=CHOOSE (3, A2, A3, A4, A5)

	A	B	C	D	E	F	G	H
1	Names of students							
2	Joy	=CHOOSE(3,A2, A3, A4, A5)						
3	Loveth	CHOOSE(index_num, value1, [value2], [value3], [value4], [value5], [value6], ...)						
4	Jasmine							
5	Anita							

- Click on Enter and the function will return the third value as **Jasmine** as shown in the table below

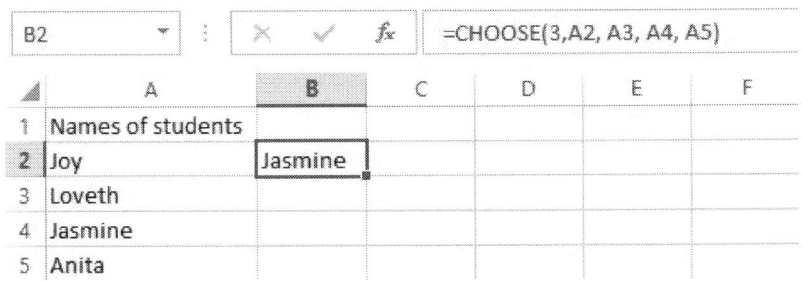

	A	B	C	D	E	F
1	Names of students					
2	Joy	Jasmine				
3	Loveth					
4	Jasmine					
5	Anita					

NOTE: Keep these in mind when using the CHOOSE function:

- When the text values in an argument are not enclosed in quotes and are not invalid cell reference, it returns #NAME? error
- #VALUE! error occurs when the index_num provided is less than 1 or greater than the given number of values or when the index_num argument is non-numeric

THE MATCH FUNCTION

The MATCH function is a tool that is used to look up a value within a range and then returns the relative position of that value within that range.

The MATCH function uses the following arguments for its operations

=MATCH (lookup_value, lookup_array, [match_type])

- **Lookup_value (Required Argument):** This is the value to be looked up
- **Lookup_array (Required Argument):** This is the data array where the value will be looked up from
- **Match_type (Optional Argument):** This argument indicates how the Lookup_value with values in lookup_array are matched together.

Match_type	Behaviour
1 or omitted	This match_type finds the largest value that is less or equal to the lookup_value. When this argument is used, the lookup_array must be in ascending order.
0	This match_type finds the first value that is equal to the lookup_value. when this argument is used, the lookup_array can be ordered anyhow
-1	This match_type finds the smallest value that is greater than or equal to the lookup_value. When this argument is used, the lookup_array must be in descending

USING THE MATCH FUNCTION

With the table below, let's find the value of Apple

	A	B	C	D	E
1					
2	Items	Value			
3	Spinach	Apple			
4	Pineaple				
5	Cucumber				
6	Apple				

To find the value of Apple;

- Select an empty cell and type in the function name and its arguments; =MATCH (B3, A3:A6,0)

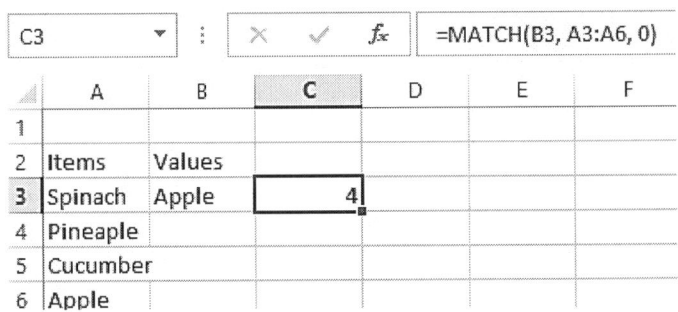

- Click on Enter and the function will return the value of Apple to be 4 as shown in the table below

NOTE: keep the following in mind when using the MATCH function

- The MATCH function is case insensitive i.e., it does not distinguish between lowercase and uppercase letters when looking up the values in the dataset
- When the MATCH function cannot find a match for the lookup_value, #N/A! error is returned
- The Function allows for appropriate and exact matching and also the use of wildcards for partial matches

The TRANSPOSE Function

The TRANSPOSE function is a tool that is used to change the orientation of a given range or array; TRANSPOSE changes a vertical range to horizontal range and vice versa.

The TRANSPOSE function uses just an argument;

=TRANSPOSE (array)

The array argument contains the range of cells to be transposed. When an array is transposed, the first row becomes the first column of the new array and the second row also becomes the second column of the new array and it continues like that.

USING THE TRANSPOSE FUNCTION

With the example below, let's change the orientation display of the array from vertical portrait to horizontal portrait using the TRANSPOSE function

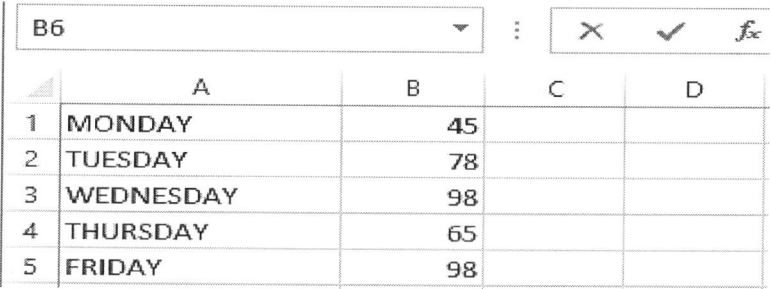

To do this, follow the procedures below:

- The first thing to do is to select some blank cells. Ensure that the cells selected are the same as the numbers of the original set of the cell but in the other direction

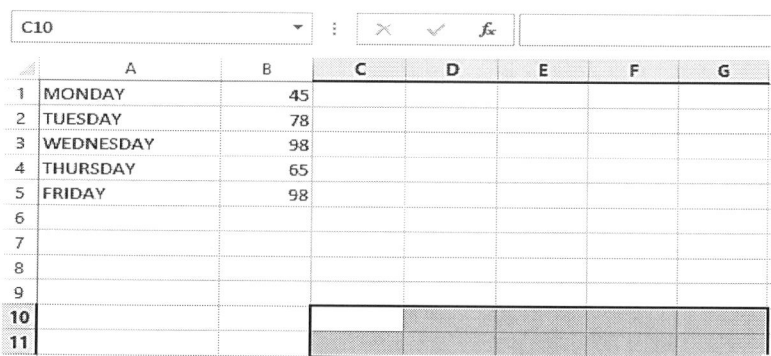

- In the selected blanks cells, type **=TRANSPOSE**

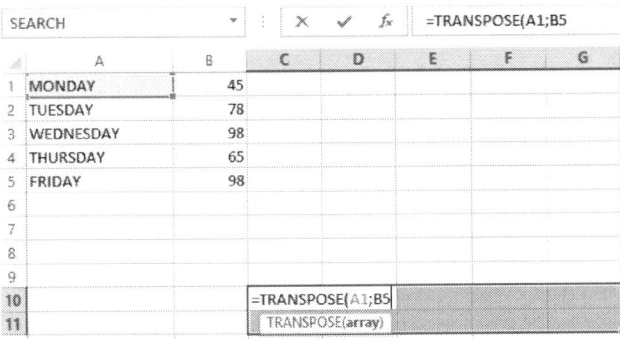

- Type in the range of the original set of cells in the TRANSPOSE function; **=TRANSPOSE (A1:B5)**

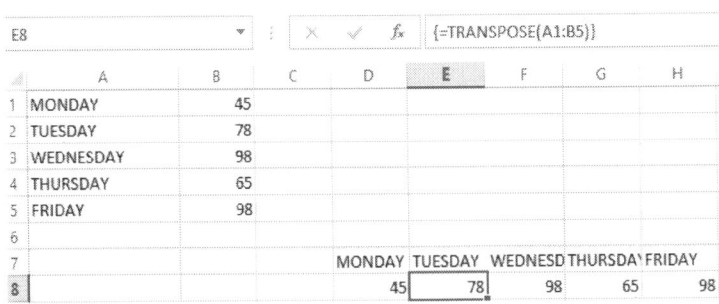

- Finally, press **CTRL+SHIFT+ENTER,** then the cell range will be transposed

NOTE: Observe the following points in mind when using the TRANSPOSE function**:**

- The TRANSPOSE function being an array function does not permit changing any part of the array it returns. However, you can still

edit the TRANSPOSE function by selecting the entire range used with the function and then make any corrections. When this is done, press **Ctrl +Shift +Enter** to save the changes made
- The TRANSPOSE location range must have the same numbers of rows and columns as the original set of cells
- The TRANSPOSE formula must be inputted as an array formula by pressing **Ctrl +Shift +Enter.**

THE FORMULATEXTS FUNCTION

The FORMULATEXT function is used to get a formula in a text form from a given reference or referred cell. With the FORMULATEXT function, you can extract a formula as a text from a cell. This function was first introduced in MS Excel 2013.

The FORMULATEXT function uses just one argument

= FORMULATEXT (reference)

- **Reference (Required argument)**: This is the reference to the cell or range of cells you want the formula as texts.

USING THE FORMULATEXT FUNCTION

With the table below, let's use the FORMULATEXT function to check the formula used to find the total score of Joy in mathematics

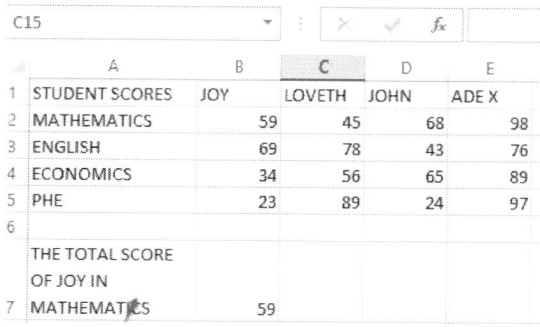

To check the formula used, using the FORMULATEXT, follow the steps below:

- Select an empty cell and type in the function **=FORMULATEXT**

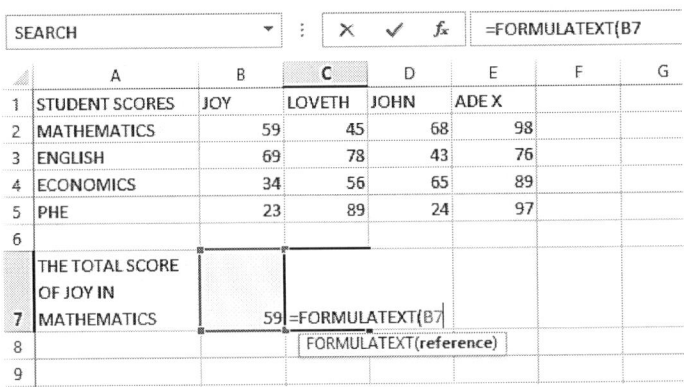

- Type the reference which is **B7** to the function; **=FORMULATEXT(B7)**

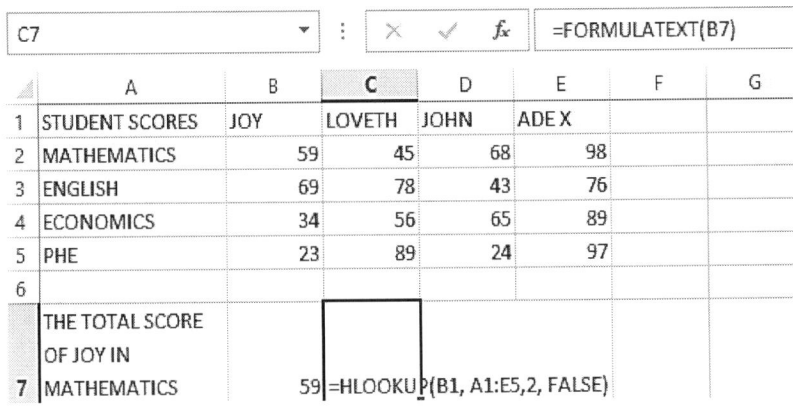

- Finally, click on enter and the formula used in the table will be displayed for you to see

NOTE: Keep the following points in mind when using the FORMULATEXT function:

- #VALUE error occurs when invalid data types are used as inputs
- The N/A error can occur due to the following reasons:
    - When you use the FORMULATEXT on a cell that does not contain a formula
    - When a reference argument is to another workbook that is not open.
    - When the formula input in the cell is longer than 8192 characters
    - When the worksheet cannot be opened because it is protected
- VBA is needed in an older version of Excel to use the formula in the cell
- The Reference argument can be used in another worksheet or workbook

THE COLUMN FUNCTION

The column function returns the column number of a given cell reference in a worksheet. It helps to give or provide the column number of a given cell reference

The COLUMN function uses one argument

= COLUMN (reference)

- **Reference (Optional Argument):** This is the cell or range for which to find the column number

USING THE COLUMN FUNCTION

In the table below, we will be using the COLUMN function to find out the column numbers of the targeted cells A4, B3, and C4

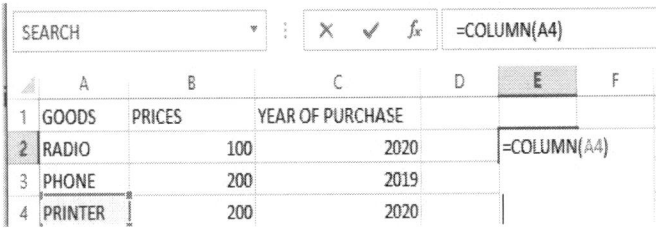

To find the column number of cell A4

- Click on a blank cell and then type the function and the cell reference you wish to know its column number **=COLUMN(A4)**

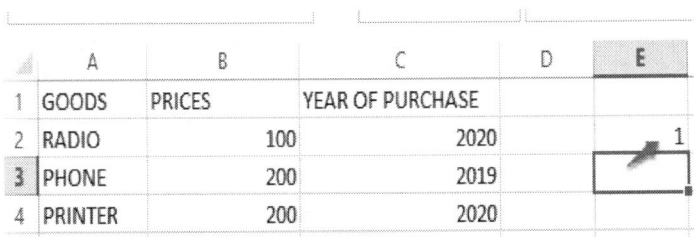

- Click on Enter and the column number will be displayed

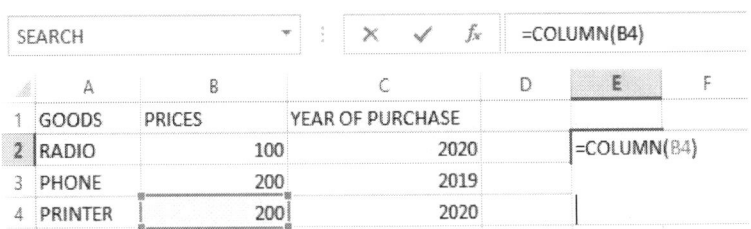

To find the column number of cell B3

- Click on a blank cell and then type the function and the cell reference you wish to know its column number **=COLUMN(B4)**

- Click on Enter and the column number will be displayed

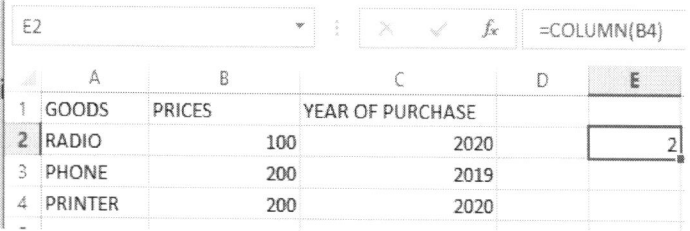

To find the column number of cell C1

- Click on a blank cell and then type the function and the cell reference you wish to know its column number =**COLUMN(C4)**

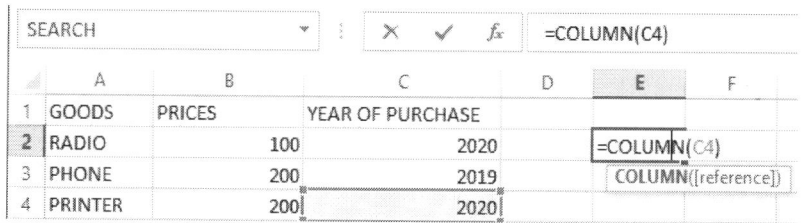

- Click on Enter and the column number will be displayed

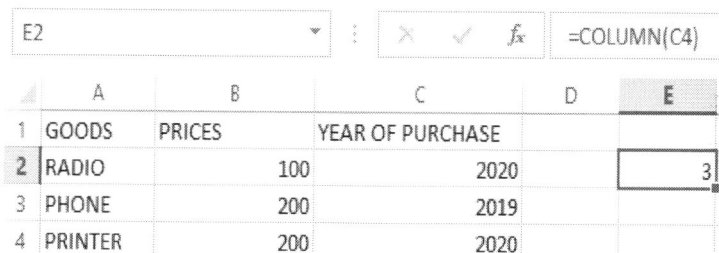

When you use the COLUMN function without specifying the reference, the function will automatically pick the column number of the cell it is inserted into =**COLUMN ()**

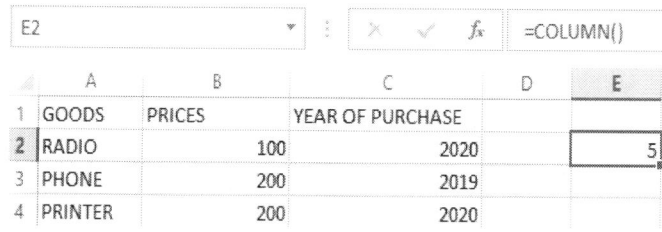

NOTE: Keep the following points in mind while using the COLUMN function

- The COLUMN function cannot include more than one cell reference or address
- The cell reference in a COLUMN function can be a single cell or a range of cells
- The reference argument in the COLUMN function is optional

THE ROW FUNCTION

The ROWS function returns the row number of a given cell reference in a worksheet. This function helps to look up and give the number of rows in a dataset or table. For instance, the formula =ROW(C6) returns 6 since C5 is the fifth row in the worksheet. To use the ROW function, all you need is to select the cell reference of the row number you wish to know.

The ROWS function uses an argument

=ROWS (reference)

- **Reference (Optional Argument):** This is the cell or range of cells to find the row numbers

USING THE ROW FUNCTION

In the table below, we will be using the ROWS function to find out the row numbers of the targeted cells A3, B4 and C3

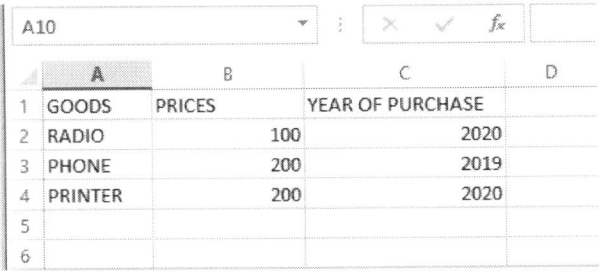

To find the row number of cell A3;

- Click on a blank cell, type the function and the cell reference you wish to know its row number =ROW(A3)

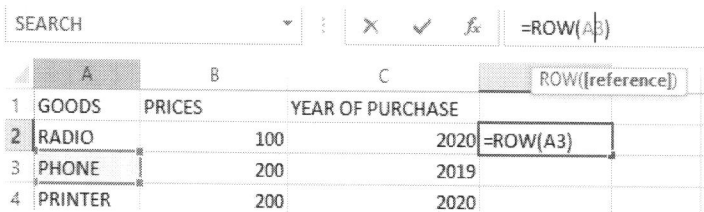

- Click on Enter and the column number will be displayed

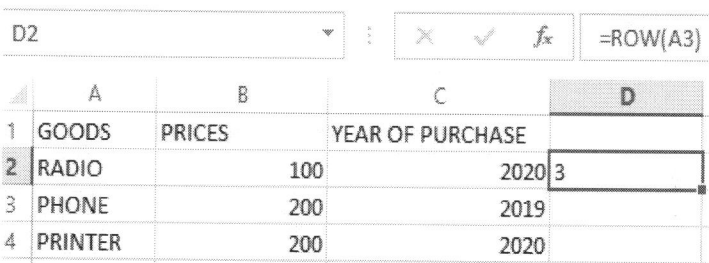

To find the row number of cell B4;

- Click on a blank cell and then type the function and the cell reference you wish to know its column number =ROW(B4)

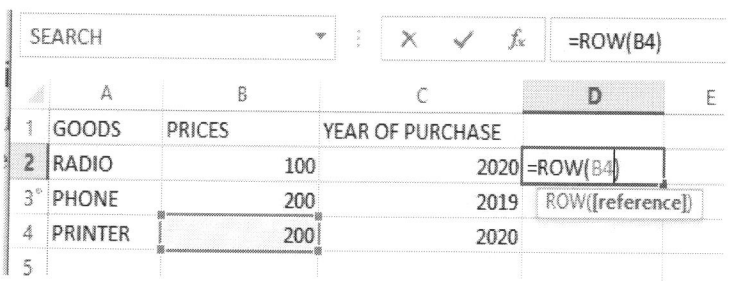

- Click on Enter and the column number will be displayed

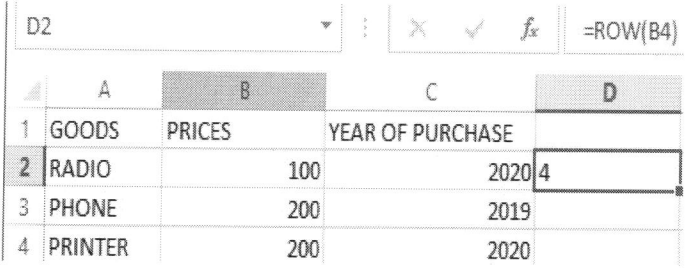

To find the row number of cell **C3**;

- Click on a blank cell and then type the function and the cell reference you wish to know its column number **=ROW(C3)**

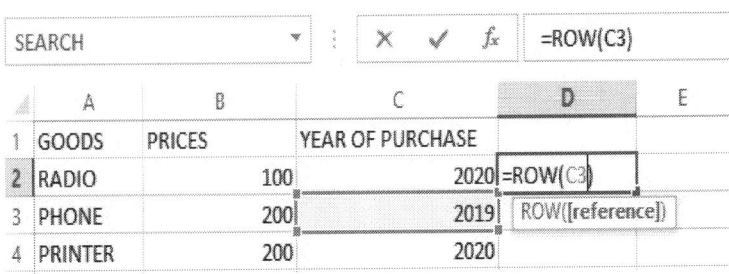

- Click on Enter and the column number will be displayed

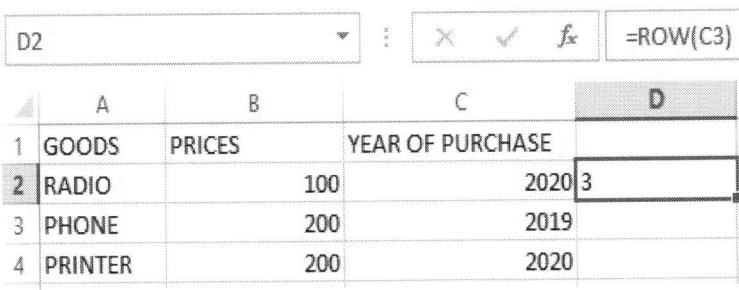

Just like the COLUMN function, you can also use the ROW function without specifying the reference. The function automatically picks the row number of the cell it is inserted into **=ROW ()**

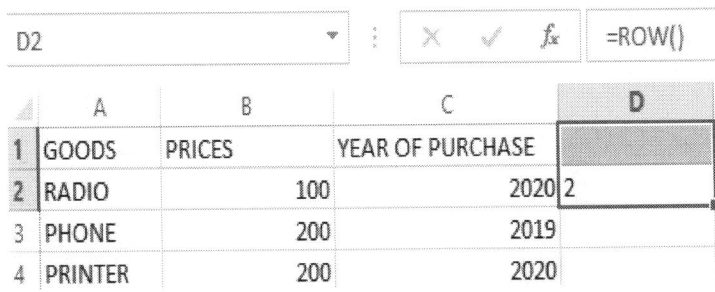

NOTE: Keep the following points in mind while using the COLUMN function

- The ROW function cannot include more than one cell reference or address

- The cell reference in a ROW function can be a single cell or a range of cells
- The reference argument in the COLUMN function is optional
- If the reference in the ROW function is entered as an array, the ROW function returns the row of numbers of all the rows in that array

THE INDEX FUNCTION

The INDEX function returns a value or a reference to a value within a table based on the intersection of rows and columns within the dataset or table. The INDEX function is mostly used with the MATCH function and can also be used in the replacement of VLOOKUP. There are two formats for the INDEX function

- Array Format
- Reference Format

The Array Format of The INDEX Function

The array format of the INDEX function is used to return the value of a specific cell or an array of cells.

The array format of the INDEX functions takes the following arguments:

=INDEX (array, row_num, [col_num])

- **Array (Required Argument):** This is the specific array or range of cells to look up From.
- **Row_num (Required Argument):** This indicates the row number of the specified array from which to return a value from. When this argument is set to zero or blank, all rows in the array will default to zero or blank.
- **Column_num (Optional Argument):** This indicates the row number of the specified array from which to return a value from. When this argument is set to zero or blank, all columns in the array will default to zero or blank.

USING THE ARRAY FORMAT OF THE INDEX FUNCTION

From the table below, we will use the array format of the INDEX function to find out the numbers of goals scored by LOVETH

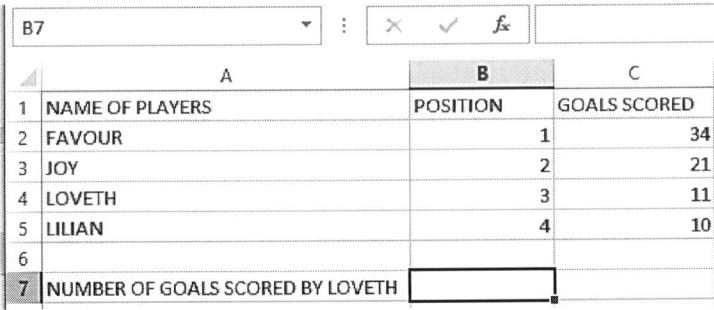

To find out the total number of scores by LOVETH, follow the steps below:

- Select an empty cell and type in the function to be used with the **array** i.e., the specified range of cells which are A2:C5=**INDEX (A2:C5**

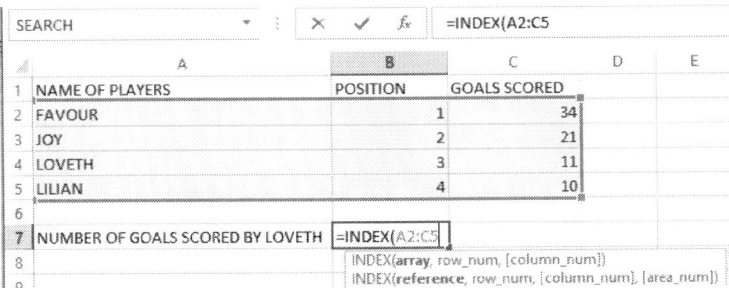

- Put in the row and column number alongside the array; **INDEX (A2:C5,3,3)**

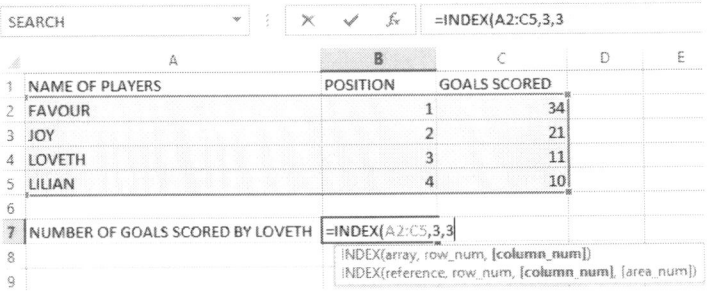

- If you have followed the steps above, the result of your operation using the array format of the INDEX function with the table will be **11**

	A	B	C
1	NAME OF PLAYERS	POSITION	GOALS SCORED
2	FAVOUR	1	34
3	JOY	2	21
4	LOVETH	3	11
5	LILIAN	4	10
6			
7	NUMBER OF GOALS SCORED BY LOVETH	11	

B7 fx =INDEX(A2:C5,3,3)

THE REFERENCE FORMAT OF THE INDEX FUNCTION

The reference format of the INDEX function returns the reference of the cell when the row_num and col_num are intersected.

The reference format of the INDEX functions takes the following arguments:

=INDEX((reference,row_num,[column_num],[area_num])

- **Reference (Required Argument):** This is a reference to one or more cells. When multiple areas are inputted into the function, each is separated by commas e.g. (A1:B2, D5:E6)
- **Row_num (Required Argument):** This indicates the row number of the specified reference from which to return a value from. When this argument is set to zero or blank, all rows in the array will default to zero or blank.
- **Col_num (Optional Argument):** This indicates the col number of the specified reference from which to return a value from. When this argument is set to zero or blank, all columns in the array will default to zero or blank.
- **Area_num (Optional Argument):** When the reference supplied is a multiple range, the area_num specifies the range in reference from which to return the intersection of row_num and column_num

USING THE REFERENCE FORMAT OF THE INDEX FUNCTION

From the table below, we will be using the reference format of the INDEX function to find out the price of mango

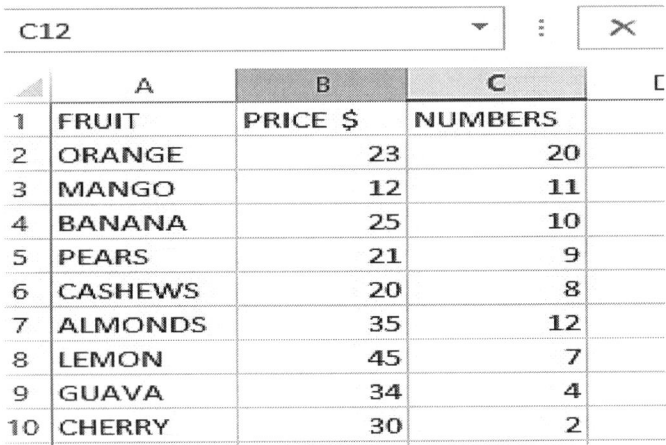

To find out the price of mango in the table, follow the steps below

- Select an empty cell and type in the function to be used with the reference i.e., the specified range of cells which is A2:C10 =**INDEX (A2:C10**

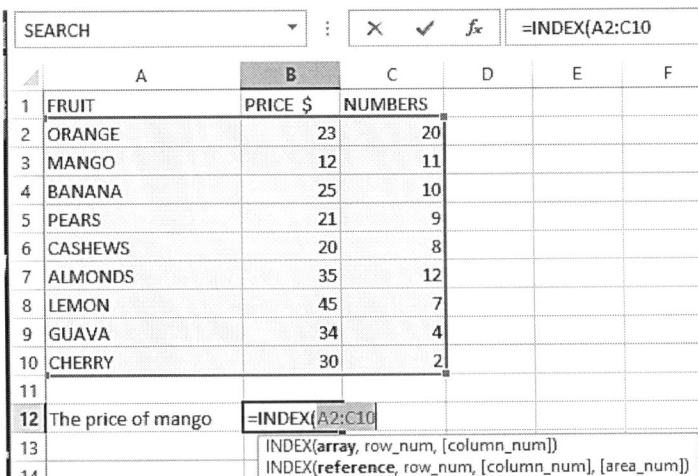

- Put in the row and column number alongside the reference; **INDEX (A2:C10,2,2,1)**

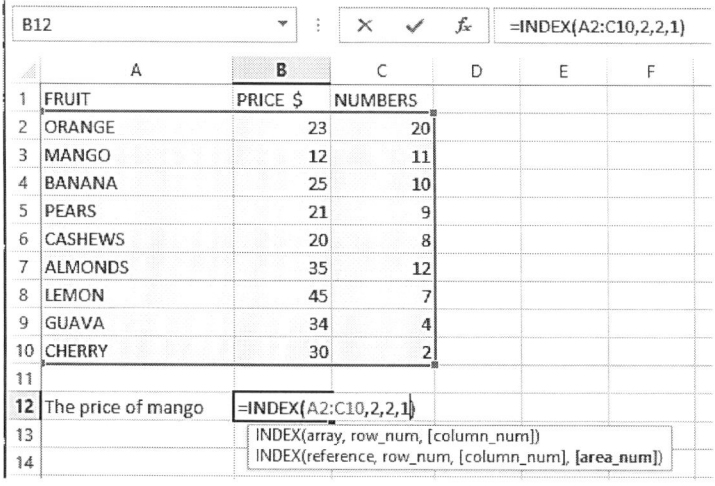

- If you have followed the steps above, the result of your operation using the reference format of the INDEX function with the table will be **12**

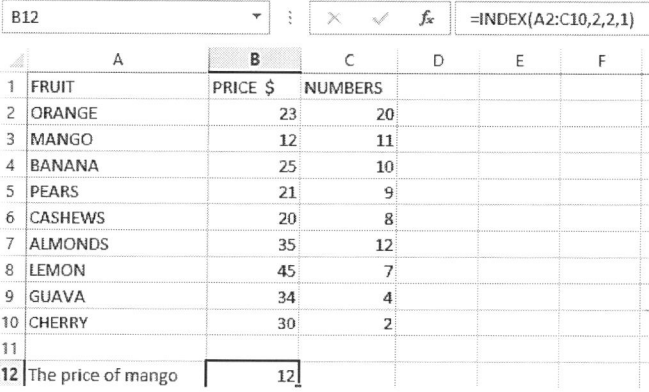

NOTE: Keep these in mind when using the array and reference format of the INDEX function:

- The INDEX function returns the value in the cell at the intersection of row_num and column_num when both the rows_num and column_num arguments are used.
- When the row_num or column_num is set to 0, the INDEX function automatically returns the array of values for the entire column or row.

- #VALUE! error occurs when the given row_num, col_num or area_num arguments are non-numeric
- #REF! error occurs:
    - When the row_num argument given is greater than the number of rows in the given range
    - When the col_num argument given is greater than the number of columns provided in the range
    - When the area_num argument is more than the number of areas provided in the range given.

CHAPTER THIRTEEN

TEXT FUNCTIONS

One of the most important functions in excel is the text function. The Text functions are used when the data you are working on has too many texts. In this chapter, we will be talking about some text functions and how they can be used and applied to the Excel worksheet.

THE FIND FUNCTION

The FIND function is used to return the position of a particular text string or subtext string within a given text string. When this text string is not found, the FIND function returns a #VALUE error

The FIND function has the following arguments

=FIND(find_text, within_text [start_num])

- **Find_text (Required Argument):** This is the text string to find or search for
- **Within_text (Required Argument):** This is where the text string will be searched from
- **Start_num (Optional Argument):** This indicates the position in the within_text where the search should begin from. When this is not applied, it will start the search at the start of the within_text string i.e., it will take on the default value of 1.

USING THE FIND FUNCTION

Using the table below, let's find the position of

i. a
ii. the
iii. love

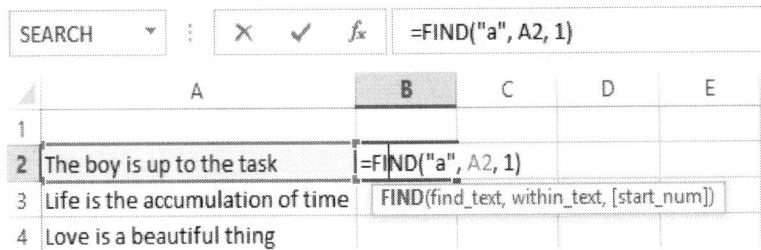

To find the position of "a" in cell A2

- Select an empty cell, type in the function and its argument =**FIND("a", A2, 1)**

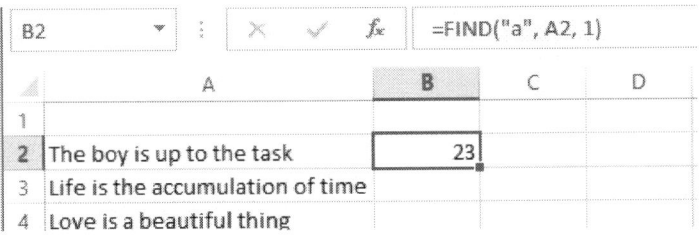

- Click on enter and the result will be 23 as shown in the table below

To find the position of "the" in cell A3

- Select an empty cell, input the function alongside with the arguments; =**FIND("the", A3, 1)**

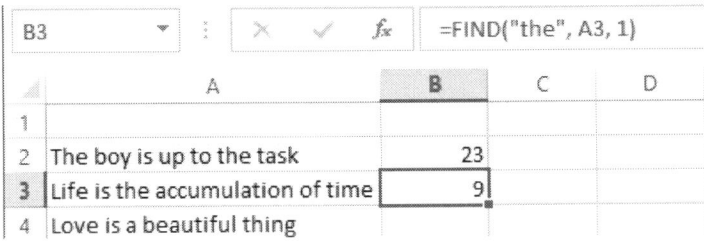

- Click on enter and the result will be 9 as shown in the table below

	A	B	C	D
1				
2	The boy is up to the task	23		
3	Life is the accumulation of time	9		
4	Love is a beautiful thing			

B3 =FIND("the", A3, 1)

To find the position of Love in cell A4

- Select an empty cell and type in the function and its argument **=FIND("Love", A4, 1)**

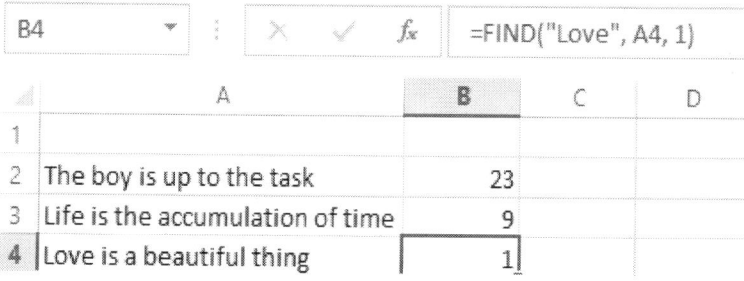

- Click on enter and the result will be 1 as shown in the table below

B4 =FIND("Love", A4, 1)

	A	B	C	D
1				
2	The boy is up to the task	23		
3	Life is the accumulation of time	9		
4	Love is a beautiful thing	1		

NOTE: Keep this in mind when using the FIND function

- The FIND function returns the location of the first instance of find_text in within_text
- #VALUE error occurs when the find_text is not found in within_text
- The FIND function is case sensitive and it does not support the use of wildcards

- The start_num is optional and when omitted, it defaults to 1
- The FIND function returns the location as the number of characters from the start of within_text.
- To search without case sensitivity, use the SEARCH function.
- To use the wildcards, use the SEARCH function

CONCATENATE FUNCTION

The CONCATENATE function is a function that allows for the joining of two or more strings to form a single string.

The CONCATENATE function uses the following arguments to carry out its operations

=CONCATENATE(text1, [text2],...)

- **Text1 (Required Argument)**: This is the first item to join and it can be in form of a text value, cell reference, or a number
- **Text2 (Required Argument)**: This is the next item to be joined with the first item. This can be up to 255 items with up to 8192 characters

USING THE CONCATENATE FUNCTION IN EXCEL

With the table below, we will be using the CONCATENATE to join some text strings into a single text string

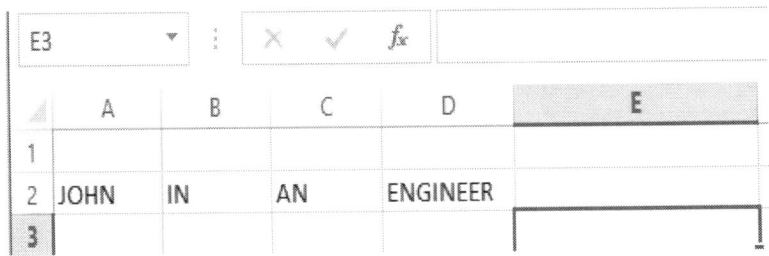

To join the texts in the table together using the CONCATENATE function

- Select an empty cell, type in the function and its argument =CONCATENATE(A2, B2, C2, D2)

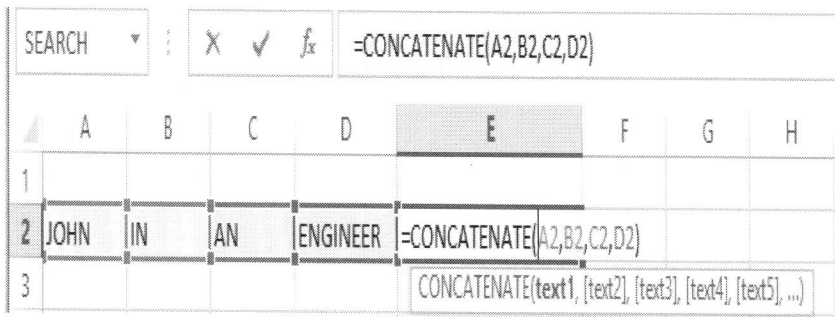

- Click on enter and the texts will be joined to form a single text string as shown in the table below

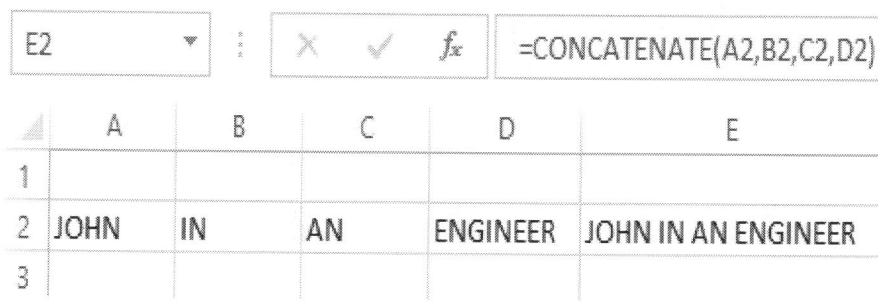

ADDING SPACE, COMMA, QUOTATION MARK, HYPHEN USING THE CONCATENATE FUNCTION

- To concatenate the text strings with space, add two double quotes in the middle of each text string

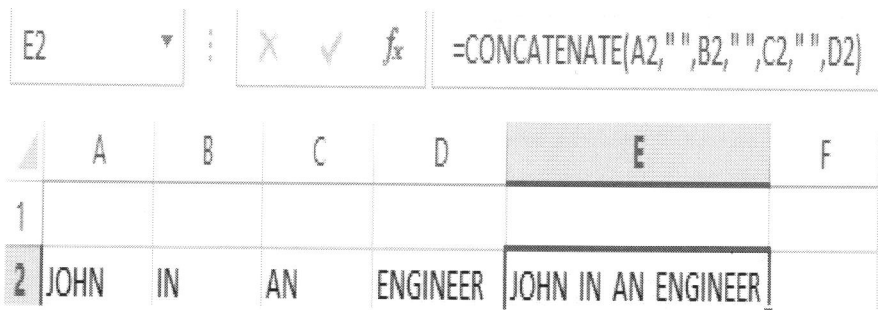

- To concatenate text strings with a comma, add two double quotes with a comma in between the two double quotes in the middle of each text string

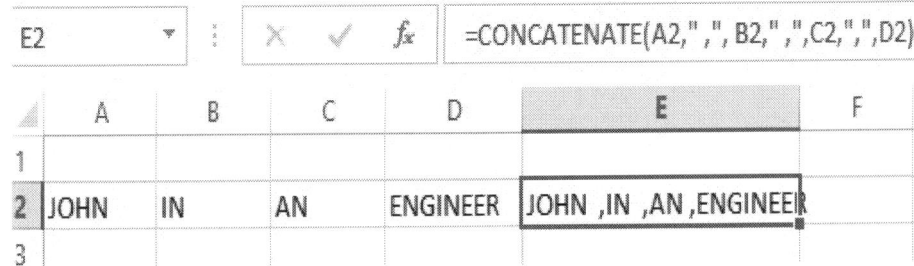

- To concatenate text strings with a quotation mark, add a comma with four double quotes before the text strings and also close it with the four double quotes

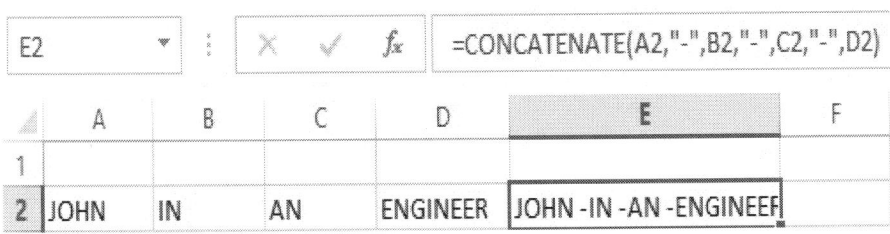

- To concatenate text strings with a hyphen, add two double quotes with a minus sign in between in the middle of each text string

NOTE: Keep the following in mind when using the CONCATENATE function

- In the CONCATENATE function, numbers don't need to be in quotation mark
- The CONCATENATE function converts numbers to text when they are joined
- The CONCATENATE function does not recognize arrays
- #NAME! error occurs when a quotation is missing from a text argument

- When one of the CONCATENATE function's argument is invalid, #VALUE! error occurs

THE TEXTJOIN FUNCTION

The TEXTJOIN function is a function that joins or combines from multiple cells or ranges with a delimiter that is used to separate each value. This is introduced in MS Excel 2016.

The TEXTJOIN function uses the following arguments for its operations

=TEXTJOIN(delimiter,ignore_empty, text1,[text2], ...

- **Delimiter (Required Argument):** This is the text string that can be either empty or with one or more characters enclosed by double quotes or a reference to a valid text string. The most common delimiters used are comma or a space separator
- **Ignore_empty (Required Argument):** This argument determines whether empty cells are included in the resulting string. Empty cells will be ignored if the argument is TRUE and empty cells will be included if it FALSE.
- **Text1(Required Argument):** This argument contains the text you wish to join together
- **Text2(Optional Required)** This is the argument additional texts you wish to be joined together

USING THE TEXTJOIN FUNCTION

Using the table below, join the texts together using the TEXTJOIN function

	A	B	C	D
1				
2	Monday			
3	Tuesday			
4	Wednesday			
5	Thursday			
6	Friday			

To join the texts in the table using the TEXTJOIN FUNCTION

- Select an empty cell type in the function and its argument =TEXTJOIN(",", TRUE, A2, A3, A4, A5, A6)
- Click on enter and the texts will be joined to form a single text string as shown in the table below

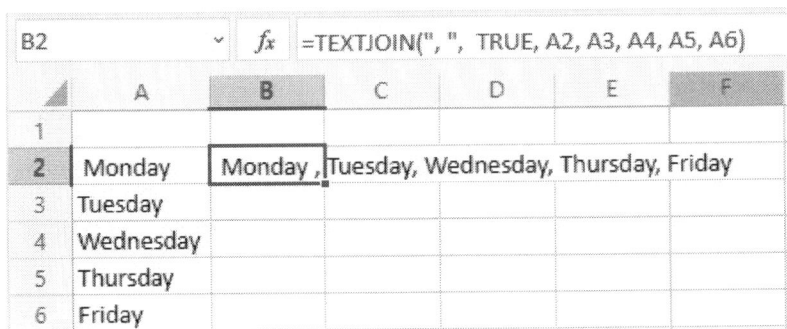

NOTE: Keep the following in mind when using the TEXTJOIN function

- #VALUE! error occurs when the resulting string exceeds the cell value limit which is 32767
- The TEXTJOIN function can take in 252 text arguments
- The TEXTJOIN function accepts delimeter
- When an older version of Excel that doesn't support this function is used, #NAME? error occurs
- #NULL! error occurs when we forget to put the comma between the text string we wish to join
- The TEXTJOIN function allows the users to use cell ranges instead of using individual cell references

TRIM FUNCTION

The TRIM function is used to remove extra spaces from a text, leaving only a single space between words and with no space character at the start or end of the text.

The TRIM function uses the following arguments for its operations

=TRIM(text)

- **Text (Required Argument):** This is the text you wish to remove the spaces from

USING THE TRIM FUNCTION

Remove the spaces in the texts in the table below using the TRIM function

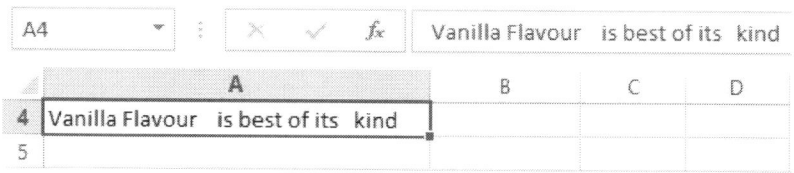

To remove the space from the text in the table;

- Select an empty cell and type in the function and its argument **=TEXTJOIN(",", TRUE, A2, A3, A4, A5, A6)**

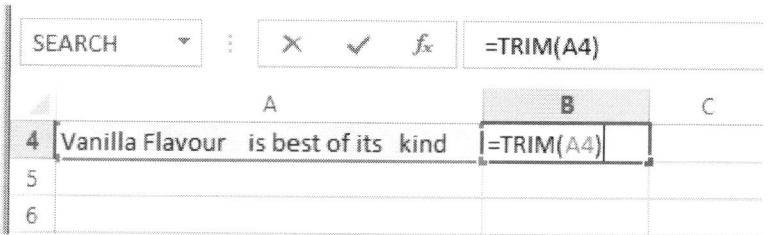

- Click on enter and the texts will be joined to form a single text string as shown in the table below

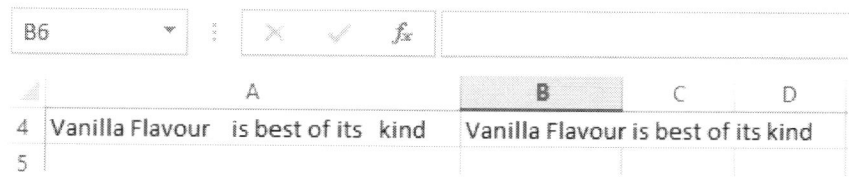

NOTE: Keep the following in mind when using the TRIM function

- TRIM function only removes extra spaces from text and leave just a single space in the texts
- TRIM function is useful for cleaning up text that comes from other applications or environment

243

- The TRIM function removes the ASCII space character from the text

THE UPPER FUNCTION

The UPPER function is one of the Excel Text function that changes texts to capital letters(UPPERCASE) without having any effect on the punctuations and numbers

This function has just one argument which is **=UPPER(Text)**

- **Text (Required Argument):** This is the text you wish to change to UPPERCASE. It can be a text string or a cell reference

USING THE UPPER FUNCTION

Convert the characters in the table to capital letters using the UPPER function

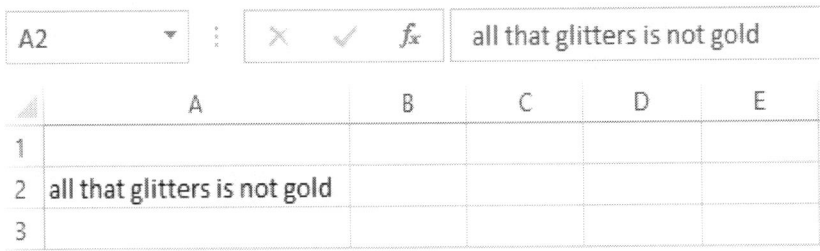

To convert text strings using the UPPER function:

- Select an empty cell, type in the function and its argument **=UPPER(A2)**

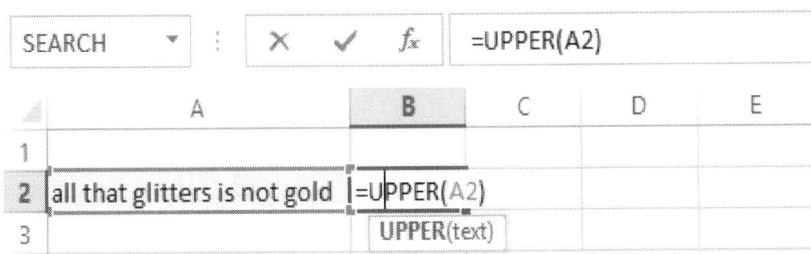

- Click on enter and the text strings will be converted to capital letters as shown in the table below

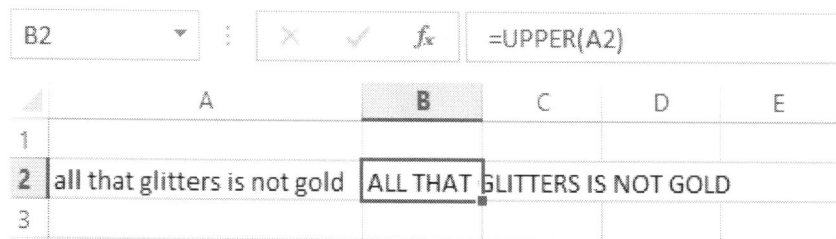

NOTE: Keep these in mind while using the UPPER function

- The UPPER function does not affect the numbers and punctuation characters
- All text characters are converted to uppercase

THE LOWER FUNCTION

The LOWER function is a function that converts text characters to lowercase and this can be a text string or cell reference

This function has just one argument which is **=LOWER(Text)**

- **Text (Required Argument):** This is the text you wish to change to lowercase. It can be a text string or a cell reference

USING THE LOWER FUNCTION

Convert the characters in the table to lower case using the LOWER function

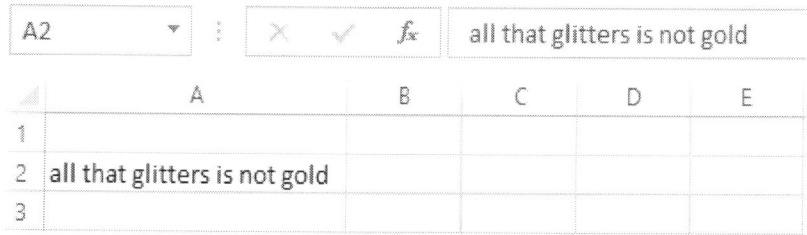

To convert text strings using the LOWER function:

- Select an empty cell, type in the function and its argument **=LOWER(A2)**

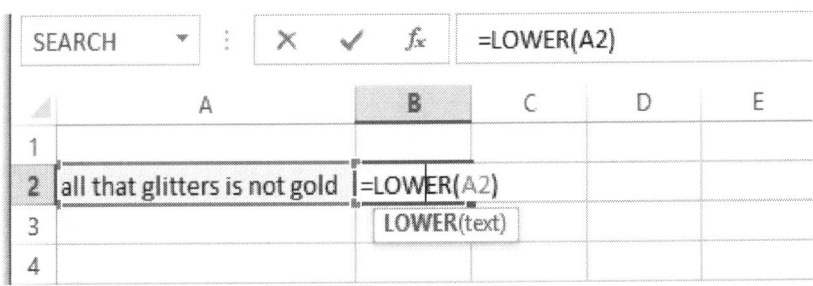

- Click on enter and the text strings will be converted to lower case as shown in the table below

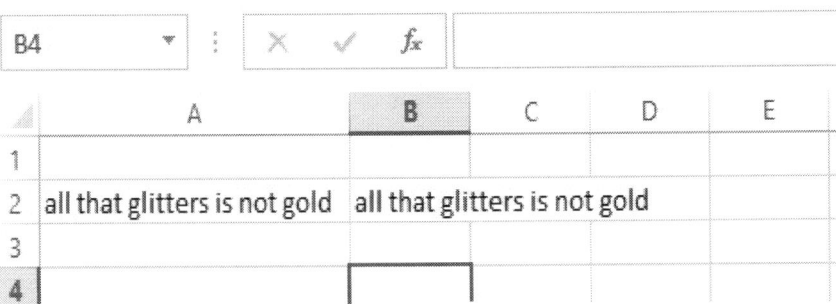

NOTE: Keep these in mind while using the LOWER function

- The LOWER function does not affect the numbers and punctuation characters
- All text characters are converted to lowercase

THE PROPER FUNCTION

The PROPER function is a function that changes texts or characters into a proper case. The first letter of each text string is written in upper case and the remaining words that precede are in lower case

The PROPER function uses just an argument which is **=PROPER(Text)**

- **Text (Required Argument):** This is the text you wish to change to a proper case. It can be a text string or a cell reference

USING THE PROPER FUNCTION

Change the text strings in the table to a proper case using the PROPER function

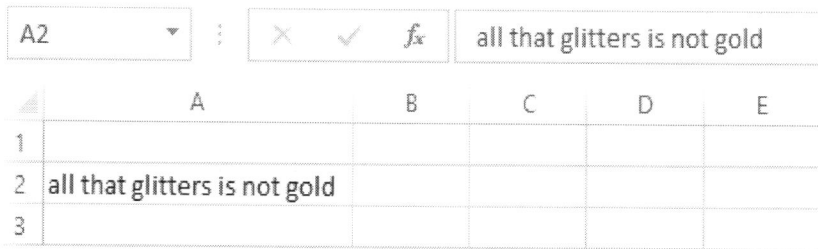

To convert the text strings to proper case

- Select an empty cell and type in the function and its argument
  =PROPER(A2)

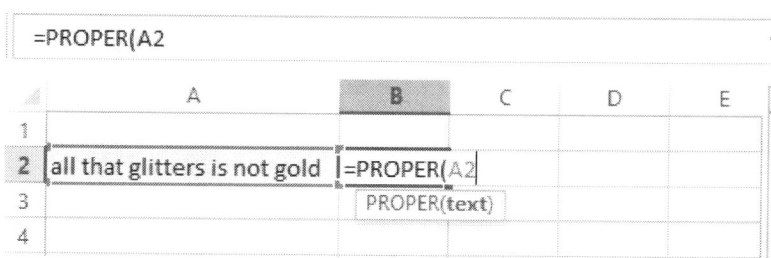

- Click on enter and the text strings will be converted to a proper case as shown in the table below

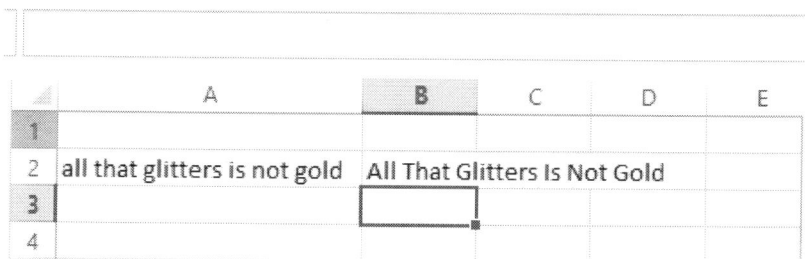

NOTE: Keep these in mind while using the PROPER function

- In the PROPER function, the first letter of each text string is converted to an upper case while the remaining words are changed into lower case

- The PROPER function does not affect numbers and punctuations

LEN FUNCTION

The LEN function is a function that returns or counts the numbers of characters in a text string excluding the number formatting

The LEN function uses an argument

=LEN(text)

- **Text (Required Argument):** This is the text you wish to find or calculate its length

USING THE LEN FUNCTION

With the table below, find the numbers of characters using the LEN function

To find the numbers of characters;

- Select an empty cell, input the function with arguments to be used=**LEN(A2)**

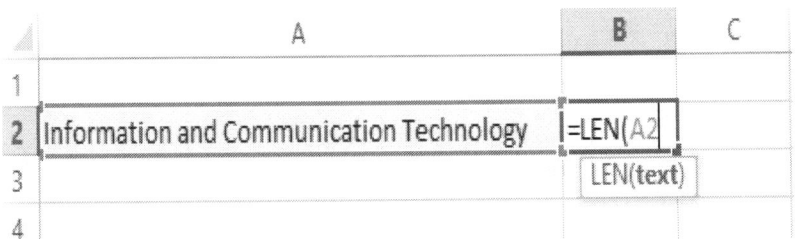

- Click on enter and the number of text strings will be 41 as shown in the table below

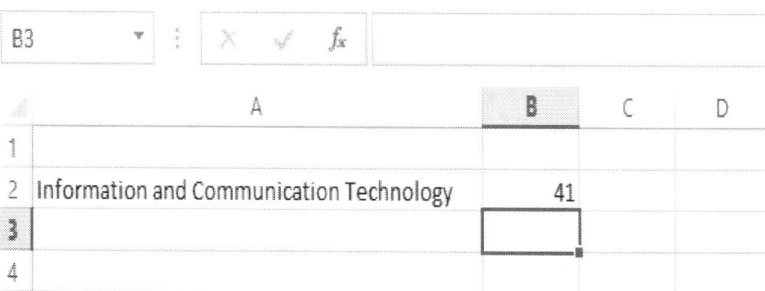

THE LENB FUNCTION

The LENB function is a function that returns the number of bytes used in representing characters in a text string.

Just like the LEN function, the LENB function uses one argument

=LEN(text)

- **Text (Required Argument):** This is the length you wish to find or calculate the length of a text string.

USING THE LENB FUNCTION

With the table below, find the length of the text strings in cell A3 using the LENB function

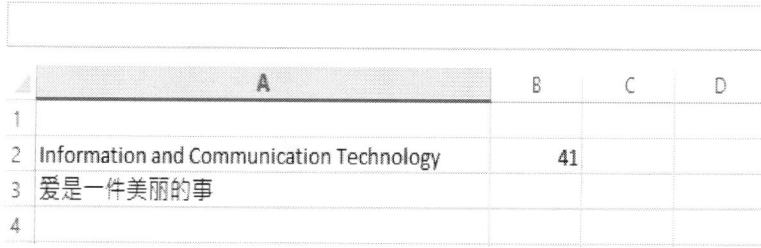

To calculate the length of characters in the text strings;

- Select an empty cell, type in the function and its argument **=LENB(A3)**

	A	B	C
1			
2	Information and Communication Technology	41	
3	爱是一件美丽的事	=LENB(A3)	
4		LENB(text)	

=LENB(A3)

- Click on enter and the number of text strings will be 8 as shown in the table below

=LENB(A3)

	A	B	C
1			
2	Information and Communication Technology	41	
3	爱是一件美丽的事	8	
4			

NOTE: Keep these in mind when using the LEN and LENB function

- Spaces are counted as characters
- The number of formatting is not included

MID Function

The MID function is a function that is used to extract a specified number of characters from the middle of the text string given.

The MID function uses the following arguments to execute its operation

=MID(text,start_num,num_chars)

- **Text (Required Argument): This is the original text to extract from**
- **Start_num (Required Argument):** This specifies or indicates the position of the first character you wish to extract the text
- **Num_chars (Required Argument):** This is used to indicate the numbers of characters to be extracted from the texts

USING THE MID FUNCTION

Extract a specified number of characters from the middle using the MID function from the table below

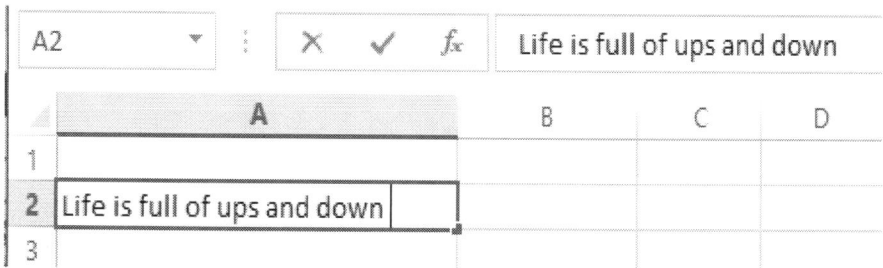

To get the specified number of characters from the middle using the MID function

- Select an empty cell, type in the function and its argument
  =MID(A2, 9,5)

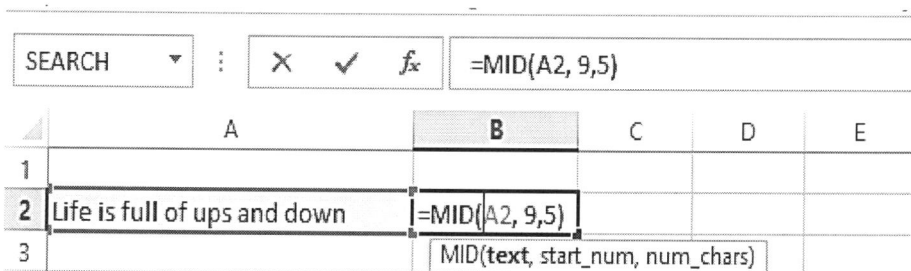

- Click on enter and the number of characters extracted from the middle will be shown in the table below

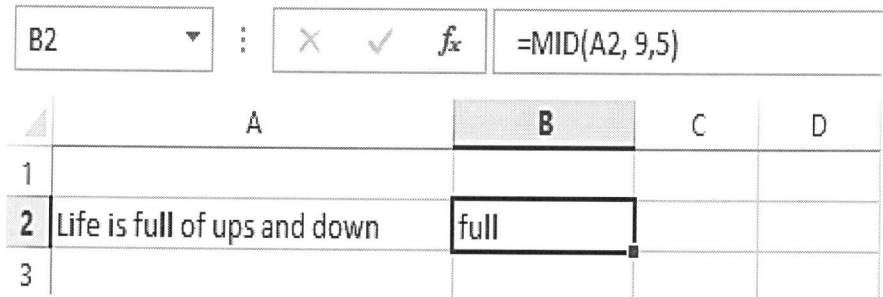

NOTE: Take note of the following when using the MID function

- #VALUE! error occurs when the num_chars is less than 0 and when the given start_num argument is less than 1
- When the MID function is used on a date, it will return the middle characters of the number that indicates that date.
- In the MID function, the number formatting is not included as a part of the string and it will not be extracted or counted
- While using the MID function, the user must specify the last parameter otherwise it will take 0 by default

THE MIDB FUNCTION

The MIDB function is a function that is used to extract a specified number of bytes from the middle of the text string given. The MID function

The MID function uses the following arguments to execute its operation

=MID B(text,start_num,num_bytes)

- **Text (Required Argument):** This is the original text to extract from
- **Start_num (Required Argument):** This specifies or indicates the position of the first character you wish to extract the text
- **Num_bytes (Required Argument):** This indicates the numbers of characters to be extracted from the texts in bytes

USING THE MIDB FUNCTION

Extract a specified number of texts in bytes from the middle using the MIDB function from the table below

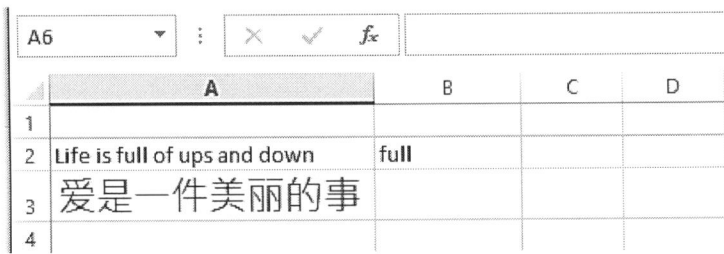

To return the specified number of text in bytes from the middle using the MIDB function

- Select an empty cell, type in the function and its argument =MIDB**(A3,3,4)**

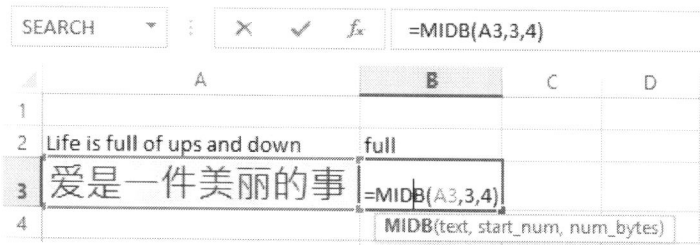

- Click on enter and the number of characters extracted from the middle will be shown in the table below

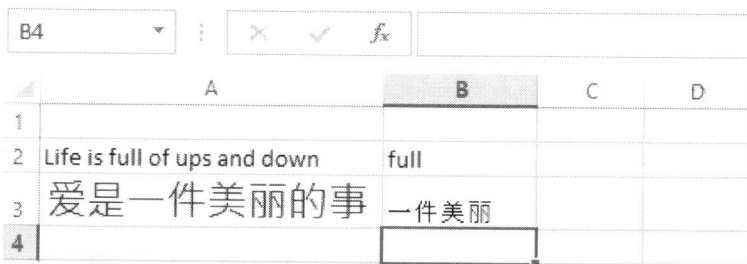

LEFT FUNCTION

The LEFT function returns a specified number of characters from the start of a text string. This function extracts characters from the left-hand side of the text.

The LEFT function uses the following arguments to execute

=LEFT(text,[num_chars])

- **Text (Required Argument):** This is the original text to extract from
- **Nun_chars (Optional Argument):** This is used to indicate the numbers of characters to be extracted from the given texts

USING THE LEFT FUNCTION

From the table below, let's extract some characters using the LEFT function

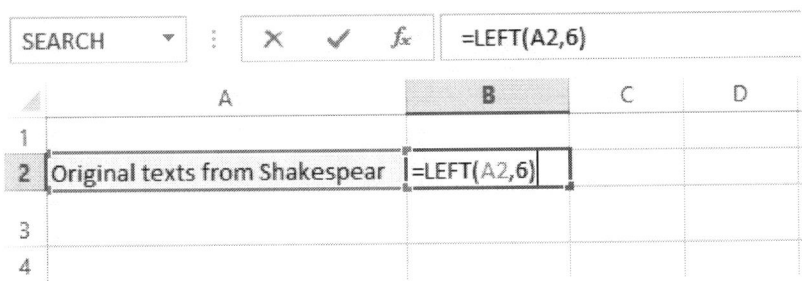

To extract the characters from the given text string using the LEFT function

- Select an empty cell and type in the function and its argument
  =LEFT(A2,6)

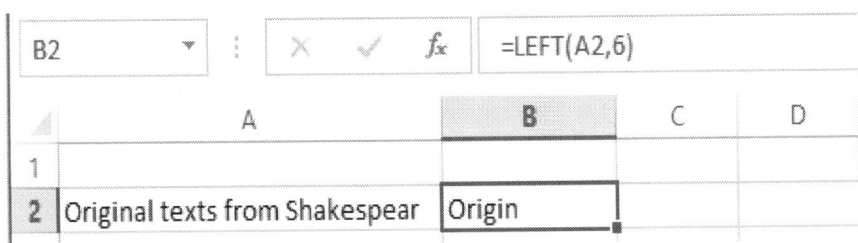

- Click on enter and the number of characters extracted from the left will be shown in the table below

THE LEFTB FUNCTION

The LEFTB function returns the left portion of a text string based on a specified number of bytes.

The LEFTB function uses the following arguments to execute its operation

=LEFTB(text,[num_bytes])

- **Text (Required Argument):** This is the text string you wish to extract from
- **Num_bytes (Optional Argument):** This indicates the numbers of characters to be extracted from the texts in bytes

USING THE LEFTB FUNCTION

Extract a specified number of texts in bytes from the left using the LEFTB function from the table below

To return the specified number of text in bytes from the left using the LEFTB function

- Select an empty cell, type in the function and its argument =**LEFTB(A2,6)**

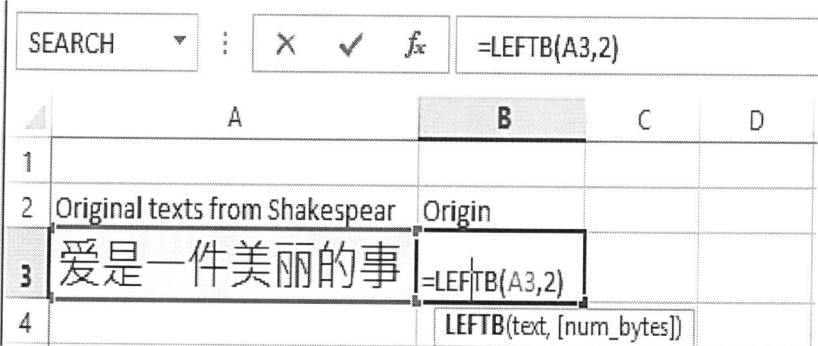

- Click on enter and the number of characters extracted from the left based on bytes will be shown in the table below

	A	B	C	D
1				
2	Original texts from Shakespear	Origin		
3	爱是一件美丽的事	爱是		
4				

B3 =LEFTB(A3,2)

NOTE: Keep the following in mind when using the LEFT and LEFTB functions

- #VALUE! error occurs when the given num_chars or num_bytes arguments is less than 0
- When the LEFT or LEFTB function is used on a date, the start character of the number that indicates the date will be returned
- If the num_chars or num_bytes is omitted, it defaults to 0

THE RIGHT FUNCTION

The RIGHT function returns a specified number of characters from the end of a text string. This function extracts characters from the right-hand side of the text.

The RIGHT function uses the following arguments to execute

=RIGHT(text,[num_chars])

- **Text (Required Argument):** This is the original text to extract from
- **Nun_chars (Optional Argument):** This is used to indicate the numbers of characters to be extracted from the given texts

USING THE RIGHT FUNCTION

With the table below, let's find some characters using the RIGHT function

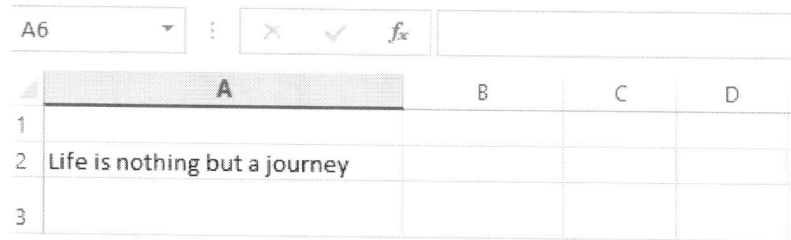

To find the character in the text string fusing the RIGHT function

- Select an empty cell and type in the function and its argument
=LEFTB(A2,4)

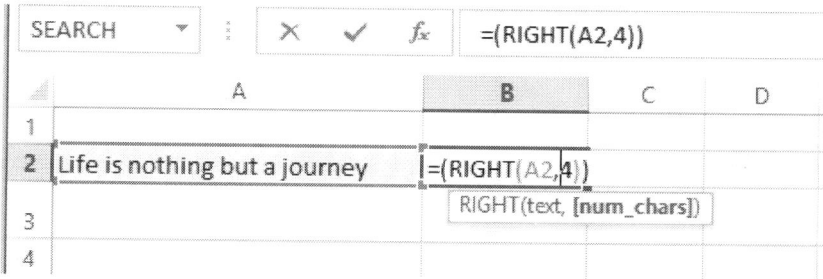

- Click on enter and the number of characters extracted from the right will be shown in the table below

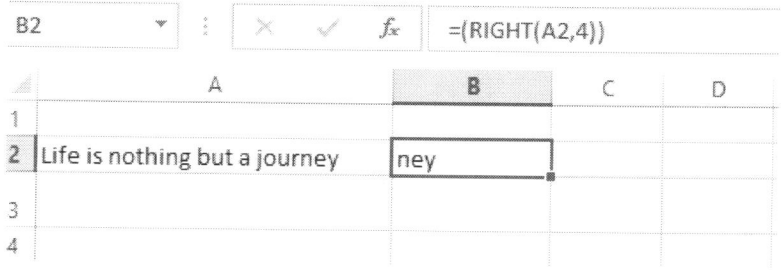

THE RIGHTB FUNCTION

The RIGHTB function returns the right portion of a text string based on a specified number of bytes.

The RIGHTB function uses the following arguments to execute its operation

=RIGHTB(text,[num_bytes])

- **Text (Required Argument):** This is the text string you wish to extract from
- **Num_bytes (Optional Argument):** This indicates the numbers of characters to be extracted from the texts in bytes

USING THE RIGHTB FUNCTION

With the table given below, find some text characters using the RIGHTB function

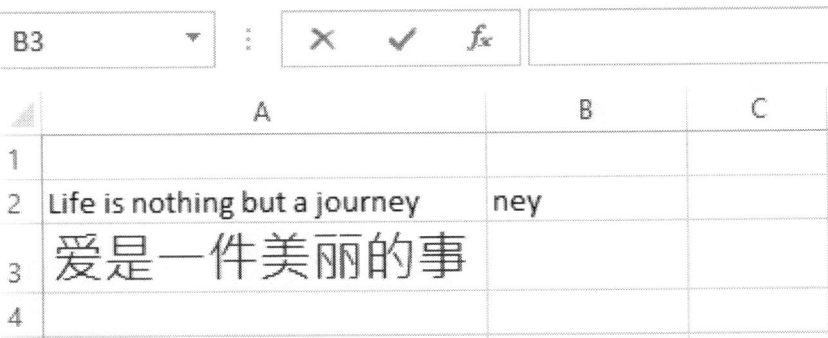

To find the characters at the right portion of the text string using the RIGHTB function,

- Select an empty cell, type in the function and its argument =RIGHTB(A3,3)

- Click on enter and the number of characters extracted from the right will be shown in the table below

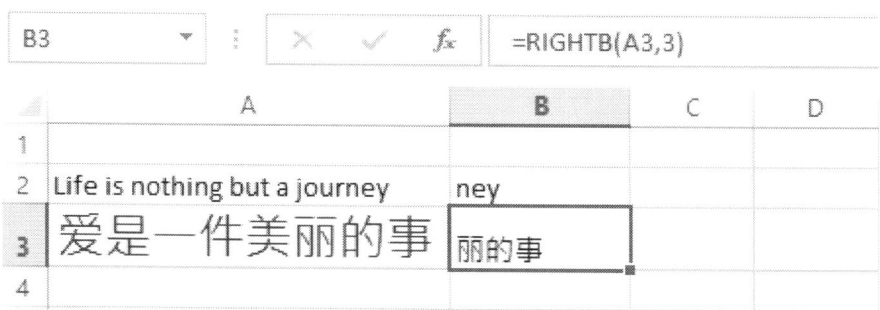

NOTE: Keep these in mind when using the RIGHT and RIGHTB function

- #VALUE! error occurs when the given num_chars or num_bytes arguments is less than 0
- If the num_chars or num_bytes is omitted, it defaults to 0
- When the RIGHT or RIGHTB function is used on a date, the start character of the number that indicates the date will be returned

CHAPTER FOURTEEN

DATE AND TIME FUNCTION

Here in this chapter, we will be discussing the date and time functions that are available in Excel and how they can be used. But before that, let me briefly explain the date format.

THE DATE FORMAT

A date is a number and just like a percentage format, it can be customized to any format of your choice. In Excel, a date is the number of days since 01/01/1900 which is the first date in excel. When you insert a date in a cell, it displays in the format dd/mm/yy.

However, there are two ways of displaying the date and they are

- Short Date
- Long Date

To locate these options on your Excel, go to the **Number Format** drop-down on the **Home menu** and then click on it

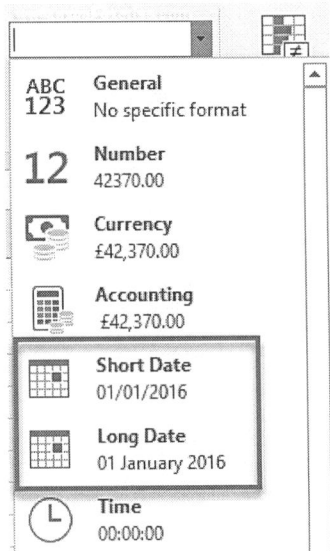

The date can be in different formats such as

- 01/01/2021
- Jan 2021
- Fri, 1 Jan 2021

DATA PARAMETER

A date has the following parameters

- d for the day
- m for the month
- y for the year

CUSTOMIZING A DATE

To customize a date on Excel, you have to open the dialog box. To open the dialog box

- Go to the **Home tab** and click on **More number** formats at the bottom of the format dropdown
- In the dialog box, select the **Custom** in the Category list and write the date format code in the **Type**

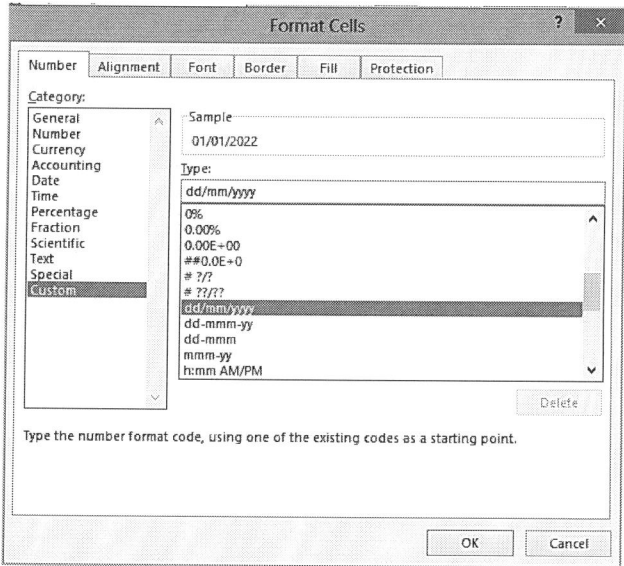

THE DAY FUNCTION

The DAY function returns the day of the date and the result is displayed in form of a serial number. The day is given as an integer from 1 to 31.

The DAY function uses this argument

=DAY (Serial_number)

- **Serial_number (Required Argument):** This is the day of the date one is trying to find. The date can be provided to the DAY function in form of serial numbers, date values from other Excel functions, and references to a cell containing dates

USING THE DAY FUNCTION

Using the table below, let's find the day in the date using the DAY function

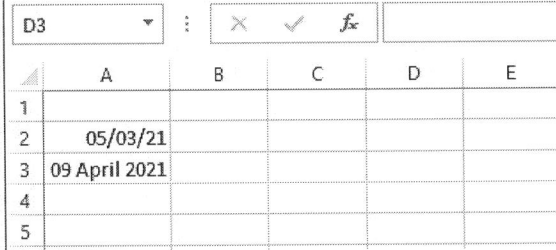

To find the day in the dates in cell A2 from the table above

- Select an empty cell, type in the function name and its arguments; **=DAY(A2)**
- Click on enter and the result will be **5** as shown in the table below

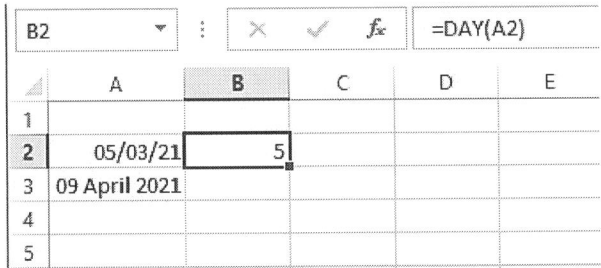

To find the day in the dates in cell A3 from the table above;

- Select an empty cell, type in the function name and the argument to be used; **=DAY(A3)**
- Click on enter and the result will be **9** as shown in the table below

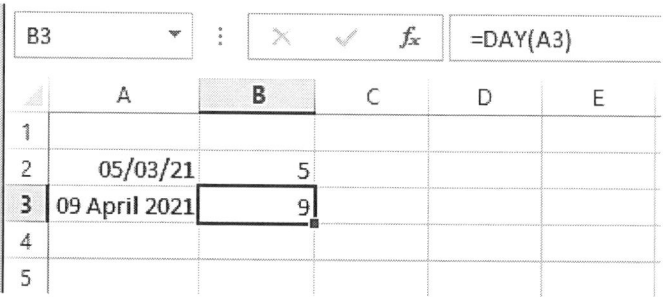

THE MONTH FUNCTION

The MONTH function returns the month of a date that is represented by a serial number. The month is given as an integer from 1 to 12.

The MONTH function uses an argument to execute its operation

=MONTH (serial_number)

- **Serial_number (Required Argument):** This is the date you wish to return the month of. The date can be a serial number, a reference to cells containing dates and date value from the Excel function.

USING THE MONTH FUNCTION

Using the table below, let's find the months in the date using the MONTH function

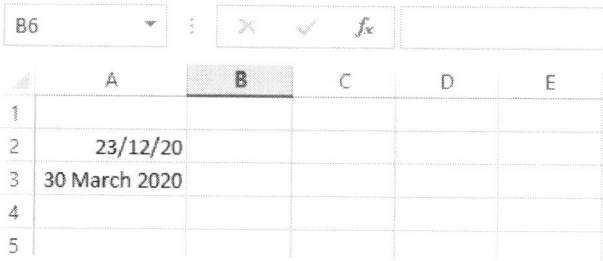

To find the month in the dates in cell A2 from the table above

- Select an empty cell, type in the function name and its arguments;
  =MONTH(A2)
- Click on enter and the result will be **12** as shown in the table below

	A	B	C	D	E
1					
2	23/12/20	12			
3	30 March 2020				
4					
5					

To find the month in the dates in cell A3 from the table above

- Select an empty cell, type in the function name and its arguments;
  =MONTH(A3)
- Click on enter and the result will be **30** as shown in the table below

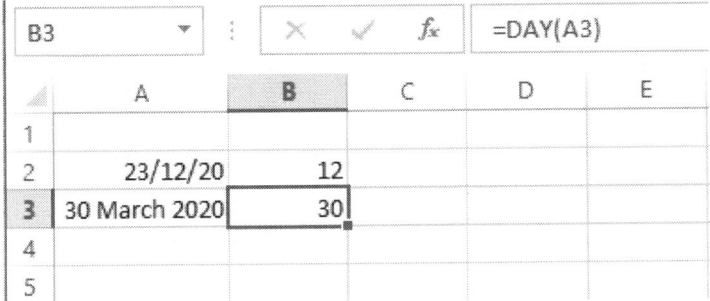

	A	B	C	D	E
1					
2	23/12/20	12			
3	30 March 2020	30			
4					
5					

THE YEAR FUNCTION

This is a function that is used for calculating the year number from a given date by returning an integer that is a four-digit number. For instance, if you use this function on a date e.g., 11/11/2020, it will return the year to be 2020.

The YEAR function uses an argument

=YEAR(serial_number)

- **Serial_number (Required Argument):** This is the date you wish to return the year. The date can be a serial number, a reference to cells containing dates and date value from the Excel function

USING THE YEAR FUNCTION

Using the table below, let's find the months in the date using the **YEAR** function

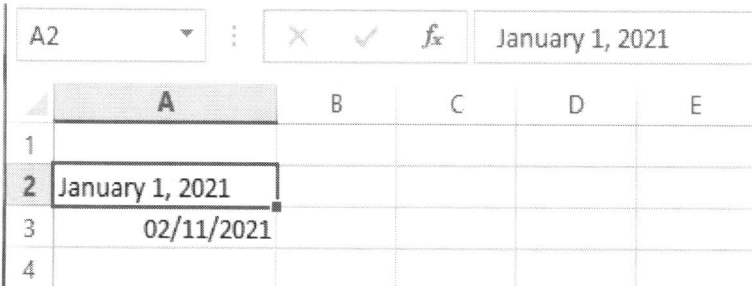

To find the year in the dates in cell A2 from the table above

- Select an empty cell, type in the function name and its arguments; **=YEAR(A2)**
- Click on enter and the result will be **2020** as shown in the table below

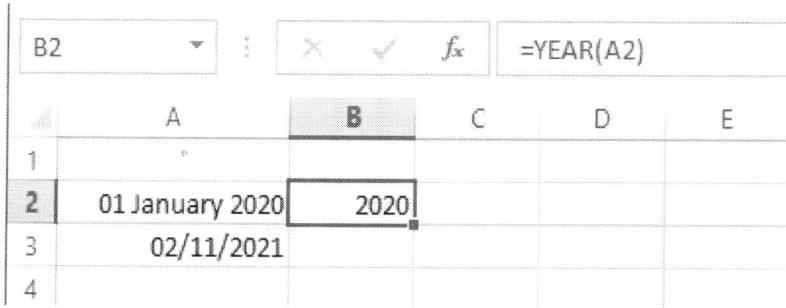

To find the year in the dates in cell A3 from the table above

- Select an empty cell, type in the function name and its arguments; **=YEAR(A3)**
- Click on enter and the result will be **2021** as shown in the table below

	A	B	C	D	E
1					
2	01 January 2020	2020			
3	02/11/2021	2021			
4					

Cell B3 contains formula: =YEAR(A3)

NOTE: Keep the following in mind when using the DAY, MONTH, AND YEAR FUNCTION

- The values returned by the DAY, MONTH, AND YEAR FUNCTION are always in Gregorian values not minding the display format of the date value supplied
- For the DAY, MONTH and YEAR function work correctly, the date must be entered using the DATE (year, month, and day) function

THE DATE FUNCTION

The DATE function is a function that creates a valid date from an individual year, month, and day components

The DATE function uses the following arguments

=DATE(year, month, day)

- **Year (Required Argument):** This is the number representing the year ranging from one to four digits.
- **Month (Required Argument):** This is the number representing the month which can be either positive or negative ranging from 1 to 12 (January to December).
- **Day (Required Argument):** This is the number representing the days of the month from 1 To 31

USING THE DATE FUNCTION

Using the table below, let's find the date using the DATE function

	A	B	C	D	E
1	Year	Month	Day	Date	
2	2019	6	23		
3	2016	7	21		
4					

To find the date in cell A2:C2

- Select an empty cell, type in the function, and followed by the arguments; **=DATE(A2,B2,C2)**

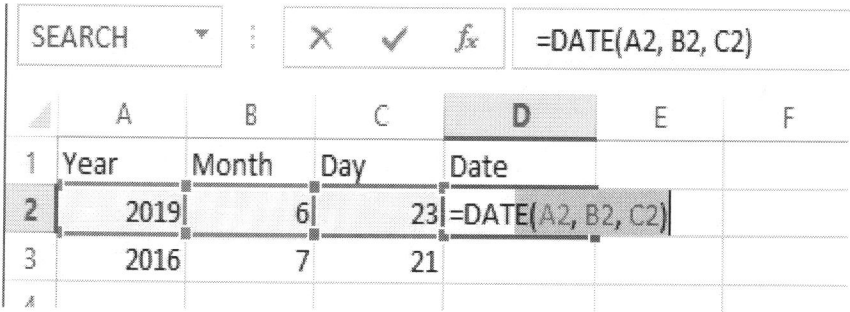

- Click on enter and the result will be **23/062019** as shown in the table below

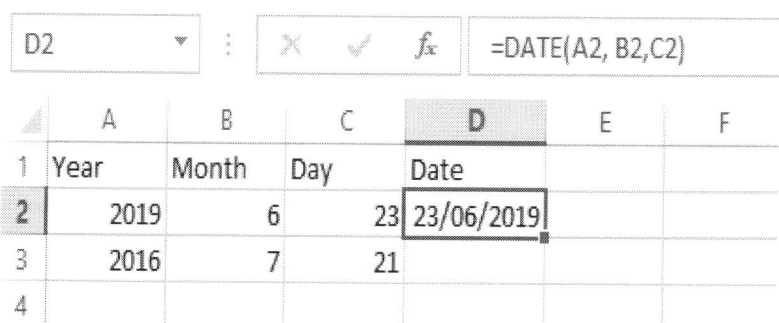

To find the date in cell A3:C3

- Select an empty cell, type in the function name and its arguments; **=DATE(A3,B3,C3)**

	SEARCH	▼	:	×	✓	fx	=DATE(A3, B3,C3)	
	A	B	C	D	E	F		
1	Year	Month	Day	Date				
2	2019		6	23	23/06/2019			
3	2016		7	21	=DATE(A3, B3,C3)			
4					DATE(year, month, day)			

- Click on enter and the result will be **23/062019** as shown in the table below

	D3	▼	:	×	✓	fx	=DATE(A3, B3,C3)	
	A	B	C	D	E	F		
1	Year	Month	Day	Date				
2	2019		6	23	23/06/2019			
3	2016		7	21	21/07/2016			
4								

NOTE: Keep these in mind when using the DATE function

- When any of the provided arguments is < 0 or ≥ 10000, #NUM! error is returned.
- When any of the provided arguments is non-numeric, #VALUE! error is returned.
- While using the DATE function, the result can be in serial numbers. However, this can be changed to date format

THE DATEDIF FUNCTION

The DATEDIF function is a function that calculates the number of days, months, and years between two dates. This function returns the numerical value that indicates the number of days, months, and years between two dates.

The DATEDIF function uses the following arguments to execute its operations

=DATEDIF(start_date, end_date, unit)

- **Start_date (Required Argument):** This is the initial date of the period or the starting date of the value of the period
- **End_date (Required Argument):** This connotes the ending date of the value of the period
- **Unit (Required Argument):** This indicates the time unit where we want the information

Unit	Returns
"Y"	The difference in complete years
"M"	The difference in complete months
"D"	The difference in complete days
"MD"	The difference in days, ignoring months and years.
"YM"	The difference in months, ignoring the years
"YD"	The difference in days, ignoring the years

USING THE DATEDIF FUNCTION

With the table, let's use the DATEDIF to find numbers of years and months between two dates

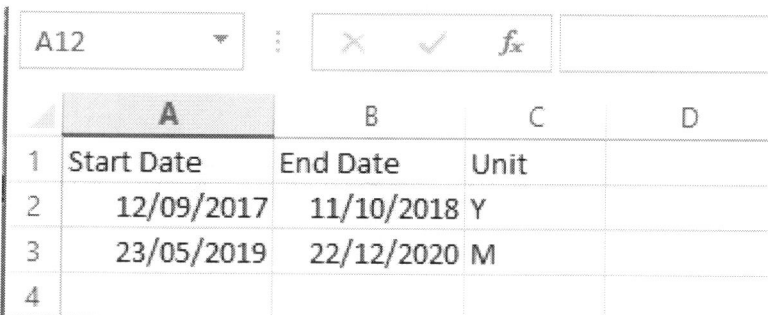

To find the difference in years between the start date (A2) and the end date (B2)

- Select an empty cell, type in the function name and its arguments; =DATEDIF(A2,B2, "y")

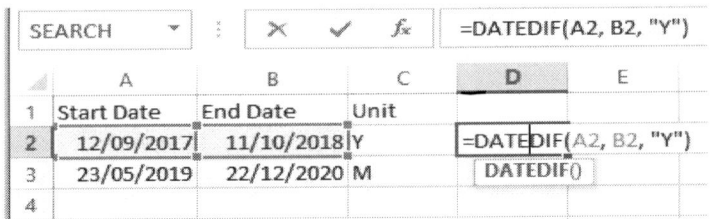

- Click on enter and the result will be **1** as shown in the table below

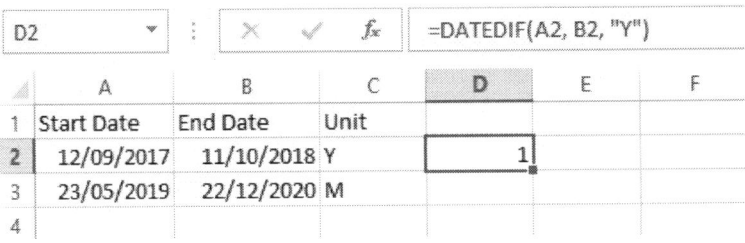

To find the difference in months between the start date (A3) and the end date (B3)

- Select an empty cell, type in the function name and the arguments to be used; =DATEDIF(A3,B3, "M")

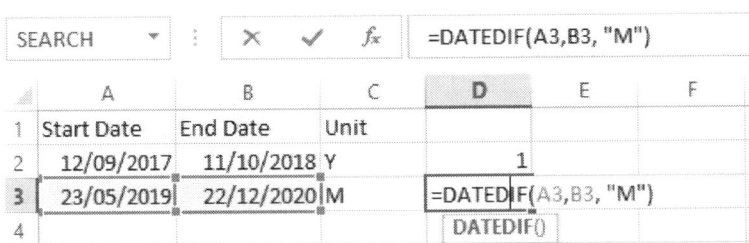

- Click on enter and the result will be **18** as shown in the table below

NOTE: Observe the following when using the DATEDIF function

- When the start_date is greater than the end_date, #NUM! error is returned
- When the date argument provided is invalid, the #VALUE error is returned

THE DAYS FUNCTION

The DAYS function is a date and time function that is used for returning the number of days between two dates. The DAYS FUNCTION was first introduced in Excel 2013

The DAYS function uses the following arguments to perform its operations

=DAYS (end_date, start_date)

- **The end_date and start_date (Required Arguments):** These are the two dates between which you want to know the number of days.

USING THE DAYS FUNCTION

Using the table below, let's find the number of days between the two dates using the DAYS function

	A	B	C	D	E
1					
2	12 July 2020	23 September 2020			
3					
4					

To find the number of days in the dates in cell A2 and B2 from the table above

- Select an empty cell, type in the function name and its arguments; **=DAY(B2,A2)**

	A	B	C	D	E
1					
2	12 July 2020	23 September 2020	=DAYS(B2,A2)		
3			DAYS(end_date, start_date)		
4					
5					

- Click on enter and the result will be **73** as shown in the table below

	A	B	C	D	E
1					
2	12 July 2020	23 September 2020	73		
3					
4					
5					

NOTE: Keep these in mind when using the DAYS function

- When both date arguments are numbers, the DAYS function uses EndDate and StartDate to calculate the number of days between both dates
- When any of the arguments is in text, the argument is treated as DATEVALUE (date_text). In this instance, the integer date is returned instead of the time component.
- #NUM! error occurs when the numeric data given for the date argument is outside the range of the valid dates
- #VALUE! error value occurs when the date arguments are strings that cannot be parsed
- #NAME? error occurs when the syntax used in the formula is incorrect.

THE EDATE FUNCTION

The EDATE function is a function used to add or subtract a specified number of months to date (the start date) and returns as serial date as the result.

The EDATE function uses the following arguments for its operations

=EDATE(start_date, months)

- **Start_date (Required Argument):** This is the starting date to use in the calculation. To enter dates in the date format, use the DATE function or other formulas or functions. For instance, use DATE (2020, 5, 24) for May 24, 2020. When dates are entered as text, the function returns error,
- **Month (Required Arguments):** This is the number of months before or after the start_date. A positive value produces a future date while a negative value produces a past date.

USING THE EDATE FUNCTION

With the table below, calculate the date using the EDATE function

	A	B	C	D	E
1	Date	months			
2	02/03/2020	12			
3	10/10/2020	-12			
4					
5					

To calculate the value of A2

- Select an empty cell and type in the function name and its arguments; **=EDATE(A2,B2)**
- Click on enter and the result will be **44257** as shown in the table below

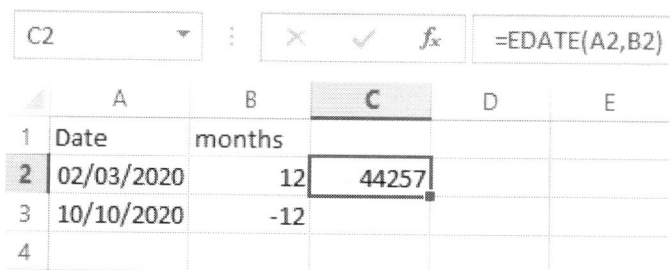

To calculate the value of A3

- Select an empty cell, type in the function name and its arguments; **=EDATE(A3,B3)**
- Click on enter and the result will be **43748** as shown in the table below

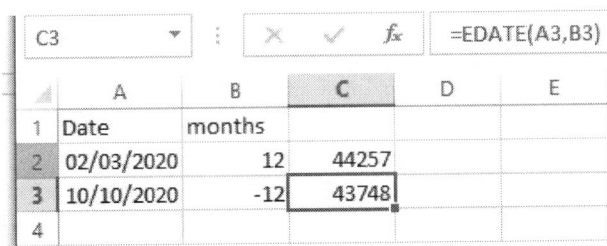

You can change the dates from serial numbers to the normal date format. To achieve this,

- Go to the **Home tab** and click on **More number** formats at the bottom of the format dropdown
- In the dialog box, select the **Date** and click on the date format you want

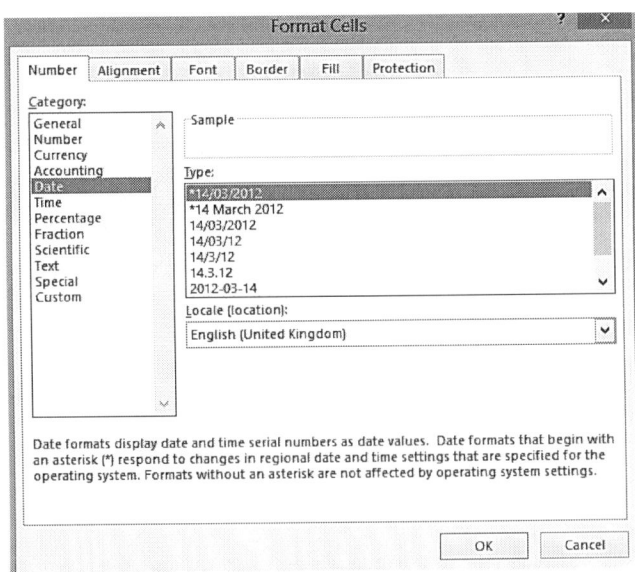

- If you follow the instructions given above, your result will be displayed as shown in the table below

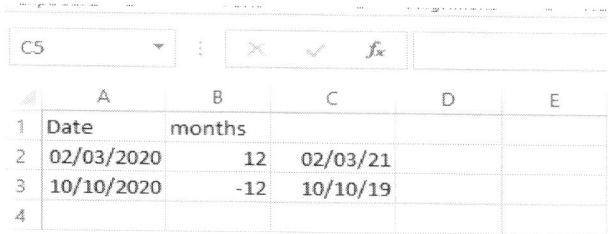

NOTE: Keep these in mind when using the EDATE function

- When the date to be returned from the calculation is not a valid number, #NUM! error occurs
- #VALUE error occurs when the start_date provided is not a valid date or when any of the arguments provided is non-numeric

THE DATEVALUE FUNCTION

The DATEVALUE function is a function that converts date stored in a text format to a serial number that Excel recognizes as its date format. The DATEVALUE is most useful when you have a worksheet containing dates in a text format that need to be filtered, sorted out, or formatted as dates or used in the date calculation

The DATEVALUE function uses the following argument for its operations

= DATTEVALUE(date_text)

- **Date_text (Required Argument):** This is the text that indicates a date in the Excel format, or a reference to a cell indicating a date in the Excel date format.

USING THE DATEVALUE FUNCTION

With the table below, let's convert the date in text format to Excel date

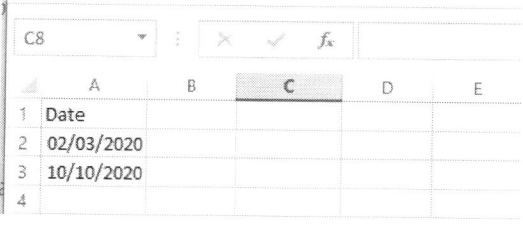

To change cell A2 to Excel date format

- Select an empty cell, type in the function name and its arguments; =EDATE("02/03/2020")
- Click on enter and the result will be **43892** as shown in the table below

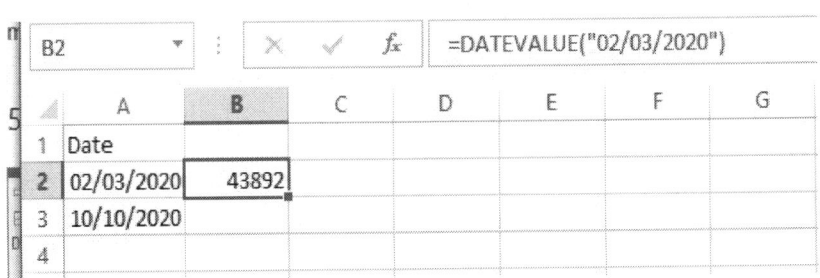

To change cell A3 to Excel date format

- Select an empty cell, type in the function name and its arguments; =EDATE(("10/10/2020")
- Click on enter and the result will be **44114** as shown in the table below

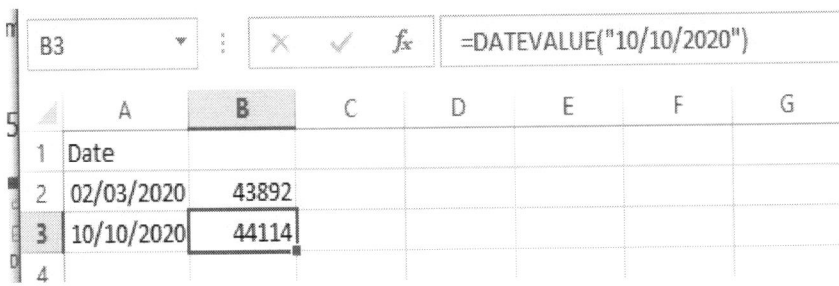

To convert date from serial numbers to date format, you can refer to the steps given in the EDATE function

NOTE: Keep this in mind when using the DATEVALUE function

- When the start_date is greater than the end_date, NUM! error will occur]
- When the value of the date_text argument falls out of the range of January! 1990 and December 31, 1996

THE NETWORKDAYS FUNCTION

The NETWORKDAYS function is a function that is used for calculating the numbers of working days between two dates in Excel. By default, the NETWORKDAYS function excludes weekends i.e., Saturday and Sunday. Not only that, this function allows you to skip a list of holidays as provided in the worksheet as dates.

The NETWORKDAYS function uses the following arguments

=NETWORKDAYS(start_date, end_date, [holidays])

- **Start_date (Required Argument):** This is the date that indicates the start date
- **End_date (Required Argument):** This is the date that indicates the end date
- **Holidays (Optional Argument):** This indicates the list of holidays that should be excluded from the workdays

USING THE WORKDAYS FUNCTION

Using the table below, let's find the number of working days using the NETWORKDAYS function

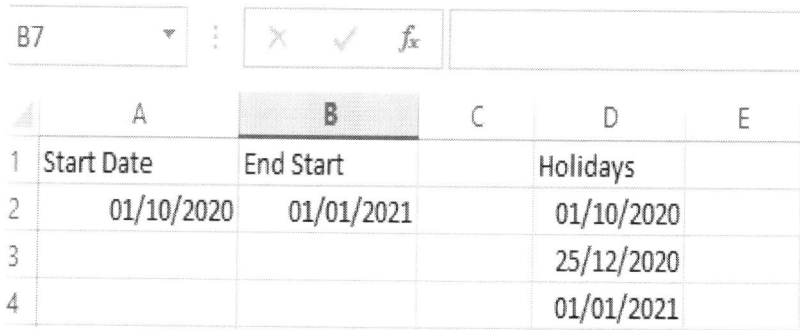

To find the number of working days

- Select an empty cell and type in the function name and its arguments; =EDATE(("10/10/2020")

	A	B	C	D	E
1	Start Date	End Start		Holidays	
2	01/10/2020	01/01/2021		01/10/2020	
3				25/12/2020	
4				01/01/2021	
5					
6	WORKDAYS	=NETWORKDAYS(A2,B2,D2:D4)			
7		NETWORKDAYS(start_date, end_date, [holidays])			

- Click on enter and the result will be **43** as shown in the table below

	A	B	C	D	E
1	Start Date	End Start		Holidays	
2	01/10/2020	01/01/2021		01/10/2020	
3				25/12/2020	
4				01/01/2021	
5					
6	WORKDAYS	64			

NOTE: Few points to observe when using the NETWORKDAYS function

- A negative value is returned when the start date is later than the end date
- The NETWORDAYS function must include both the start date and end date when calculating the workdays.
- When any of the provided arguments is not a valid date, #VALUE! error occurs
- To use weekends apart from Saturday and Sunday, use the NETWORKDAYS.INTL function
- The NETWORKDAYS function calculates workdays ignoring any time values

THE NOW FUNCTION

The NOW function is a function that is used to show the current date and time in an Excel worksheet. This function uses no argument and requires empty parentheses.

=NOW()

USING THE NOW FUNCTION

Let's use the NOW function to find the current date and time. To do this

- Select an empty cell and type in the function name and its arguments; **=NOW()**

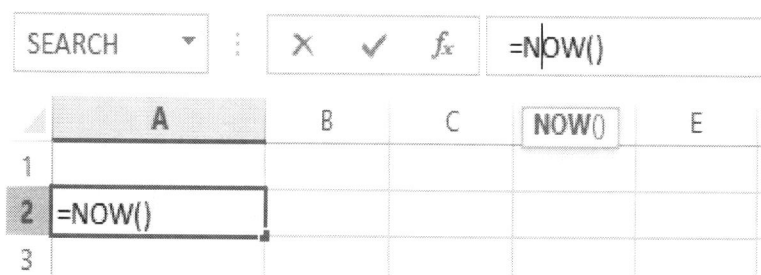

- Click on enter and the current date and time will be displayed

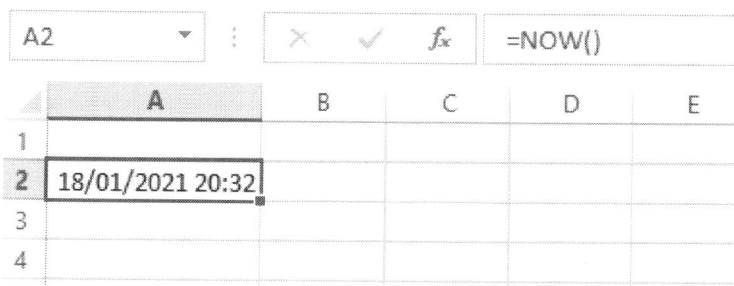

NOTE: Observe the following when using the NOW function

- When the provided serial number is not a valid Excel time, it returns a #VALUE! error
- To display date only, format the cell with a date format that only displays the date or

THE TODAY FUNCTION

The TODAY function is a function that returns the current date in an Excel worksheet. This updates from time to time whenever the worksheet is opened or changed by the user. This function uses no argument

=TODAY()

USING THE TODAY FUNCTION

- When you use the TODAY function. It gives you the current date; **=TODAY()**

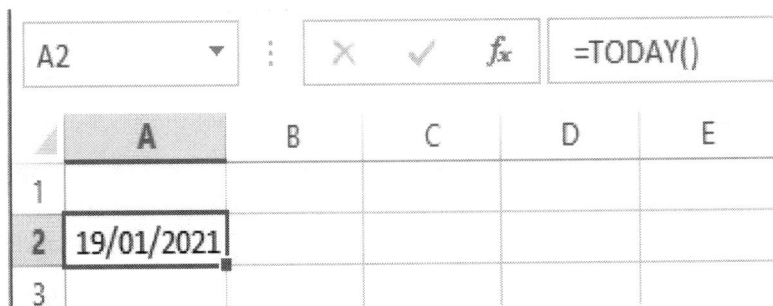

- When you use the add 15 days to the TODAY function, it adds 15 days to the current date; **=TODAY()+15**

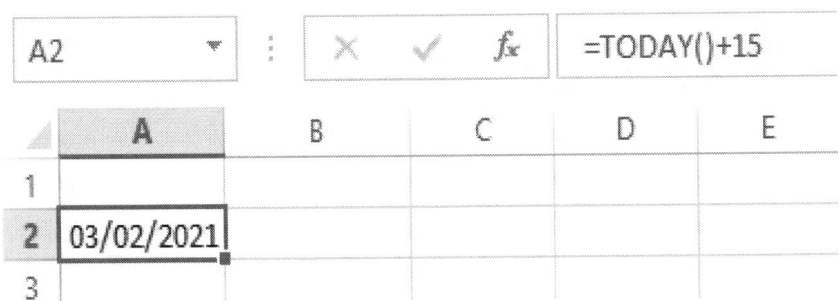

- When you use the WORKDAY function with TOADY function, it adds 30 workdays to today's date; **=WORKDAY(TODAY()30)**

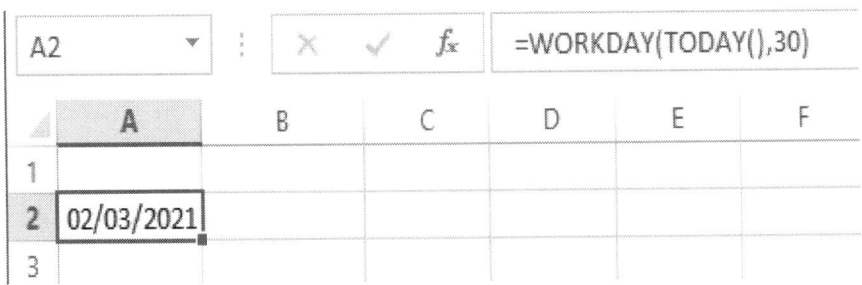

When you add the MONTH function to the TODAY function, it will return the current month of the year (1-12). Now that we are in January, the result will be returned to 1; **=MONTH(TODAY())**

[A screenshot showing cell A2 with formula =MONTH(TODAY()) and value 1 in cell A2]

NOTE: keep the following in mind when using the TODAY function

- In case you don't want the date to change, enter the current date using the keyboard shortcut; **Ctrl + ;**
- To get the current date and time, use the NOW function

THE TIME FUNCTION

The TIME function is a function that is used to create time using individual hour, minute, and second components

The TIME function uses the following arguments for its operations

=TIME(hour, minute, second)

- **Hour (Required Argument):** This time value can start from zero (0) to 32767 indicating the hour. When the value exceeds 23, it will be divided by 24 and the remainder will be treated as the hour value.
- **Minute (Required Argument):** This also starts from 0 to 32767 indicating the minutes. When the value is greater than 59, it will be converted to hours and minutes.
- **Second (Required Argument):** This ranges from 0 to 32767 indicating second. When the value is greater than 59, it will be converted to hours, minutes, and seconds.

USING THE TIME FUNCTION

From the table, let's use the TIME function to extract the date

	A	B	C	D	E
1	Hour	Minute	Second		
2	4	23	23		
3	12	34	2		
4					

To extract the time in cell **A2:C3**

- Select an empty cell, type in the function name and its arguments;
  =TIME(A2,B2,C2)

=TIME(A2,B2,C2)

	A	B	C	D	E	F
1	Hour	Minute	Second			
2	4	23	23	=TIME(A2,B2,C2)		
3	12	34	2	TIME(hour, minute, second)		
4						

- Click on enter and the time will be extracted to be **4:23 AM** as shown in the table below

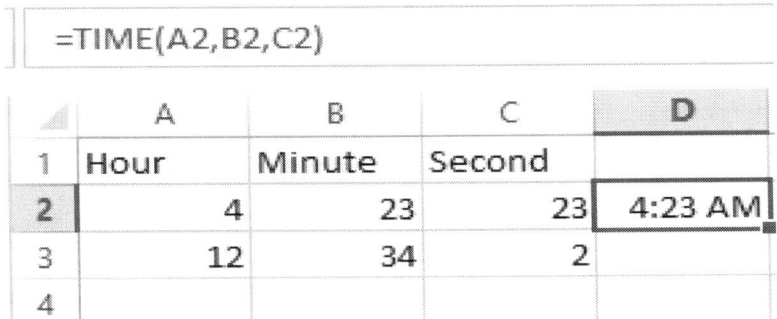

To extract the time in cell A3:B3

- Select an empty cell, type in the function name and its arguments;
  =TIME(A2,B2,C2)

	A	B	C	D	E	F
1	Hour	Minute	Second			
2	4	23	23	4:23 AM		
3	12	34	2	=TIME(A3,B3,C3)		
4				TIME(hour, minute, second)		

- Click on enter and the time will be extracted to be **4:23 AM** as shown in the table below

=TIME(A3,B3,C3)

	A	B	C	D	E
1	Hour	Minute	Second		
2	4	23	23	4:23 AM	
3	12	34	2	12:34 PM	

NOTE: Keep these in mind when using the TIME function

- When the hour arguments provided are evaluated to a negative number, #NUM! error is returned
- When any of the arguments provided is non-numeric, #VALUE! error is returned

CHAPTER FIFTEEN

THE EXCEL POWER QUERY

WHAT IS POWER QUERY?

Power query is a business intelligence tool in Excel that allows you to extract or import data from different sources, transform them and reshape the data and produced the desired result on the worksheet.

WHERE IS THE POWER QUERY LOCATED?

The **Power Query** is an add-in. This is downloaded and installed in Excel 2010 and 2013 which appears as a new tab in the ribbon tagged as Power Query. In Excel 2016, 2019, Office 365, and Excel 2020, the Power Query comes automatically with them and it is found in the Data tab as q group names Get & Transform

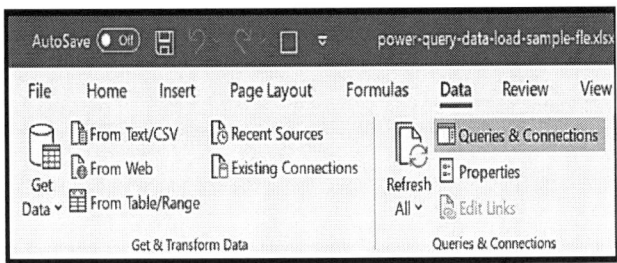

What Can Power Query Do?

The Power Query can do the following operations:

- To import data from multiple log files.
- To create a custom view over data.
- To carry out data cleansing operation.
- To gather data into Power Pivot from new data sources such as Facebook, XML, etc.
- To search and connect data from a large variety of sources.
- To merge and redefine data sources to match your data analyses criteria or requirements.

SOURCES OF POWER QUERY DATA

You can get data for the Power Query in the sources below;

- Excel or CSV file
- Text File
- Web Page
- XML file
- Folder
- SQL Server database
- Microsoft Azure SQL Database
- Access database
- Active Directory
- Microsoft Exchange
- SharePoint List
- Hadoop File (HDFS) etc.

IMPORTING DATA SOURCE USING POWER QUERY

Here, I will be showing you how to import data source using the Power Query. Most importantly, how to import data from Excel workbook, CVS, or text file.

IMPORTING A SINGLE DATA SOURCE FROM THE WORKBOOK

- From the **Data tab**, go to **Data** and select **Get Data**.
- Then go to **File** and select Workbook.

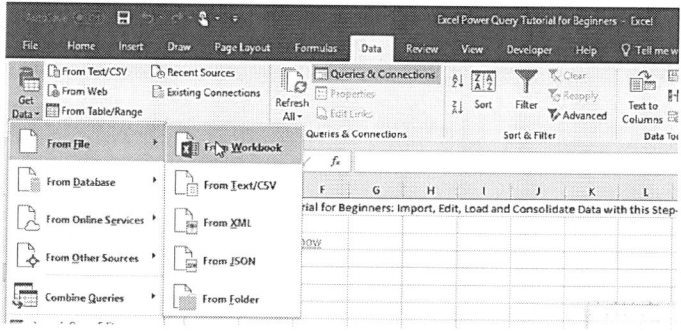

- In the **Import Data dialog box**, select the workbook and double click on it.

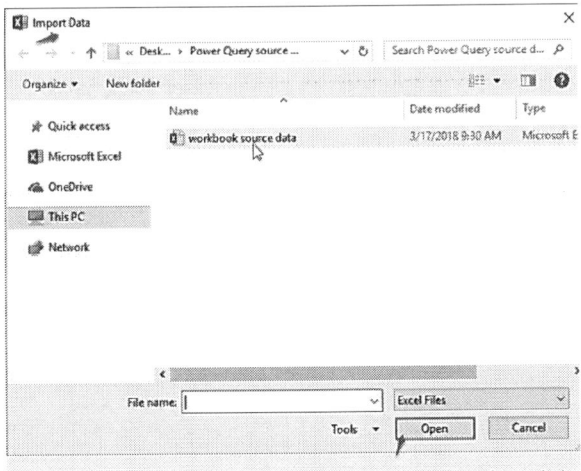

- In the **Navigation dialog box**, click on the data source you wish to work with.
- Then click on **Load**

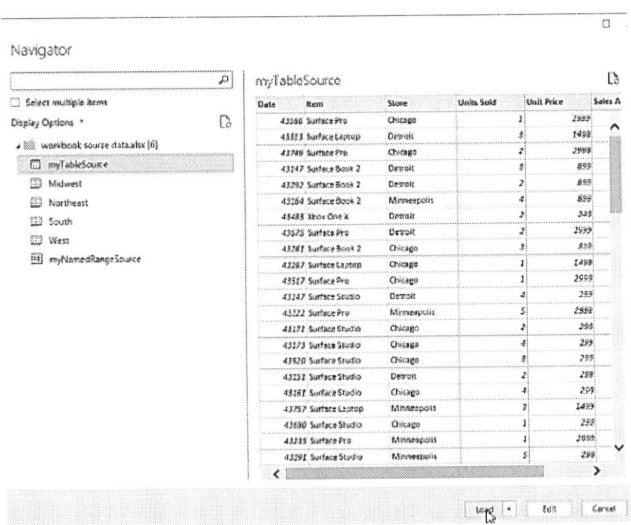

IMPORTING DATA FROM MULTIPLE DATA SOURCES IN A WORKBOOK

- From the **Data tab**, go to **Data** and select **Get Data**.

- Then go to **File** and select Workbook.

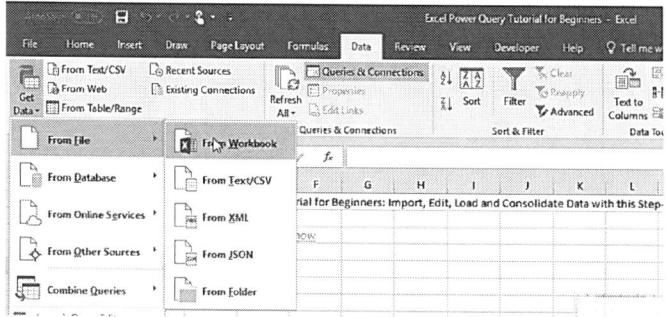

- In the **Import Data dialog box**, select the workbook and double click on it.

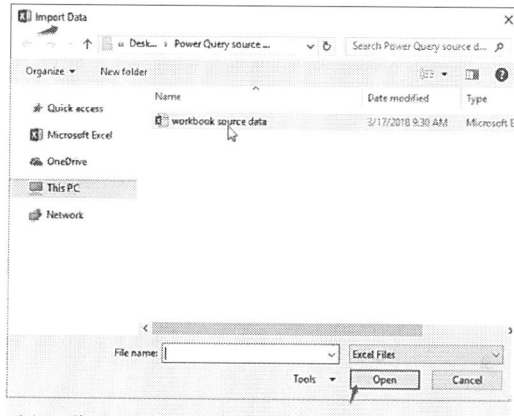

- In the **Navigation dialog box**, click on Select **multiple items**
- Then click on **Load**

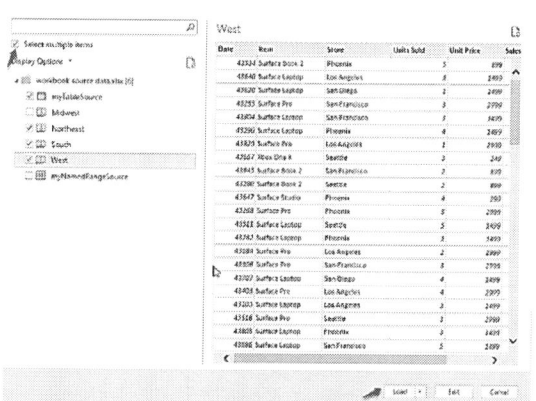

IMPORTING DATA FROM A CSV FILE

- From the **Data tab**, go to **Data** and select **Get Data**.
- Then go to **File** and select **Text/CVS**

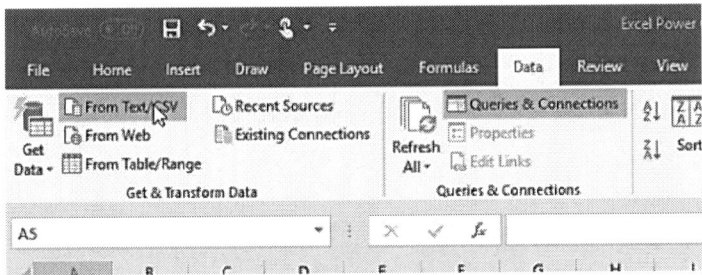

- In the **Import Data dialog box**, select the **CVS File** and click on **Import**

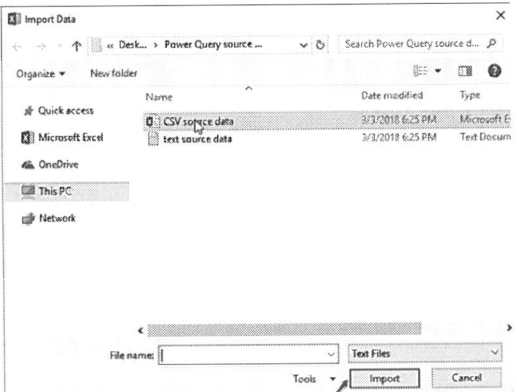

- In the dialog box named CSV file, click on **Load**

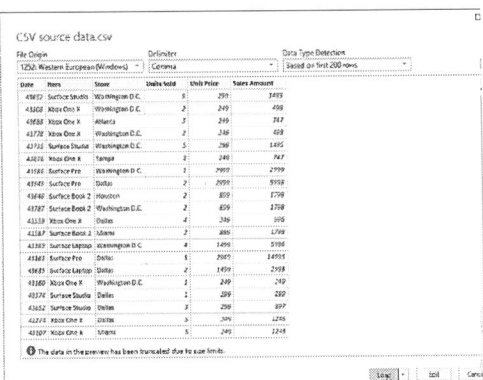

IMPORTING DATA FROM A TEXT FILE

- From the **Data tab**, go to **Data** and select **Get Data**.
- Then go to **File** and select **Text/CVS**

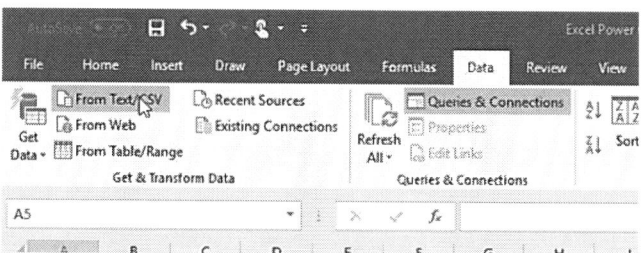

- In the **Import Data dialog box**, select the **Text File** and click on **Import**

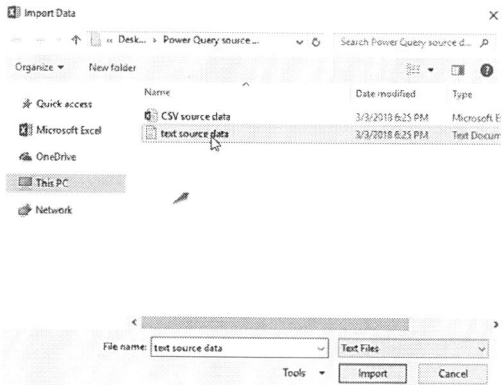

- In the dialog box named Text file, click on **Load**

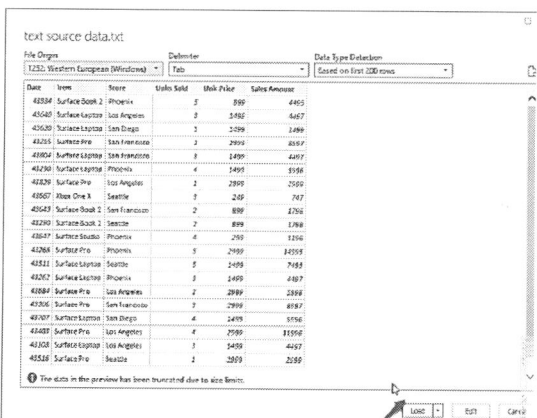

POWER QUERY EDITOR

The power Query Editor displays when you want to load, edit, and create a new query. The Query Editor when displayed has 4 main divisions; The Ribbon, Formula bar, Preview pane, and Query Setting task pane. The operation is done above such as importing data from Text File, CSV, etc. are done in the Power Query Editor.

To launch the Query Editor;

- Move to the Data **tab**, Select Data, and select **Get Data**.
- Then launch the **Query Editor**.

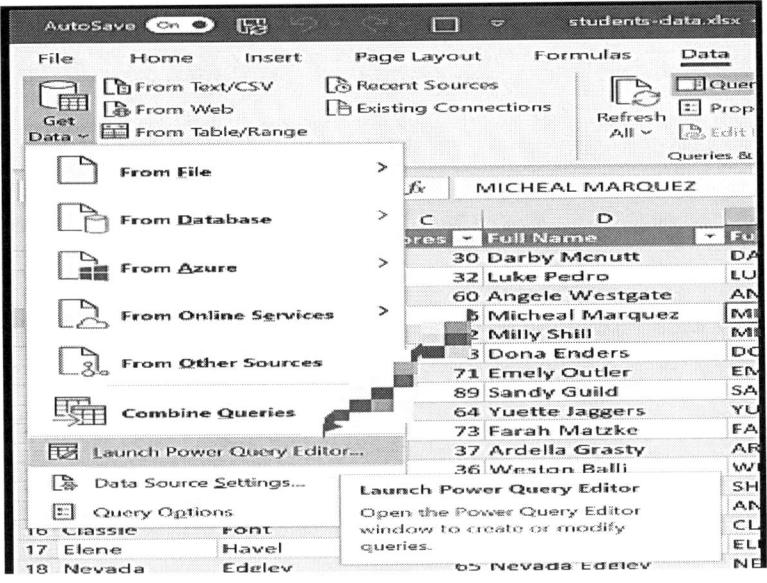

CHAPTER SIXTEEN

EXCEL SHORTCUTS, TIPS & TRICKS

Imagine there is a shortcut to getting to a particular place in just 5 minutes and initially, the journey should cost you not less than an hour, I am sure you will opt-in for that shortcuts. To make the use of Excel especially that of 2020 easier, faster, and convenient to use, we will be taking ourselves to learn some tips and tricks which will come in handy as you begin to get yourself more accustomed to the use of this app.

EXCEL SHORTCUTS

EDITING SHORTCUTS

Keys	Functions
F2	To edit cell
Ctrl + C	To copy
Ctrl + V	To paste
Ctrl + X	To cut
Ctrl + D	To fill down
Ctrl + R	To fill right
Alt+ E+ S	Paste special
F3	To paste the name into a formula
F4	Toggle reference
Alt +Enter	To start another new line within the same old cell
Shift + F2	To insert or edit a cell comment
Shift + F10	To display a shortcut menu
Ctrl + F3	To define the name of a cell
Ctrl + Shift + A	To insert arguments names with parentheses for a function after typing a function name in a formula
Alt + I + R	To insert a row

Alt + I + C	To insert a column

FORMATTING SHORTCUTS

Keys	Functions
Ctrl + B	To bolden
Ctrl + I	For italics
Ctrl + Z	To undo
Ctrl + Y	To repeat the last action
Ctrl + A	To select all cells
Ctrl + 1	To display or bring up the format cell menu
Ctrl + Shift + !	For number formatting
Ctrl + Shift + %	For percent format
Ctrl + Shift + #	For date format
Alt + h	To increase decimal
Alt + h + 9	To decrease decimal
Alt + h + 6	To increase indent

NAVIGATION SHORTCUTS

Keys	Functions
Arrow	To move from one cell to the next
F5	Go to
Ctrl + Home	Go to cell 1
Home	To go to the beginning of a row
Shift + Arrow	To select the adjacent cell
Shift + Spacebar	To select an entire row
Ctrl + Spacebar	To select an entire column
Ctrl + Shift + Home	To select all to the start of the sheet
Ctrl + Shift + End	To select all to the last used cell of the sheet
Ctrl + Shift + Arrow	To select the end of the last used row/column

Ctrl + Arrow	To select the last used cell in rows/columns
PageUp	To move the screen up
PageDown	To move the screen down
Alt + PageUp	To move the screen to the left
Alt+ PageDown	To move the screen to the right
Ctrl + PageUP/Down	To move the next or previous worksheet
Ctrl + Tab	To move to the next worksheet while on the spreadsheet
Tab	To move to the next cell

FILE SHORTCUTS

Keys	Functions
Ctrl + N	New
Ctrl + O	To open
Ctrl + S	To save workbook
F12	Save As
Ctrl + P	Print
Ctrl + F2	To open the preview print window
Ctrl + Tab	To move to the next workbook
Ctrl + F4	To close a file
Alt + F4	To close all open Excel files

PASTE SPECIAL SHORTCUTS

Keys	Functions
Ctrl + Alt + V+T	Paste Special formats
Ctrl + Alt + V+V	Paste Special values
Ctrl + Alt + V+F	Paste Special formulas
Ctrl + Alt + V+ C	Paste Special comments

RIBBON SHORTCUTS

Keys	Functions
Alt	To show ribbon accelerator keys
Ctrl + F1	To show or hide the ribbon

CLEAR SHORTCUTS

Keys	Functions
Delete	To clear cell data
Alt+ h + e + f	To clear cell format
Alt+ h + e + m	To clear cell comments
Alt+ h + e + a	To clear all data formats and comments

SELECTION SHORTCUTS

Keys	Functions
Shift + Arrow	To select a cell range
Ctrl + Shift + Arrows	To highlight a contiguous range
Shift + PageUp	To extend selection up one screen
Shift + PageDown	To extend selection down one screen
Alt + Shift + PageUp	To extend selection left one screen
Alt + Shift + PageDown	To extend selection right one screen
Ctrl + A	Select or highlight all

DATA EDITING SHORTCUT

Keys	Functions
Ctrl + D	To fill down from cell above
Ctrl + R	To fill right from cell left
Ctrl + F	To find and replace
F5 + Alt + s +o	To show all constants
F5 + Alt + s +c	To highlight the cell with comments

DATA EDITING (INSIDE A CELL) SHORTCUTS

Keys	Functions
F2	To edit the active cell
Enter	To confirm a change in a cell before opting out of that cell
Esc	To cancel a cell entry before opting out of that cell
Alt + Enter	To insert a line break within a cell
Shift + Left/Right	To highlight within a cell
Ctrl + Shift + Left/Right	To highlight contiguous items
Home	To move to the beginning of the cell contents
End	To move to the end of a cell content
Backspace	To delete a character from left
Delete	To delete a character from the right
Tab	To accept autocomplete suggestion
Ctrl + PageUp/Down + Arrows	For referencing a cell from another worksheet

OTHER SHORTCUTS

Keys	Functions
Ctrl + ;	To enter date
Ctrl +:	To enter time
Ctrl + '	To show formula
Ctrl +]	To select an active cell
Alt	To drive menu bar
Alt + Tab	To open the next program
Alt + =	To autosum

EXCEL TIPS AND TRICKS

HOW TO USE IDEAS

If you are looking for suggestions on how best to display your Excel data, use Ideas as an inspiration. To do this:

- Click anywhere on the table

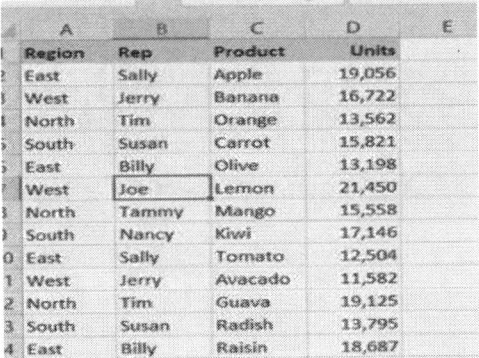

- Go to the Home tab and choose Ideas

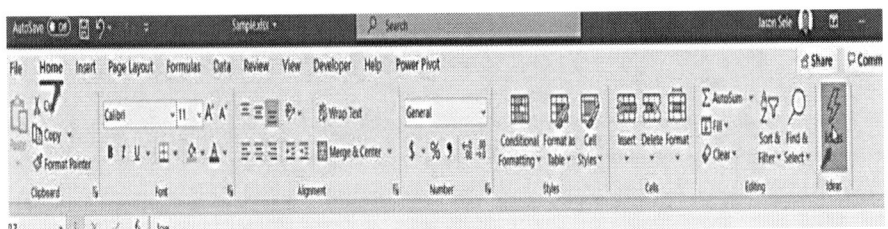

- The ideas will pop up any graph suitable to display your data, then click on insert.

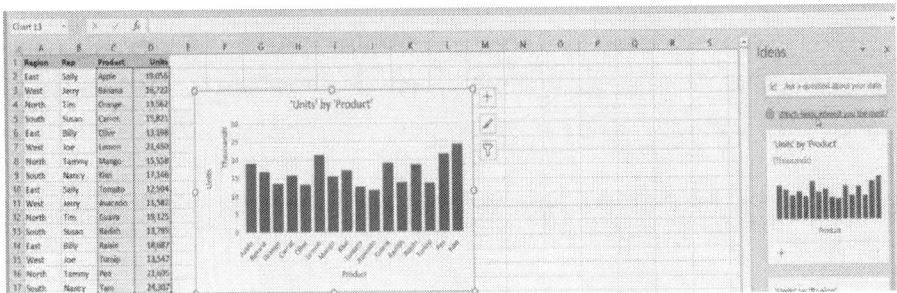

HOW TO REMOVE BLANKS FROM A WORKSHEET

If you want to remove a bunch of empty cells in a set of data,

- Highlight the whole list of data

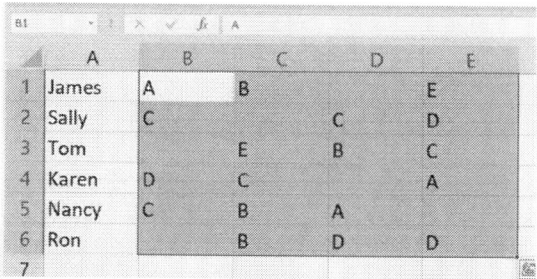

- From the Home tab, go to Find and Select

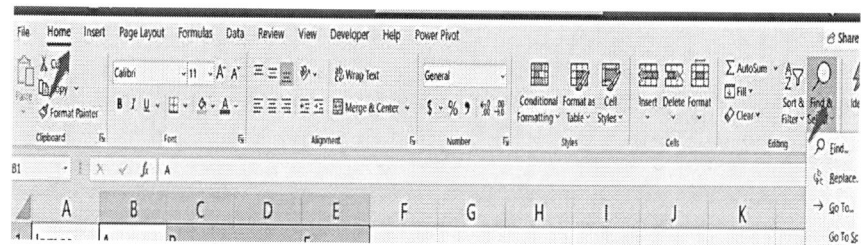

- Click on Go to special

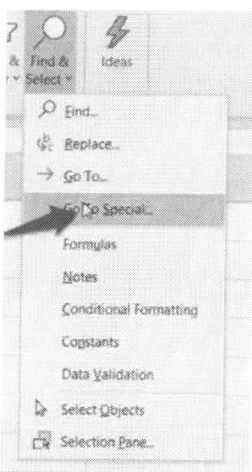

- Then click on Blank and press Ok

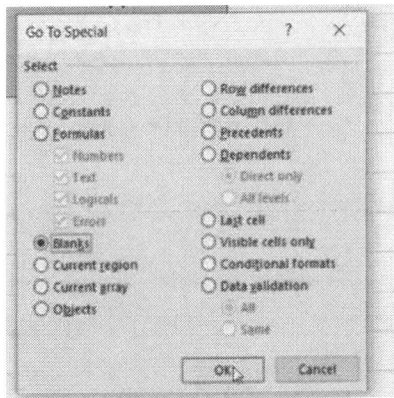

- Here in the next page, the blank cell will be highlighted

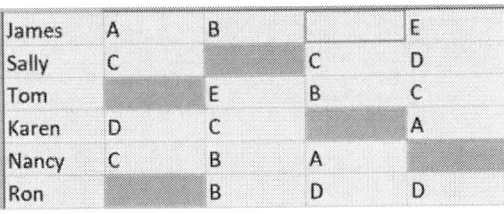

- To delete, right-click on any of the empty cells and select Delete

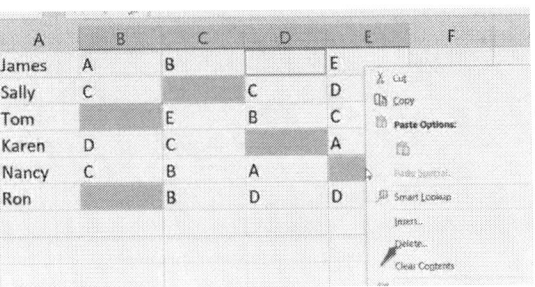

- In the Delete option, select Shift cell left and the blanks cell will be deleted.

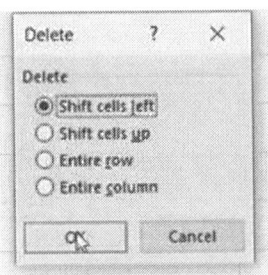

HOW TO REMOVE DUPLICATE DATA FROM EXCEL WORKBOOK

If you have a list of data in Excel and you want to remove the duplicates, do the following:

- Hight light the data

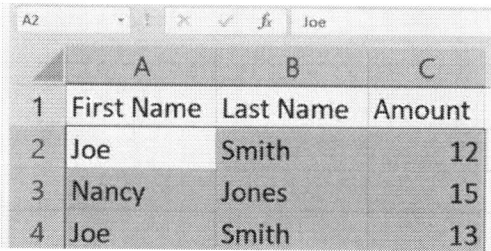

- From the Data tab, select Remove duplicate

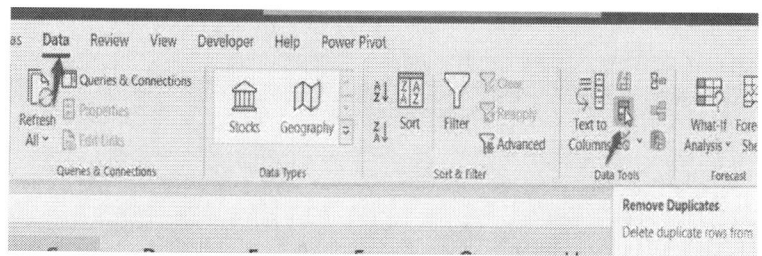

- Click on the options that come up depending on the one you want and click on Ok

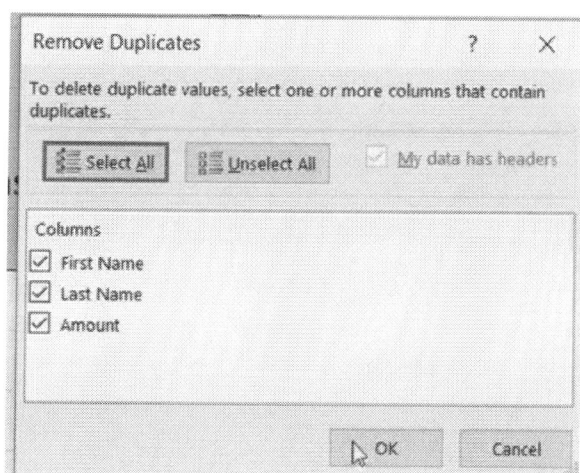

- Here in the worksheet, the change is effected

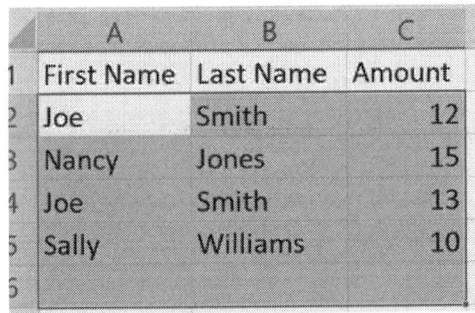

TRANSPOSING ON YOUR WORKSHEET

Transposing allows you to switch the rows and columns on your table and to get this done,

- Highlight the table, right-click, and select copy

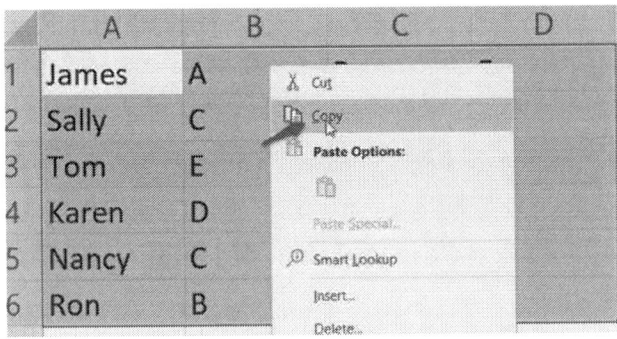

- Select the new location, right-click on it and select Paste Special

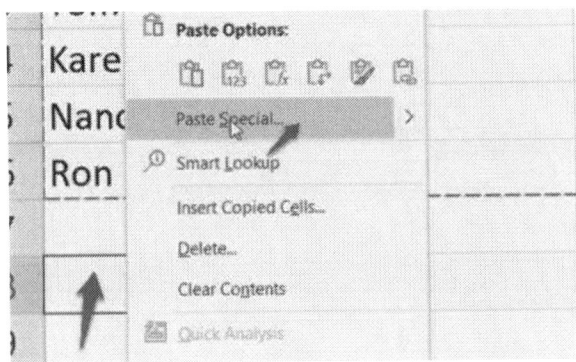

- Select the Transpose and click on Ok

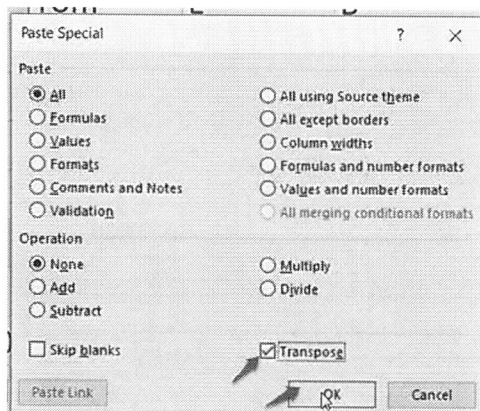

- Here in this, the changes will be effected

James	Sally	Tom	Karen	Nancy	Ron
A	C	E	D	C	B
B	C	B	C	B	D
E	D	C	A	A	D

HOW TO ADD TEXT TO COLUMNS

you can copy texts into your column from a different source by applying the following instructions:

- Copy the data into an Excel worksheet

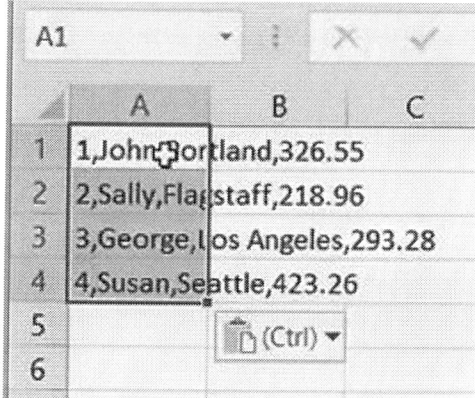

- Go to Data and select Text to column

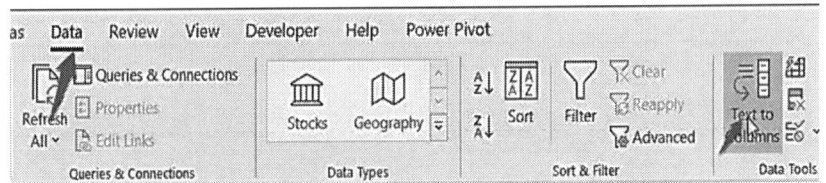

- Go to the pop-up window and select Comma, check for the preview at the lower part of the pop-up window, and click on Finish

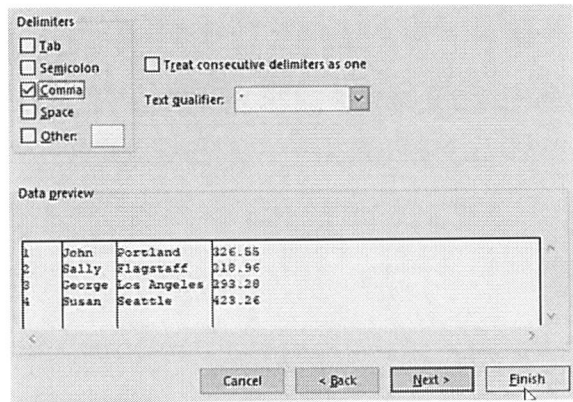

HOW TO INSERT SCREENSHOT TO YOUR EXCEL WORKBOOK

To insert images from other application to Excel worksheet,

- Go to the Insert tab and click on Screenshot

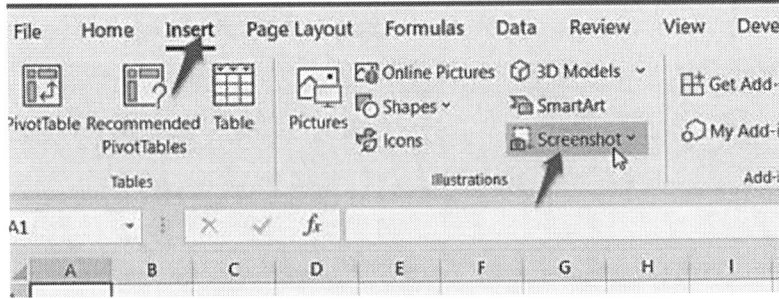

- From the Screenshot tab, select the image available

- Here, the selected image will be displayed on the Excel worksheet

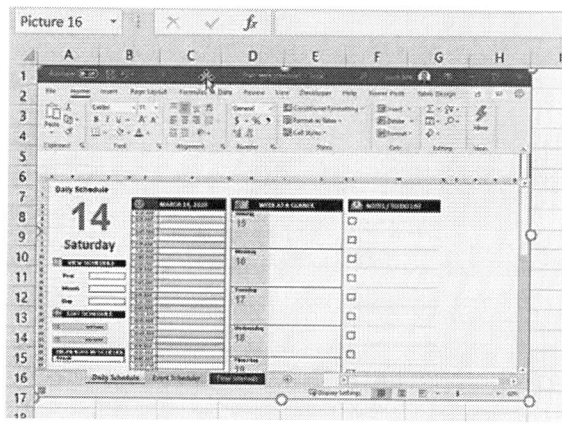

HOW TO INSERT MULTIPLES ROWS

Rather than inserting rows one by one in your worksheet, you can insert three to four rows at once and this helps to save time. To add multiple rows:

- Select as many rows as you want and right-click

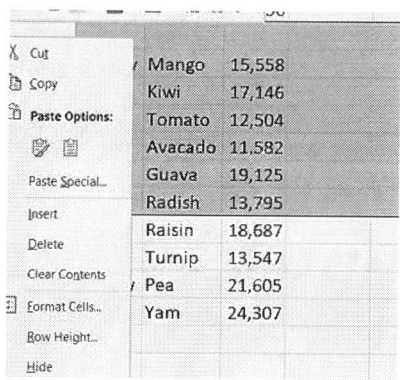

Click on insert and new rows will be added

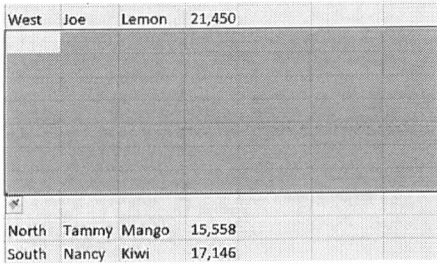

NOTE: The steps above can be applied when adding multiple columns in a worksheet.

HOW TO CREATE PEOPLE GRAPH

Peoples' graph is a kind of graph that is created with a simple two-column table. To do this:

- Go to the Insert tab and click on Transform col data into a cool picture which will bring up a default people graph

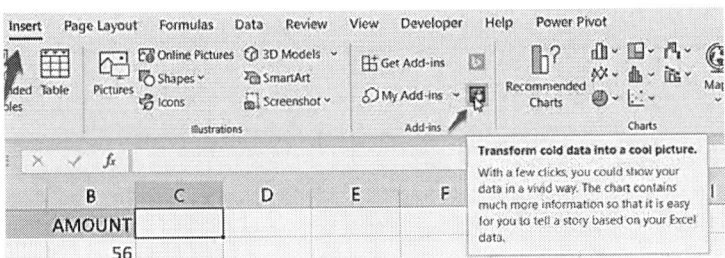

- When the default graph appears, move to select your data

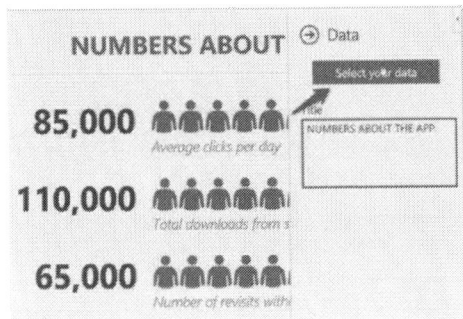

- Go to the simple two-column table to highlight your data and click on Create

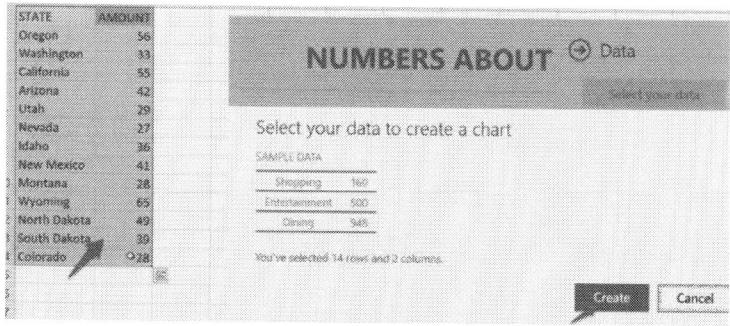

- The changes are seen here in this page

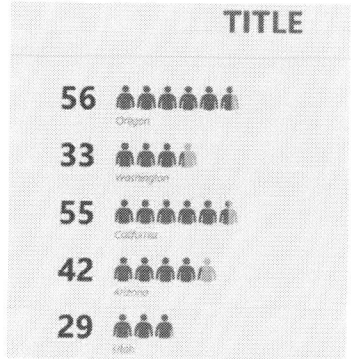

HOW TO HIGHLIGHT TEXT AND NUMBERS

To highlight only numbers in a worksheet;

- Select the whole data in the table

Sr No	Product	Cost	Country
1	Product 1	$247.00	USA
2	Product 2	$168.00	France
3	Product 3	Canada	UK
4	Product 4	$129.00	$156.00
5	Product 5	$133.00	India
6	Product 6	USA	$227.00
7	Product 7	$156.00	France
8	Product 8	India	$578.00

- Press F5 and a window will pop up and then click on Special

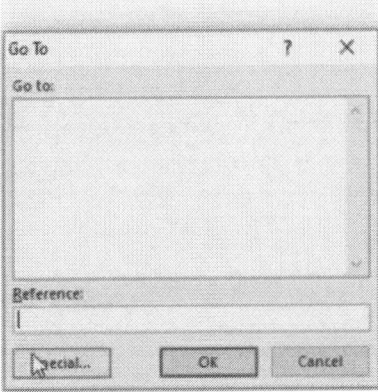

- Select Constants, tick on Numbers and click on Ok

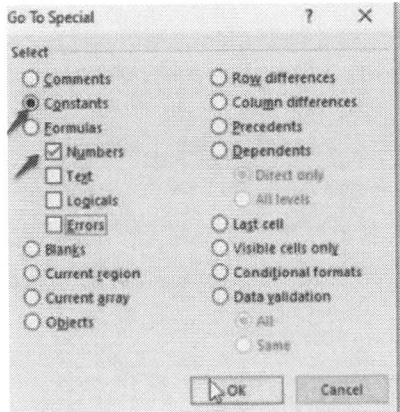

- Here on this page, the numbers will be highlighted

Sr No	Product	Cost	Country
1	Product 1	$247.00	USA
2	Product 2	$168.00	France
3	Product 3	Canada	UK
4	Product 4	$129.00	$156.00
5	Product 5	$133.00	India
6	Product 6	USA	$227.00
7	Product 7	$156.00	France
8	Product 8	India	$578.00

Then go to the fill color to apply to the highlighted numbers

Sr No	Product	Cost	Country
1	Product 1	$247.00	USA
2	Product 2	$168.00	France
3	Product 3	Canada	UK
4	Product 4	$129.00	$156.00
5	Product 5	$133.00	India
6	Product 6	USA	$227.00
7	Product 7	$156.00	France
8	Product 8	India	$578.00

To highlight only texts,

- Select the whole data in the table

Sr No	Product	Cost	Country
1	Product 1	$247.00	USA
2	Product 2	$168.00	France
3	Product 3	Canada	UK
4	Product 4	$129.00	$156.00
5	Product 5	$133.00	India
6	Product 6	USA	$227.00
7	Product 7	$156.00	France
8	Product 8	India	$578.00

- Press F5 and a window will pop up and then click on Special

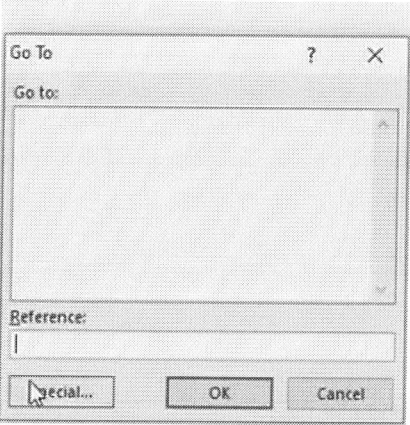

- Select Constants, tick on Texts and click on Ok

307

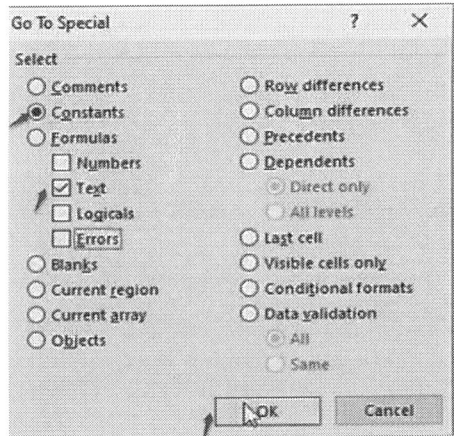

- Here on this page, the texts will be highlighted

Sr No	Product	Cost	Country
1	Product 1	$247.00	USA
2	Product 2	$168.00	France
3	Product 3	Canada	UK
4	Product 4	$129.00	$156.00
5	Product 5	$133.00	India
6	Product 6	USA	$227.00
7	Product 7	$156.00	France
8	Product 8	India	$578.00

- Go to the fill colour to apply to the highlighted numbers

Sr No	Product	Cost	Country
1	Product 1	$247.00	USA
2	Product 2	$168.00	France
3	Product 3	Canada	UK
4	Product 4	$129.00	$156.00
5	Product 5	$133.00	India
6	Product 6		$227.00
7	Product 7	$156.00	France
8	Product 8	India	$578.00

HOW TO HIGHLIGHT CELLS THAT HAVE FORMULAS

To select or highlight the cells that have formulas;

- On the table that contains all the cells, press Ctrl + G
- Right here, a window will pop and click on Special

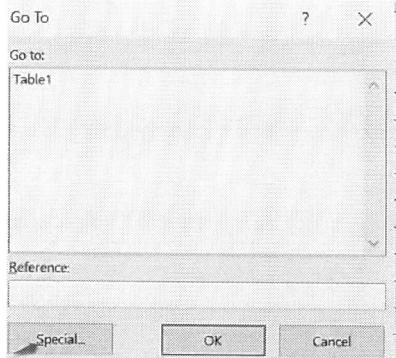

- In the next window that pops up, select Formula and press Ok

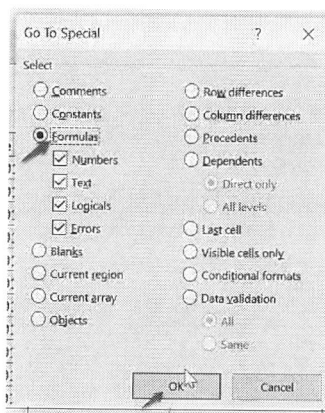

- Here in this page, the cell with formulas with be highlighted

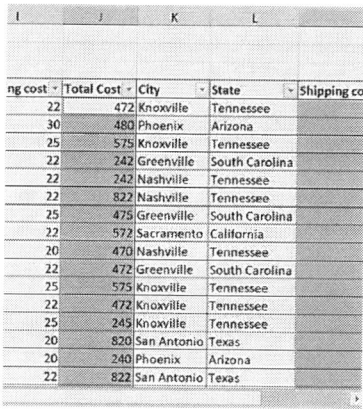

HOW TO GET DATA FROM THE INTERNET

You can get live data into your Excel worksheet and to get this done, all you need to do is,

- Open your internet browser and go to the website you need to get the data

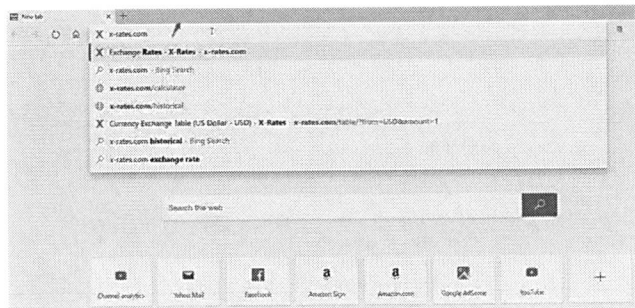

- Copy the URL link from the website

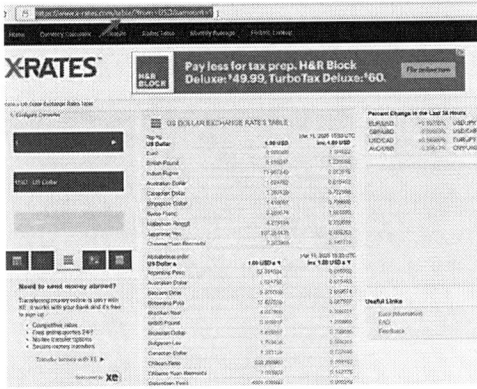

- Go back to Excel, go to Data and select from Web

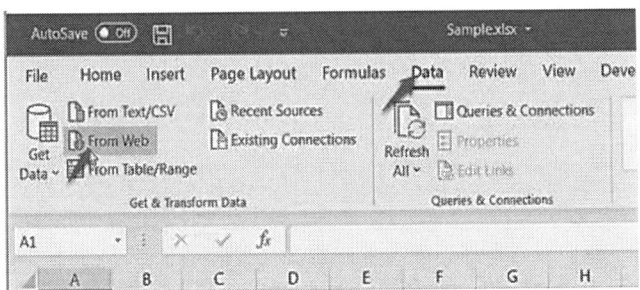

- Paste the copied URL and select Ok

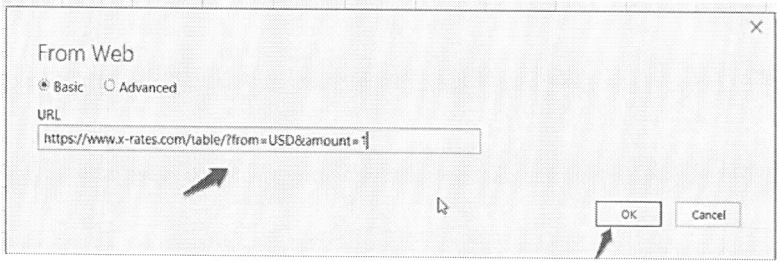

- A window pops up showing you the list of data on the web page, select the data you want and then click on Load

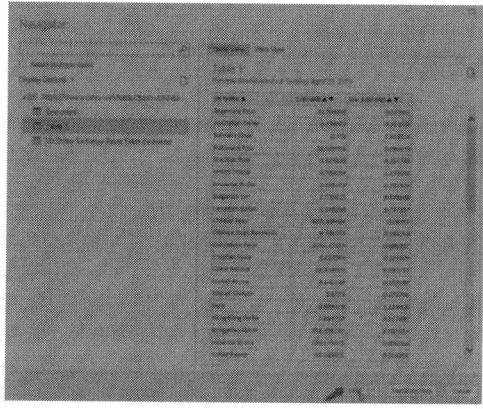

- Finally, on this page, the data is displayed on the Excel Worksheet.

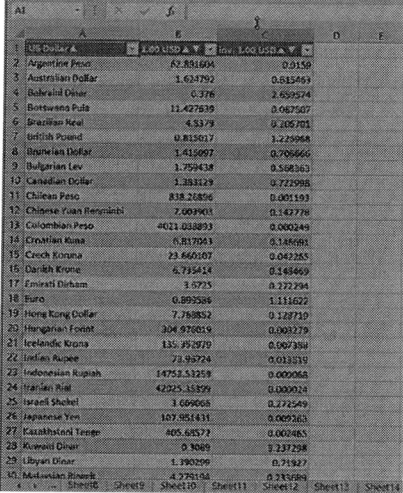

RENAMING A SHEET WITH A DOUBLE CLICK

There are various ways to rename sheets in Excel and the easiest of them all is by double-clicking on the sheet, and then rename it

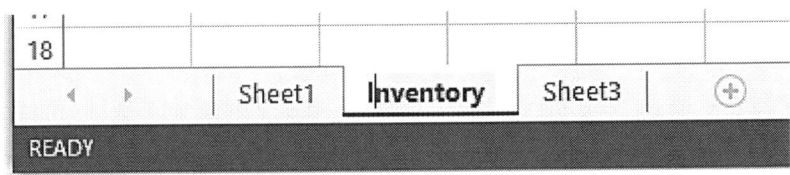

CHANGING THE CASE OF A TEXT

Certain functions are used to change the case of a text. For Example, the UPPER function capitalizes all the characters, the LOWER function changes the text to lower case while the PROPER function capitalizes the first character of a text.

FORMING A TEXT WITH &

With the sign & you can join the texts in different columns into a single cell. Let's join cell A2, B2, C2, and D4 to form JOYUSA23F in cell F2

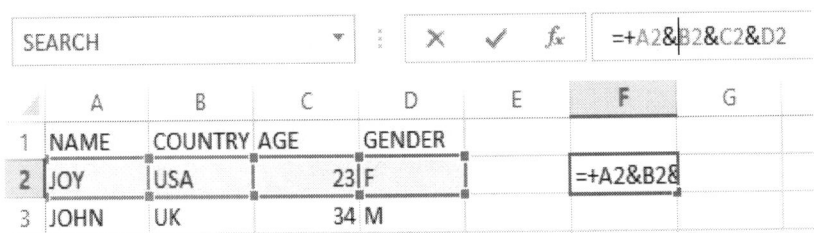

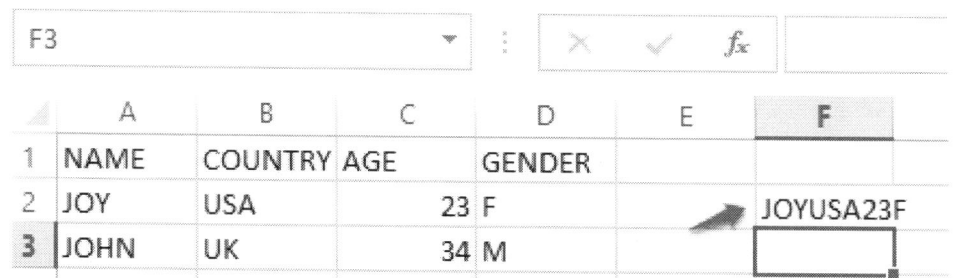

HOW TO MAKE EXCEL SHOW LEADING ZERO

When a value starts with zero, Excel will automatically delete the zero. To avoid this problem, add a single quote mark before the zero as shown in the table below.

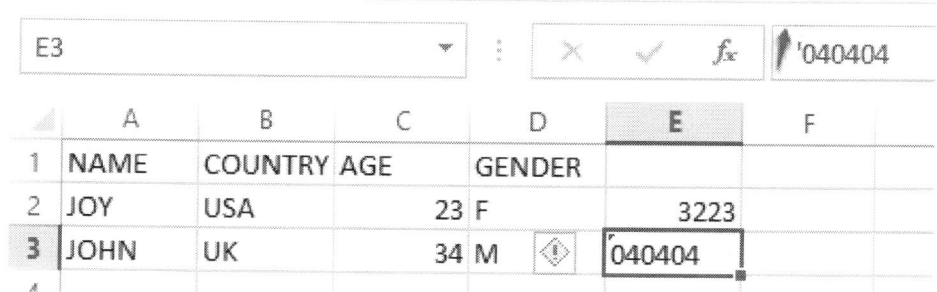

EXTENDING FORMULA DOWN

You can extend the formula from a cell by dragging the + cross at the lower bottom corner of the cell and move to the other cells

CHANGING HOW ENTER WORKS

When you click on **Enter** by default, it moves you down to a cell. You can change the method of how Enter works in another direction. To do this,

- Go to **File** and move to **Options**
- Click on the **Advanced** tab and go to **Edit Options**

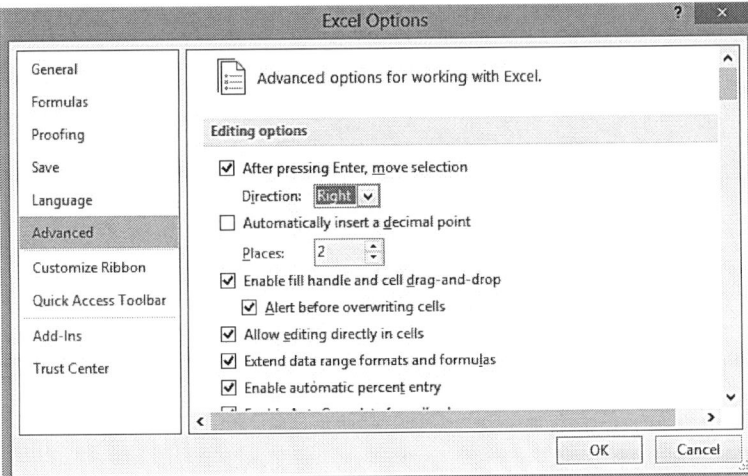

QUICK SELECT FORMULAS

This feature can help save time when trying to input formulas into the cells. As you begin to type the formula, you can scroll down to choose out of the suggested formulas and use the Enter to select the formula automatically.

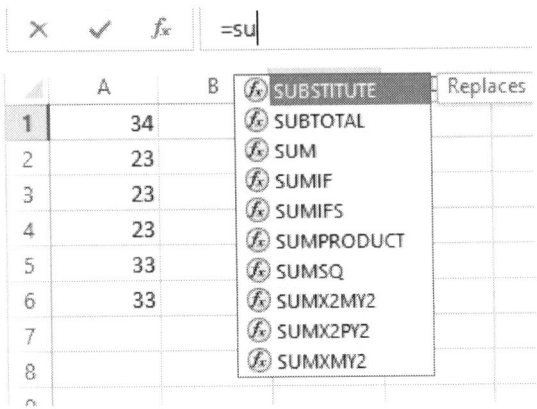

DISABLING THE EXCEL START SCREEN

Probably you hate it when you open your Excel program, only to be welcomed with Excel Start Screen. To disable the Start Screen,

- Go to **File** and move to **Options**
- Go to **General** and move **to Start-up options** to disable the Excel Start Screen
- Then click on Ok

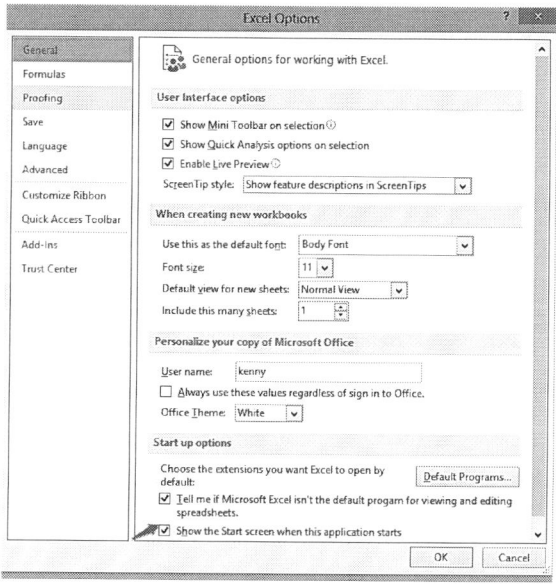

ACTIVATING CURRENT DATE AND TIME

You can insert the current date and time by using the NOW function by using the date and time from the system.

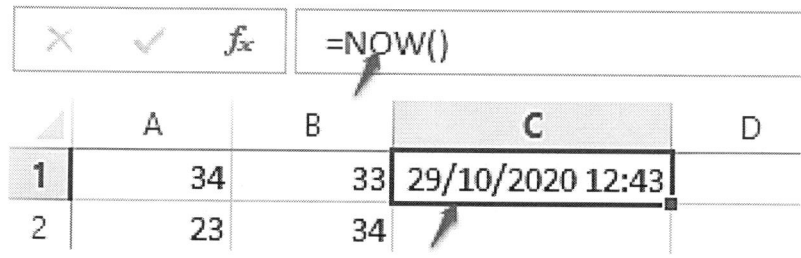

CUSTOMIZING THE STATUS BAR

When you right-click on the status bar, there are a lot of features available you can add.

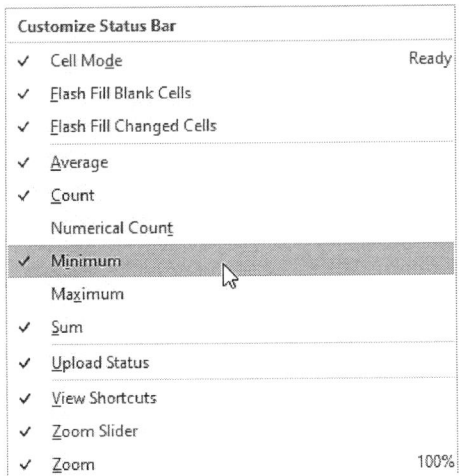

DELETING ERRORS CELLS

To get rid of cells with error values;

- From the **Home tab,** go to **Editing and** click on **Find & Replace**
- Go to **Go To Special and in** the **Go To Special** dialog box, select **Formula** and then tick **Errors**

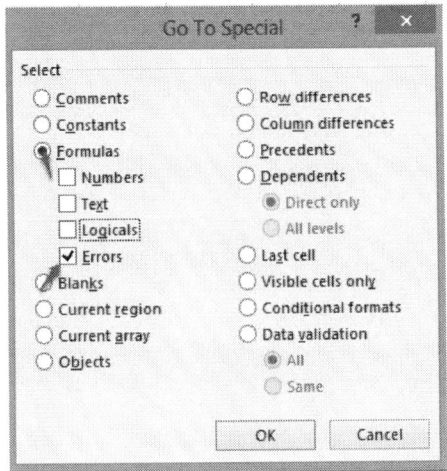

STRIKING THROUGH TEXTS IN EXCEL

To strike through texts in Excel, all you need to do is first select the cell and then press **Ctrl + 5**

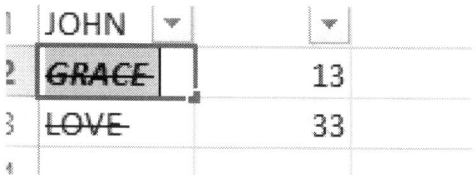

HOW TO CLEAR FORMATTING

You can clear any formatting from a cell or a range of cells. To do this;

- From the **Home tab,** go to **Editing**
- Select **Clear** and click on **Clear Format**

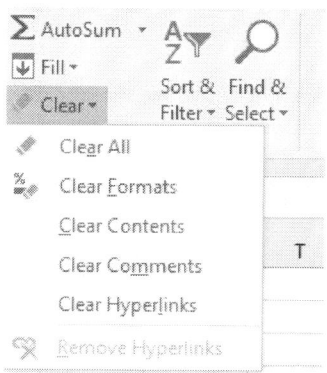

SHARING DATA ONLINE ON EXCEL

You can share excel data or documents online. By implication, you can collaborate with another person to work alongside with you on the Excel worksheet. Not only that, you don't have to go around with your computer, you can choose to save your data to OneCloud and make reference to it anytime, anywhere.

To share Excel file online;

- From the File menu back view, go to Share.
- Then choose any of the options that pop up (**Invite People, Email, and Save to OneDrive**).

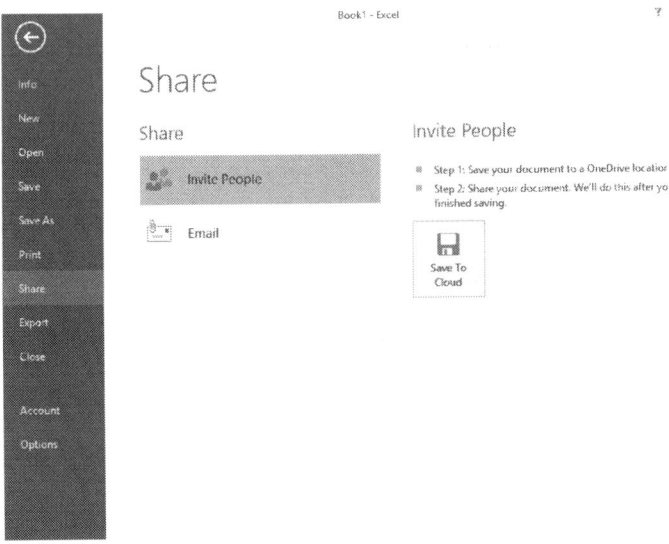

NOTE: To save your data or files on **OneCloud**, you must have Microsoft Account on your computer.

CONCLUSION

Having gone through this book, I am sure you must have realized how important and useful Microsoft Excel is to the organizations in the world especially that of 2020 coupled with the features it entails.

As a businessman or woman, Excel is meant solely for you; You don't want to waste your time doing what you could have done in little or no time with Excel 2020 you can do well to recommend this to your family and friends even your colleagues at work.

As a student, there are a lot of added advantages you get to see by taking your time to learn how to use this app, you never can tell where you will find yourself in the future. Moreover, it is dangerous to live in this world without any basic knowledge regarding the use of Microsoft Excel.

With Excel 2020, you are on your way to taking your business, career, etc. to another height.

Was this book helpful to you?
Are you satisfied with the contents of this book?
If yes, I would like to hear from you, please kindly leave a review for this book after purchase. Thanks.

ABOUT THE AUTHOR

My name is James Jordan, I am an author who is passionate about my customers' satisfaction and always puts my customers' needs at the front line. I am a content writer and a publisher who drives passion in providing solutions to people in online businesses.

Follow my author page for updates on my other books.

One of the things that makes an author do more is getting customers' feedback and reviews.

Kindly leave a feedback after reading this book.

I will really appreciate it.

James Jordan

Made in the USA
Coppell, TX
05 March 2021